D0585936

MY ALPHABET

MY ALPHABET

A LIFE FROM A TO Z

NICK HEWER

**SIMON &
SCHUSTER**

London · New York · Sydney · Toronto · New Delhi

A CBS COMPANY

First published in Great Britain by Simon & Schuster UK Ltd, 2018
A CBS COMPANY

Copyright © Last Gasp Productions Ltd, 2018

The right of Nicholas Hewer to be identified as the author
of this work has been asserted in accordance with the
Copyright, Designs and Patents Act, 1988.

3 5 7 9 10 8 6 4 2

Simon & Schuster UK Ltd
1st Floor
222 Gray's Inn Road
London WC1X 8HB

www.simonandschuster.co.uk
www.simonandschuster.com.au
www.simonandschuster.co.in

Simon & Schuster Australia, Sydney
Simon & Schuster India, New Delhi

The author and publishers have made all reasonable efforts
to contact copyright-holders for permission, and apologise
for any omissions or errors in the form of credits given.
Corrections may be made to future printings.

A CIP catalogue record for this book
is available from the British Library

Hardback ISBN: 978-1-4711-6706-5
Trade Paperback ISBN: 978-1-4711-6707-2
eBook ISBN: 978-1-4711-6708-9

Typeset in Palatino by M Rules
Printed and bound by CPI Group (UK) Ltd, Croydon, CR0 4YY

Simon & Schuster UK Ltd are committed to sourcing paper
that is made from wood grown in sustainable forests and support the Forest
Stewardship Council, the leading international forest certification organisation.
Our books displaying the FSC logo are printed on FSC certified paper.

To Catherine, who righted this old boat,
caulked the hull, took the helm and steered me
into safer and kinder waters. With much love.

CONTENTS

Never try to eat the elephant all at once

A

The Apprentice

Life in the Sugar shaker

Long after leaving *The Apprentice*, there are still two questions that punctuate my daily life, and they are both asked by strangers in the street, on trains, in airport queues, coffee shops, hotel foyers and even while taking a pee in the gents. They are, firstly, 'Was being on *The Apprentice* fun?' and, secondly, 'So, what's he like?'

Everybody thinks that being on *The Apprentice* must be the biggest laugh ever, and for a long time it was enormous fun, but I've got to tell you that it became an absolute nightmare, at least for this old chap. Can you imagine anything worse than trailing around after six or eight ego-crazed wannabes, day after day, writing everything down, everything they say, not missing a trick and taking it all seriously? Truth is, any fool can do what Margaret and I did, or Baroness Karren Brady of Knightsbridge and Claude Littner do, because it's not difficult: all you have to do is possess fairly good secretarial skills and a modicum of

1

business sense – and a huge dollop of stamina. The real talent and worth of the show is when Lord Alan Sugar silently appears through that glass door, enters the boardroom and gets to work on dissecting the task in hand, discovering who was responsible for the failure, or indeed, success of the task in question.

It was the stamina that did it for me. Which is why I packed it in, because after ten years I'd had enough. I was exhausted and bored and irritable and I thought: Right, I'd better get out of this before I become a nuisance. Additionally, it was beginning to put a strain on my relationship with my wonderful partner Catherine. While she is the soul of patience and generosity, I was starting to fret at never being able to get home during the lengthy shoot, for it was pretty much 24/7. On a show as big as *The Apprentice*, when most of the action takes place out on the road, the logistics are formidable. And, once you're signed up, you belong to the producers, who can be tough to deal with. I missed one family funeral as I could not be spared, and when Catherine's wonderful and much-loved mother Helen, who was living with us, passed away, I just made it to the funeral in our village church, but there was a car waiting with the engine running to take me back to London. I had barely ten minutes to join the other mourners at the house before I was whisked off. Amazingly, this didn't seem strange at the time.

I had tried to withdraw after Series 9 but got talked out of it, though I told Patrick Holland, the talented and civilised then-managing director of Boundless, producers of the show, during the filming of the final in Series 10 that this would definitely be my last. Also, I missed Margaret. We had both stumbled into this unlikely adventure at the same time, and I enjoyed her funny, generous, warm-hearted, obstinate, competitive and uncompromising self.

In one of the first episodes, when we were sitting in the board-room with Sir Alan (as he then was), waiting for the return of some of the losing team, Margaret barked out: 'THAT LIGHT UP THERE IS BLINDING ME AND I WILL NOT CARRY ON UNLESS IT IS EXTINGUISHED.' A hushed voice came back from the gallery: 'We're sorry it's so bright, Margaret, but if we turn it off, we will be filming you in darkness.' She replied, in stentorian tones, 'Perfect! That's absolutely fine by me.'

The three of us sat there in silence, waiting for something to happen. Who would break first? After a couple of agonising minutes, Margaret said, 'Well, perhaps we could turn it down a bit and that *might* just make it tolerable.' And so, without making any adjustment at all, the lighting supervisor said, 'Right, is that better now, Margaret?' 'Yes, I think I can manage that,' she answered crisply. Dear Margaret, her temper is as fast and fiery as her heart is big.

I remember one incident when filming under the Heathrow flight path, with all the candidates lined up in front of their Chrysler Voyagers. She and I were invited to step out of the warmth of our vehicle to get in position for an important set-piece shot. We were instructed to take our place on a patch of damp grass and to do so quickly as the planes were stacking up over Heathrow and we would soon be drowned out.

Well, that was enough to fire up Margaret's legendary temper. 'GRASS? I never stand on GRASS. I have feet to con-sider.' With that, she turned and marched back to the warmth of her Chrysler. I hurried after her. 'Margaret, calm down,' I murmured. 'You looked and sounded like Mussolini just then.' 'I did?' She sounded hurt and we both resumed our places for the shot. Thereafter, she would call me up at the end of a long day's filming and admit that she'd had 'another little Mussolini moment today'. That's what makes Margaret special: she can make fun of herself, such an important quality in a person.

But let's be fair. It wasn't all so bad, not by a long chalk. Through Alan and *The Apprentice*, I enjoyed meeting interesting and sometimes extraordinary people whom I would not have encountered in the course of a normal day. Many were iconic figures, but, strangely, they almost all fell from grace, in short order, not long after I met them. I met Tony Blair, no longer a blazing light; Rupert Murdoch, who fell heavily to earth; Sir Philip Green, by now less the King of Retail than the Sir Shifty of tabloid fame; Alastair Campbell, whom I always rather liked, but who was unable to shake off the taint of Blair's idiotic and illegal war in Iraq; Piers Morgan, the big bad boy of the British tabloid media, always poised for another piece of disastrous judgement while at the same time taking on some brave and decent fights, like his unpopular US gun control campaign.

There were also some memorable moments 'on the road'. Bearing in mind that I was part of 120 episodes and had witnessed the glories and the horrors of more than 150 candidates, you'll forgive me if I limit myself to just a few behind-the-scenes antics that have stayed with me over the years.

The all-nighter. This was a task that started in the evening and ran on until the boardroom meeting the following morning, a little piece of Japanese game-show torture devised by the production team to test the stamina of the twentysomething-year-old candidates, but little thought was given to me and Karren (I can't remember whether Margaret was ever subjected to this ordeal). As the senior citizen, I was surely the one who felt it most keenly. My all-nighter parties were a distant memory, and I found it impossible to recreate the 'party Nick' of old as I staggered around in the dark from one venue to another. I vaguely remember a task involving sausages – the making thereof, and the selling thereof the following morning – which found us at London's Smithfield Market, and then somewhere south of the river with a giant mincing machine extruding (eventually) something recognisably sausage-like, and finally to Leadenhall Market at dawn to set up stalls and sell the product to City workers.

Still on the subject of food, a rather more enjoyable daylight expedition occurred when Margaret and I crossed into mainland Europe – not by ferry, as everyone else on the production team had to do, but by Eurotunnel. 'I NEVER SAIL, I AM A VICTIM OF SEVERE SEASICKNESS,' barked Margaret, 'SO WE SHALL HAVE TO DRIVE.' And so it was that we found ourselves in the magnificent, vast market square at Arras in northern France for the 'cheese' task as it became known.

Aficionados of *The Apprentice* will recall that the teams were tasked with buying English produce and, in an attempt to kick-start an export market, take their selection direct to the finicky French consumer. Paul Callaghan, an ex-army officer, took it upon himself to purchase a breeze block-sized lump of processed cheddar from that well-known British cheese emporium, Costco (was it not Charles de Gaulle who moaned, 'How can you govern a country which has 246 varieties of cheese'?). Unsurprisingly, as the French streamed past the candidates' stalls, which were festooned with Union Jacks, Paul's masonry was viewed with utter disdain. Not to be defeated, he set about frying some British sausages behind the stall on a small contraption based on a little cooker he had used in training in Snowdonia while serving with HM's armed forces. The sausages were silent, there was no hint of a sizzle, a fact remarked upon by a beret-wearing Frenchman who looked down on

Paul's lukewarm kitchen effort while urinating beside it against the wall of what appeared to be Arras Cathedral.

It was time to leave and, scouring the market, I alighted upon a stand selling surely the noisiest cheese in Europe, making Stinking Bishop look like a whimpering child in a primary school. I popped half a kilo in a plastic bag and joined Margaret at the door of our Chrysler Voyager for the trip back to London. The strength of my cheese preceded me by about 5 metres. 'You are *not* bringing that into the vehicle.' 'Oh, Margaret,' I protested. 'I'm sorry,' came the reply. 'I shall have to put my foot down. I am allergic not only to the French but in particular to French cheese.' Again, I protested, 'Oh, Margaret.' 'I have spoken,' she said conclusively, and disappeared into the darkness of the Voyager.

Not wishing to cast my purchase into the nearest dustbin, I decided to secure the plastic bag to the rear of the vehicle so that it would travel home without causing an international incident. I clambered in beside Margaret and closed the door. As I sat down, she gave a small sigh of gratitude. Alas, when we got back to London, all that was left of my precious cargo were two scraps of plastic bag handle, so I must assume that in some corner of a foreign land there lies a squashed half-kilo of cheese, a victim of the centrifugal force of a bend taken at speed. (This brings to mind a trip to West Africa with the charity Street Child, when a visit to a distant village was rewarded with the gift of a goat which, relying on the reputation of surefootedness enjoyed by our caprine friends, was placed on the roof-rack of our 4×4 with a string around its neck to ensure it didn't bolt. We could hear its clip-clop hooves on the roof as we drove back to Freetown, but a sharp turn in the road prompted a pitiful bleat as the unhappy goat shot off, its string halter having snapped, and landed untidily in the bush some 30 metres behind us. Amazingly, young Billy was captured after a short chase, reintroduced to his lofty perch, and ended up some days later in the pot.)

Lack of stamina notwithstanding (my plaintive cries about all-nighters were eventually heard, and some hours of kip could be grabbed by myself and Karren at a Travelodge or similar), we had great times, and I well remember the time that *The Apprentice* hired the parade ground of what was, at the time, the home of the Royal Army Medical Corps, next to Tate Britain on London's Embankment. It was for a BBC Comic Relief special and the parade ground was turned into a fairground with a host of celebrities manning the attractions. They turned up in droves: McFly, Piers Morgan, John Terry and Ashley Cole, both then in their prime, Trinny Woodall, Simon Cowell, Jo Brand, Gary Barlow, Chris Evans, Maureen Lipman. I found myself standing back to admire the massive scale of the event and the skill of the producers in putting such a thing together, when suddenly I turned to find Sir Clement Freud, who though small had an inordinately large head and rather watery doleful eyes. Looking at me, he said, 'I watch that show you're in. You don't do a bad job.'

Knowing that he had the reputation of being a crude, acerbic wit, I determined to play safe. 'Why, Sir Clement,' I replied, 'I take that as a great compliment, for in truth I am a complete fraud. Any idiot could do what I do.' He sneered and turned to leave, saying, 'No, I am a complete *Freud.*' It was a good reply but sadly, as the years passed, it turned out that he was indeed a complete fraud, exposed as a predatory abuser. Another icon falls.

To get us to this point in the story, we have to roll the clock back to 1983, when my relationship with Alan Sugar began. The phone rang in the office and my secretary said, 'I have a Malcolm Miller on the phone.' She put him through, and he announced himself as, 'Malcolm Miller, marketing director of Amstrad. You will have heard of us.' I demurred for a second or two and then said, 'Of course I've heard of you.'

'As you know we're at the cheap end of the hi-fi business,' Malcolm continued. 'But our founder Alan Sugar has determined that the time is right to move into the home computer business, and we understand that your company's good at launching products, so we'd like you to come and see us.'

'Sure, I'd be happy to do that. But why don't you come to Covent Garden, we're surrounded by some of the best restaurants in London and you might enjoy it.'

'No, I can't do that because we're not allowed to leave the office, so you'd have to come to us. We're in Garman Road, Tottenham.'

'*Really?*'

'Yes, we can't leave the office.'

I reluctantly hauled myself off to Garman Road, to a cardboard-strewn office-cum-warehouse, where Malcolm, a young marketing director, told me that Amstrad, the go-go company of the early 1980s, was planning to move heavily into the home computer market, which at the time was dominated by Atari, Commodore and Sinclair. Malcolm showed me a couple of Amstrad's prototype computers and explained that Amstrad was going to do what Amstrad and its founder Alan Sugar had become famous for, namely entering a market with an amazing offer at a price well below the competition, supported by heavyweight TV advertising campaigns.

The offer was that the Amstrad would come with a monitor, something that none of the competitors had considered. In those days, this was unheard of: all one could buy was a system unit, which you plugged into your dad's television set in order to play Space Invaders, and when he came back from work he'd give you a thick ear because he wanted to watch the news and you'd have to unplug it and plug it back in again when the programme was over.

Amstrad was going to bundle a system unit and a monitor – a real computer, like the ones most people only saw at the airport when they were queuing to board their charter flight to the Costa del Sol from Luton. And here was Amstrad, about to sell the same thing, for the same price or cheaper than Atari, Commodore and Sinclair, who were only selling system units. It was possible because Alan Sugar would drive down the component costs by buying in huge volume, giving him a price advantage, but it was the monitor that was the marketing clincher, as well as proof of his marketing genius.

Malcolm asked me to get back to him with a proposal as to how Amstrad might launch this product in a creative but, critically, cost-effective way, and I told him he could count on me. I went back to the office, which was pretty busy at the time, and very rudely and unprofessionally I didn't do anything about it. Malcolm kept chasing me, and Nicky Bedford-Davis, my secretary, who was taking the calls, upbraided me, 'You've really got to do something about this, it's very embarrassing.' And eventually I groaned, 'Oh God, this is awful. I've got no ideas at all and I don't understand this computer business anyway. But I'd better go and apologise to him for my lack of professionalism, and eat humble pie, so can you order me a taxi?'

I got in the taxi and went back to Garman Road, and, on the

way, I had one of the two brainwaves I've ever had in my life. What does this computer actually do? Well, it's got colour, it's got sound, arithmetical function, music and many other functions. The market is for children aged eight to ten, who use it to play games (there was virtually no other software available at the time). How about we find children with names that fit the functions? When I got to Malcolm's office, I fibbed again. 'I've been thinking long and hard about your problem,' I said. 'What we're going to do is find a group of schoolchildren, each of whose names will exemplify or explain a function of your computer. We'll hire somewhere with an academic connection, perhaps the Great Hall of Westminster School, and we'll invite the media, the retail trade, the trade press and the City.' And we did it: working with my colleague Tim Sutton we found a Ravel, a Monet, an Archimedes and so on. We couldn't find a child called Shakespeare, so we had to make do with a forty-eight-year-old William Shakespeare who was a worsted woollen merchant from Manchester.

Till now, I hadn't actually met Alan Sugar, the rising star in the City who had floated his company on the London Stock Exchange in 1980, making himself a multimillionaire at the age of thirty-three. There was one stage when I was in a briefing meeting at Garman Road, and a door eased open silently and what appeared to be half a bearded chin came around the doorframe and then quickly retreated. That was Alan Michael Sugar, apparently just seeing what was going on. I was to learn quickly that nothing escapes his notice – he knows everything that goes on within his companies.

He was at the launch, of course, and he gave a presentation on the technical and marketing aspects of the CPC 464, as it was designated, including a sure-fire headline when he described the Sinclair competitor as a 'pregnant calculator'. On the way out, as he passed me, he let out what I can only describe as a little grunt. Malcolm, who was beside me, whispered, 'That's *amazing*! You got a grunt.'

'Is that good?'

'Some people wait eighteen months for a grunt. So that's a *very* early sign of acknowledgement. It's Alan's version of a round of applause.'

The launch was a huge success. The share price pretty much doubled the next day, and this one machine, the CPC 464, selling for £199 and then £299 with a colour monitor, became a huge phenomenon not just in the UK but all over Europe, where it was distributed by Amstrad's wholly owned subsidiary in France and by a growing number of distributors across the continent. Alan had been the darling of the City – the barrow-boy made good – for a while; he was certainly on his way before we launched this. But he was now the poster boy for British business success, and the plaudits flowed in.

The following year, by which time I'd got to know him and gained a bit of traction, Alan told me he was developing a word processor, codenamed Joyce (after his long-suffering secretary at the time), and he wanted us to launch it. It was a word processor with a monitor and LocoScript software, and it killed the UK typewriter market stone dead. It cost £399, whereas an IBM golf-ball electric typewriter cost £1,000. There were other word processors and personal computers available but they were not for the small business market. In fact, I'd just laid out a staggering £13,000 on a Canadian Wordplex system for my office. I remember telling Alan that I wished he'd told me about Joyce three weeks earlier as it would've saved me a good deal of money.

This £399 Amstrad word processor was obviously going to be a big deal. No sooner had we launched it than everybody had one on their desk. You couldn't walk down Tottenham Court Road, then the mecca of electronic retailing, without being knocked down by somebody coming out of a shop with a huge box and falling into a taxi.

Amstrad was really growing apace now. I think my attention and imagination were captured by Amstrad, Alan Sugar and his team because there was always a sense of excitement, of rapid product development and also of controversy and argument. If you like the smell of cordite and the sound of gunfire, Alan Sugar's your man.

And then came Alan's next product, a personal computer. IBM had launched the PC in 1980, followed by clones made by Olivetti, Siemens, Grundig and others. These PCs all did exactly the same as the IBM model; so did the Amstrad PC 1512, but where all the others cost £2,000, this cost just £399. Once again bringing in Willie Martin and Neil Christie, who had handled the set theme, design and graphics of the previous launches, we unveiled it before an international audience of 1,200 people at the government's Queen Elizabeth II conference centre in Westminster and Amstrad soared to another level.

Within two years, Amstrad had 36 per cent of the European small business/home PC market. It was huge; the company was now worth about £1.2 billion, profits were around £160 million, turnover £860 million. It was really booming, and Alan was now Britain's pre-eminent entrepreneur, fêted by politicians and the City alike. And he was making a lot of money. I was having a great time, too, with a lot of international travel, setting up a network of PR companies across Europe and travelling out to the consumer electronic shows in Hong Kong,

Chicago, Atlanta and all over Europe. I was given pretty much a free hand. Alan was great fun to be with, and I was astonished by the way his entrepreneurial nose could sniff out a winner.

And then, sometime in 1989, I went to see Alan in his office in Brentwood and found him in a depressed state. Amstrad had just launched the first big professional PC, the PC 2000, for the likes of British Steel and British Airways – a computer for the big-league corporate market. No sooner were the computers plugged in, they were crashing. He'd called in the boffins from Cambridge and Oxford and they had torn the machines apart but couldn't understand what was going wrong. An emergency meeting was called to decide what to do. Amstrad could bluff it out and replace them, and try to fix the problem, or Alan could recall them. He recalled them. You've seen what happened to Toyota and Volkswagen: recall, and the competition shoots you in the head. And that's what happened, and that really was the end of Amstrad's ambitions to be a global computer company.

It was a very difficult time because, as I remember it, the company was left holding about £350 million of unwanted inventory, and Lloyds Bank was getting uneasy, but Alan managed to ease the remainder out into the international market – an extraordinary feat, given the circumstances. He sued the companies that had supplied the faulty parts for the PC 2000, and in one suit in London, Amstrad was awarded £98 million. I joined him that night for dinner, and Alan said to his wife, Ann, 'Well, we've had an interesting day. We won in court and we got £98 million.' Ann replied, 'Oh, that's nice. Now eat your soup before it gets cold.' That's the great thing about her, she keeps his feet on the ground.

That crash was very bad, but it was followed by a stroke of great luck. One day, the phone rang in Brentwood and Alan's secretary, Frances (long-suffering Joyce had retired), said, 'I've got Rupert Murdoch on the phone.' Story goes, Alan replied, 'I suppose he's somebody who says he went to school with me?' 'Actually, no, he's the man who owns *The Times* and the *Sunday Times* and the *News of the World*.' When Alan is focused on something there is no escape, but why should he care about Rupert Murdoch, who'd never crossed his radar? Alan doesn't know what he doesn't need to know. There's only so much room in his brain, why clutter it up with useless, irrelevant information? If it does matter to him, he knows it backwards. Up till then, Murdoch didn't matter to him. But that was about to change.

He went to see Murdoch, who told him he had a big rocket down in French Guiana, called Ariane, on top of which was a satellite called Astra, bristling with transponders. Any minute now they were going to light the fuse and blast it off and position Astra way up there in a geostationary position over Zaire, from where Murdoch's transponder, Sky Television, was going to beam a footprint all over Europe.

'What's that got to do with me?' Alan asks.

'Well, you're rated as the best man at mass-market electronics so I want you to make the dishes and the system units that will receive my signal and squirt it into television sets.'

'How many would you want?'

'Uh, I don't know, let's say 100,000 pieces per month from about March?' (It is now September 1989.) 'But this isn't an order – you'll be selling to retailers like Dixons, that's where you'll make your margin.'

Alan goes back to the office and speaks to Bob Watkins, Amstrad's long-time technical director, who's just recovering from a near-nervous breakdown after the disaster of the PC

2000. 'Bob,' says Alan, 'we're in the satellite business.' 'But,' says Bob, 'we don't know anything about it.' Alan brushes this off. 'That doesn't matter. We'll find out about it.'

When Amstrad first got into the PC market, Alan and Bob's team took the lid off a couple of PCs and peered into the back, only to discover there was pretty much nothing there – basically, a few boards and electronic bits and the rest was empty. It was all a load of hokum: make it big (hence 'pregnant') and charge a bigger price. Same thing when Alan got into the satellite business. Alan and Bob got in the people who made the dishes (mainly for embassies and government installations), and asked them to quote for a small dish, about 3 feet wide. The experts, like all experts, made a serious face and said it was going to be very expensive: there was the curvature of the steel to be taken into account, the delicacy of the component parts, yadda yadda yadda. 'Yeah, yeah,' said Alan. 'How much?' 'Somewhere in the region of £75,' came the reply. So, they got thrown out and Alan said, 'Bob, get in the people who make dustbin lids. They're the same size, what's the difference? All we're trying to make is a dustbin lid and add a few bits.' They came in, and were also sent on their way, and finally the contract went to a firm called Concentric who made hubcaps for cars: you get a big piece of metal, and a big press comes down and boom! there's your dish, and you screw the LNB cable socket and a bracket into it and that's it. That was the beginning of the great satellite revolution.

Perhaps the sweetest example of Alan's entrepreneurial flair came a few years later, in 1993. He was tipped off about a technically brilliant but commercially naive Danish mobile phone manufacturer called Dancall, which was on the brink of bankruptcy. Alan chartered a jet and flew straight to Aalborg, where he was met by a team of Dancall employees who were keen to subject him to a long storyboard presentation. As he recalls it in his autobiography, *What You See Is What You Get*, 'I cut them short and asked them to walk me round the factory and the engineering department and show me what was going on. Having spent so long in the industry, I could sniff out a good factory simply by walking round, seeing how things are made and talking to the engineers. What I saw was a pot of gold.'

Bearing in mind that Dancall was going into liquidation any minute, he had to move fast. He called the engineers together and told them to stay fast as a group, not to split off looking for other jobs, because he was going to buy the company. He was back a week later with a cheque for £6 million.

During the next two years, £10 million was invested and Dancall got to understand a bit about urgency, component buying, cost control and risk-taking. The engineers, now given some product guidance and leadership, set to and rapidly produced the prototype that Alan had called for, namely a Worldphone, a triple-band mobile that could operate in the UK, Europe and the US – a world first. It was launched at Europe's premier electronics exhibition, the Hanover Fair, and I busied myself to ensure that Dancall's cutting-edge innovation was splashed on the daily exhibition newspaper's front page. By 10:30 a.m. there was a restless queue waiting to get on the stand to see the triple-band Worldphone.

Not long afterwards, Alan pulled off a spectacular deal when he sold Dancall to the German firm Bosch for £95 million. All because he had the courage to bet on his nose.

And so things rolled on. My PR company was doing fine; I was still working with Alan, now mostly on Tottenham Hotspur, which he bought in 1991, and which turned into a total nightmare (*see* T: TOTTENHAM). But I was thinking I really should get out of all of this carry-on. I found someone to buy my business in 1998, and suddenly I was a free man. But Alan asked me to stay on, as did another long-term client, the Secretariat of the Aga Khan, and I accepted. All I needed was a portable computer, a phone and a passport. I travelled a lot and it was wonderful: a Jewish entrepreneur on one hand, an Imam on the other, and me in the middle, a Catholic Anglo-Irish boy brought up in the edgelands of Swindon. We trundled along happily until 2004, when I said to myself, Right, I'm out of here. And that was that. Alan planned secretly with my partner Catherine to host an extravagant surprise sixtieth birthday party for me at the Dorchester Hotel for a hundred friends, family and the Amstrad-related people whom I liked so much, after which I took off to our house in France and started to imagine my future now that I had retired.

That was February, and it was a gloomy time for me as I struggled to adjust to retirement, the psychological dimensions of which I had totally neglected to consider. The future, as I now imagined it, was a rather drear and barren landscape with the odd bit of tumbleweed blowing across it. Come March, I get a call from Alan. 'Where are you?' 'I'm in London.' 'Well, get yourself up to the Dorchester for three o'clock and bring a pencil, I need to talk to you about something.' I get up there and Alan tells me about a programme called *The Apprentice*, which features an iconic figure called Donald Trump. It's an entertainment show, he explains, but the bedrock of it is business.

A few years earlier, I had run a national project for Alan called You Can Do It Too, at the behest of Gordon Brown, then at the Treasury, and sponsored by Lloyds Bank. It saw Alan rocketing all over the UK on a weekly basis at his own expense to talk to university students about business and the wonders of running your own enterprise. The days of mass employment had gone – no more British Steel, no more British Rail, no more coal mines – so Alan was fronting an initiative to promote business and incentivise youngsters to consider starting their own business, and explaining the advantages of apprenticeships. He was devoted to this mission and was still doing it, and enjoying it, but now he scented a chance to do it on television because he'd heard that the BBC was about to commission a British version of *The Apprentice*.

That's why we were in the Dorchester Hotel. Alan wanted to front the show, and in a couple of minutes the show's producer, Peter Moore, was coming in and we had to persuade him that Alan was the right man for the job. Truth be told, Alan's star had faded – there were new kids on the block like Philip Green and easyJet's Stelios Haji-Ioannou. Alan had been through the nightmare of Tottenham, which took so much of his time and energy, causing Amstrad to falter, and so he was no longer pre-eminent as the man of the moment. Philip Green was, and the word was that the BBC wanted him.

So, we had a tea-and-cakes meeting with Peter at the Dorchester, at three in the afternoon on a grey March day and, to complete the desultory scene, it was raining outside. The whole set-up was inauspicious. We all agreed to keep in touch with one another and that was that.

Alan's version of this is different to mine, saying the deal was already done. He has a very good memory (perhaps, occasionally, with a bit of VAT on top), but my clear recollection is that when Peter left we both agreed it hadn't gone terribly well, and my second stroke of genius (ever) was to say to Alan: 'Look, you can't exemplify what Trump exemplifies, sitting in here in the gloom. You told me he's got helicopters and huge jets and he lives in palaces, and we're sitting here eating macaroons. It's not what you'd call show business, is it? You've got planes, so send a plane up and we'll put Peter and his team on it – we'll kidnap them and take them to your beachside villa in Marbella, we'll lock them in and not let them out until the deal is done.'

It worked a treat. When Alan's really concentrating, he's the most charming, amusing, smart, convivial, understanding, *dominant* character you could meet. And he was like this for the whole weekend, and by the end he was saying, 'Now, what we're going to do is this, the first task is this ...' He was mapping out the whole thing, and they were saying, 'Yeah, that's a great idea, Sir Alan.' We put them back on the plane at Malaga and they knew they had their man.

Just before the door closed, Peter Moore turned and stuck his head out of the plane, saying, 'What about your advisors? Nick would do.' I just laughed. I stayed on for a couple more days with Alan and Ann, and he kept saying, 'I don't know what your problem is. What's wrong with you?' I hummed and hawed and then he said, 'I'll sort out the fee.' At this point, I really hadn't considered the question of money. Funny thing is, in all the years I'd worked for him, I'd never got a fee increase to talk of, and here he was acting as my agent. It was so exquisite that I couldn't not agree.

'What about the woman advisor?' I asked.

'Margaret.'

'That's not Margaret Mountford from Girton College, Cambridge, is it? Margaret who's got a first-class honours degree in law? Margaret the Graeco-Roman scholar, chairman of the Hellenic Society? *That* Margaret? She's not going to do a vulgar TV programme!'

'Leave it with me,' said Alan.

So that's how it started. We all three waltzed into it with no idea what we were doing. There were no briefings about how to do it; we just made it up as we went along under the truly brilliant Peter Moore and his production team. And it worked. It was commissioned by Roly Keating for BBC2 and then it was promoted to BBC1, under the guiding hand of the channel's controller, Jana Bennett. As I understand it, the BBC had originally been offered the rights by its creator, Mark Burnett, a former British paratrooper and Falklands veteran who had also created the hugely successful show, *Survivor*. But the BBC had spiked it, dumped it in the out-tray. Then somebody at Talkback Thames (an independent company founded by Mel Smith and Griff Rhys Jones) heard about it, went to Burnett, and bought it. Talkback Thames then went straight to the BBC and said, 'We've got this property called *The Apprentice*, do you want to commission it?' And the BBC lot scratched their heads – 'Hang on, this rings a bell'.

I'm often asked: why are the candidates so stupid? Put it another way: are the people in *The Apprentice* Britain's brightest business hopefuls? The answer, clearly, is no, of course they're not. That's not the point. Because if you went to the Saïd Business School in Oxford, or to Yale or Stanford, and got the cleverest business graduates, first of all they'd likely be Chinese, and second they'd all have Hungarian economic theories in their back pockets and none of us would understand what the hell they were talking about, so complex would it be. And at this point, the commissioning editor would be led out of his office and placed against a wall to be machine-gunned, because fifteen people are watching it on BBC13 at six in the morning.

It's all about numbers (after thirteen years, it's punching five, six million viewers on the night, plus catch-up). And the secret is, everybody out there *knows* they can do better: the bloke on the squashy sofa in Strathclyde who's getting hammered on Stella and is shouting at the screen that he can do better than they can. And yet, in every one of those tasks, the business planks associated with it are submerged in this soup of entertainment – all the business elements are there, but the candidates simply haven't got the time to enact them. Not only are they not brilliant, but they're on an impossible deadline, which means they make mistakes and that makes great viewing.

Actually, I couldn't do what *The Apprentice* candidates do, nor could most people because the pressure is extraordinary. But in its way, *The Apprentice* does accurately reflect the highs and lows of the real business world, and for that, I think – no, I know – it's truly worthwhile. Is the greed and jealousy and shouting and grandstanding a good thing? That's debatable, for sure, but it's entertainment: if nobody watches, nobody learns. Everybody is trying to get their camera time, everyone wants to be noticed, and the best way to do that is to argue. They're all egotists, and they have to be because otherwise they wouldn't survive a minute. I wouldn't have survived a minute as a candidate; I'd have run home to Mother.

There were wonderful characters and there were some shockers among the candidates. Let me just bring out the great Stuart Baggs, from the Isle of Man, who described himself as 'Baggs the Brand'. When accused in the boardroom by Sir Alan of being a one-trick pony, he famously blustered, 'I'm not a one-trick pony, I'm not a ten-trick pony. I've got a whole field of ponies, waiting to literally run towards this [job].' Visibly unconcerned at being charged by the Baggs ponies, Alan let out a dry, 'Oh, really?' and moved the conversation on. All of us connected with *The Apprentice* were greatly saddened to hear of the young Mr Baggs's sudden death in 2015 from an asthma attack. Alan, who has a reputation for being tough and unemotional, but is in fact full of paternal concern for those he knows, was particularly distressed.

What was my role and that of Margaret, Karren and Claude? To charge around after the candidates, scribbling everything down, and having gutter picnics while Alan was back in the office earning another million. On the day of the boardroom, we would go into a briefing session and unload all our notebooks on Alan, who would boil it all down to a single page of A4 with a line down the middle: Team A, Team B. It could take three hours. He wants to know everything. He has not seen one inch of film, yet in his head he's got to visualise everything that's happened over the previous three days. Then we'd all stagger out and head for the boardroom, and the producers might try to persuade Alan to get rid of a certain candidate they're not impressed by, but Alan is completely unpersuadable. He makes up his own mind, he plays it dead straight and never tells anyone, including his sidekicks, what he's going to do. In fact, he doesn't know what he's going to do until he does it.

We'd take our seats in the boardroom, the candidates would file in, and the tension was palpable. There were six cameras behind us, three behind the mirrors, one in the roof. There was no script, just Alan's sheet of A4 with the line down the middle. It always amused me that he had highlighted every line (thus slightly defeating the purpose of a highlighter?). The advisors' job is to keep it all on track, because Alan hasn't seen anything and the candidates lie, so they need to be kept truthful.

He then sends the winning team off to have a miserable treat (in the early days, they used to be whisked off to a volcanic spa in Iceland; now they get to go bowling in Stratford), while the losing team go off to have their cup of coffee in a Styrofoam cup. They come back, there's a fight, and three are left standing. And now Alan, who would've made a brilliant criminal prosecutor, gets to work. The trick is to make each of the final three appear equally culpable. That's the jeopardy of it: you don't want the guy on the squashy sofa in Strathclyde to know who's going to get fired. I know when Alan is about to fire somebody because he starts to breathe a little more heavily just before he points the finger.

They then leave the boardroom and pick up their wheelie bags in the anteroom (which the cockier ones don't bother to pack because they think they're going to get through). Towards the end of the process, when there were only about five left, Margaret and I would go out and try to cheer them up. Some of them would be in tears, not necessarily because they'd been fired, but because they were out of the bubble they'd been living in for months.

They really are sequestered: when they arrive, independently, from different hotels, they're searched by ex-army people, and the boys have their eyeliner taken away (yes) and the mobile phone, and the money they've secreted in their socks; they have no internet access; they get one phone call a week for eight minutes, under supervision. They go into that cauldron and the pressure is really extraordinary. The production crew like to play their own private games, and they can be quite witty: in one series, they had a big fish tank in the living room of the candidates' house, stocked with a fish for every candidate, and every time somebody got fired they took a fish out, and nobody ever noticed.

The Apprentice works. It's very easy to sit there at home and think, What a mess they've made of that task. But the tasks are more difficult than they seem: the candidates are always being distracted by the production team, who pull them out of the middle of a brainstorm to ask them to do a piece to camera, so their concentration has been broken, and they've got so much to do in such a short time. I couldn't create a product and launch it in two days; most people couldn't. But there are occasional flashes of genius: we've had advertising agencies say to us, 'Can you give us that team? Our lot couldn't have done a better job in three months.'

At the time when the banks were unstable and nobody was lending any money, we had one task that proved you could start a business with very little, as long as you had focus and a real passion for what you were doing. That's what *The Apprentice* is all about. We once hired a van and gave each team £500 and set them loose to collect and sell scrap metal, and the winning team came back with a £700 profit. Certainly, you're more likely to be successful if you've got a TV crew with you – you're much less likely to get a punch on the nose for trying to drive down the price – and it helps to have a car driving you across London, but I still believe that the way the tasks are modelled does have a real educational value.

Several products developed on *The Apprentice* have gone into production and are very successful. All the winning candidates are now making money including a non-winner, ahem, Katie Hopkins. She showed herself to be an extraordinarily good presenter, I mean, she had it. Unfortunately, she's gone on to use it to create havoc. I remember saying to her, after the *You're Fired* show: 'I can see you, with your ruby red lips shaped for sin, dressed in a white trouser suit. You're just going to be unpleasant, and that's a short road that comes to an abrupt end.' And that's exactly the direction she followed. But you run out of road eventually, because you've got to all but kill somebody if you want to be more and more extreme; you've got to keep mounting up the pressure. Where does that take you?

People ask me all the time why the BBC doesn't do a programme on whatever happened to the winners, but the corporation's compliance department – which is about twice the size of the Russian army – won't allow that because, they argue, it would be construed as promoting Lord Sugar's businesses. It's daft. In one of the very early episodes of the show, some-body from Compliance intervened on set and said, 'I'm terribly sorry, Sir Alan, but we can't allow an Amstrad phone on your desk in the boardroom because that would be considered as promoting your product.' He said, 'Right, so whose boardroom is this?' 'Yours, Sir Alan.' 'And what does my company make?' 'Phones, Sir Alan.' 'Yeah, so do you think that in real life I would have a Philips phone on my desk?' Meanwhile, Chrysler appeared to be selling the BBC six or eight brand-new people carriers every year, at full whack. Chrysler must've thought it was Christmas.

The Apprentice has been running for thirteen years and there's more to come. Am I proud of it, even though I'm no longer part of it? Yes, very. Pretty much every school in the country and every company of any size has now got an *Apprentice*-style competition running. And if you think about it, all the TV elimination programmes followed *The Apprentice*, and spin-off programmes too. Its continued popularity is down in large part to a group of the most talented, hard-driving producers and directors – people such as Peter Moore, Michele Kurland, Mark Saben, Claire Walls and the brilliant Andy Devonshire. But at the very heart of the programme and its phenomenal success is Alan Michael Sugar – sharp as a scalpel, quietly generous, loyal to a fault, gloriously impatient, and with a wit on him that could knock down a wall. For all this and more, I'm grateful to him.

B

Boyhood

Gloom at The Grange, occasional bright spells

I don't know whether Nursey Rogers was trying to drown me or just punish me, but I remember being terrified, aged three, as I went down for the third time and the bath water surged over my head. From this position, I could see Nursey above me in her red knitted hat, but I couldn't tell whether she was smiling. This, possibly deranged, woman was summoned to The Grange from her home in faraway Melksham whenever Mum was trundled off to the Cheriton Nursing Home in leafy Westlecot Road, where the worthies of Swindon went to give birth. I also remember lining up with my brothers so that Nursey could give us our weekly enema – further evidence of her sadism? Or perhaps it was the fashion at the time.

Grandpa bought The Grange in the early 1930s. It is a three-storey, Edwardian red-brick house on the edge of the Old Town of Swindon, fronted by a stable yard complete with looseboxes, a garage with a hayloft and various outbuildings; at the rear, a large garden and orchard. Mum and Dad moved in when Grandpa retired from his veterinary practice in the late 1940s, and I think the move and taking over the practice was a major headache for Dad. Suddenly, he acquired all the expense of running a large house and the people whom Grandpa had always employed.

Among them was Ted Clark, Grandpa's groom, always dressed in his long brown dustcoat, whose function now was to act as a yard man: feeding the dogs, cleaning the shoes, sweeping the yard and generally helping out. If you wanted him he was always in the saddle room, a cosy little den furnished with a pot-bellied stove; there were Dad's and Grandpa's old riding boots standing upright on the bench and one could clearly see the worm holes drilled through the leather and into the wooden boot trees. I remember Dad once telling me that riding boots must be close-fitting, and he always advocated wearing ladies' stockings laced with talcum powder. Nice and tight, he explained. Interestingly for us boys, above the boots were hung some large leg bones of famous racehorses wrapped in brown packages with their names written in pencil on labels.

Clark was, I think, constantly at odds with Poole the gardener, who lived during the day in or around his potting shed. A tall, sallow, unfriendly man, he was also a kleptomaniac and his potting shed was festooned with his trophies. Like a magpie, he collected anything shiny and interesting. He had a large greenhouse where he grew flowers for the house and cultivated arum lilies, a favourite at funerals, which he would present to my mother on whom he had something of a crush. Every morning he would bring her polished vegetables from the kitchen garden. In later years, she claimed that she had been frequently surprised, when gazing out of the kitchen window into the garden, to see a sudden movement among the bamboo or the dahlias, which would be parted to reveal Poole's sallow features peering at her.

The top floor of The Grange was a self-contained staff flat occupied by the wonderful Mrs Beasley, who helped Mum in the house. Burt, her husband, had had a bad war somewhere in the Far East, and was unable to work. He always seemed to be short of breath, and I rarely saw him stand. I would sit at his knee transfixed by wartime stories, never taking my eye off the little regimental badge pinned to his lapel that I coveted with all my heart.

Margaret the maid, who came from Faringdon, was courted by the wildly exotic Frank, an American air-force man who drove an Austin 7, wore a leather jacket smothered in USAF badges, and chewed gum. Margaret, a large and simple girl, slept next to the boys' bedroom. On one occasion when our cousins from Dublin were staying, Cousin Patrick and I knocked on her door one evening when my parents were out to dinner. 'We're coming in!' we announced, and entered the darkened room. 'Margaret, please pull down your nightie.' To our amazement and growing horror, she did so without hesitation. It was at that point that we produced from underneath our dressing gowns our favourite Dinky toys – something of a relief for her – and we proceeded to drive them round her ample bosom (one each), making all the right noises as each car changed to a lower gear to make the ascent.

Poor Margaret was discovered late one night, trapped in the unblinking headlights of my parents' returning car, on the mounting block in the yard, with the ever-attentive Frank at work, and shortly afterwards we tearfully bade her farewell.

One end of the house contained Dad's office, run by the

very prim Miss Bedwin, which also contained a dispensary and a surgery, and as we grew up the practice expanded until it became Hewer, Spriggs and Wilson, the largest practice by far in the area, covering north Wiltshire and parts of Gloucestershire and Oxfordshire. It was into this household that the five Hewer children – David, me, Fergus, Stella and Annabelle – grew up, fussed over by Mother and in awe of a somewhat distant father.

I know I had an idyllic childhood, because in 1991 I wrote about it in a speech for my parents' fiftieth wedding anniversary, which was celebrated with a big party in a marquee at The Grange. From this vantage point on the lawn, I was able to point out the steeple of the nearby church, in whose shadow two of our grandparents lay buried. This is Christ Church, which houses the great bells that John Betjeman celebrated in his poem 'Summoned by Bells' – or, in our case, deafened by bells tugged by teams of visiting ringers who would pole up every weekend and create an appalling racket before pushing off home again. As a child, and even when visiting later, the first hellish peal would see me heading for the cellar.

It was Betjeman too who stood on the hill and looked down on new Swindon and saw what he described as a town of 'brick-built breeding boxes'. So, there you have it, a childhood squeezed between the bells and the breeding boxes. But in that small space, bells permitting, my parents provided a home in which my brothers and sisters could enjoy a quite special childhood, just post-austerity and just pre-designer flared jeans.

Dad was stern and head of the house, Mum was the fixer who sorted out the problems. Their roles were brought into force at an early age for me. I remember wonderful stolen moments heating the poker red-hot in the fire in the breakfast room and then pressing the end into the wooden fireplace surround. The hissing sound and the curl of smoke was a great pleasure for me, but the burn mark in the wood was a worrying problem and permanent evidence of my mischief. Caught red-pokered one day, I remember Dad bringing in the big guns in the form of his father, known as Faz, and they gave me a terrific telling-off until I was delivered into the arms of Mum, who took the heat off me and explained why it was wrong and why it was dangerous. She always had the time to explain things, and was a model of compassion and fairness.

I remember some of us children having to kneel with her in silent prayer the day that the teenager Derek Bentley was hanged in Wandsworth prison, and I remember her tears on the day that Stalin's death was announced. I said, 'Why are you crying?' And she replied, 'Uncle Joe is dead.' As it happened, we had an Uncle Joe, so I replied, 'I didn't know he was ill.' 'You stupid boy,' she answered. 'Not *that* Uncle Joe, we're talking about Uncle Joe Stalin.' One can't be right every time.

While Dad would immerse himself in the practice, Mum would take a broader view of the world. She was a great storyteller, recounting the Celtic myths and tales of her own childhood and youth in Northern Ireland and as a liberal arts undergraduate in Dublin. She would read to us from books beyond our years, and quickly stamp on bigotry or petty bias. She was a force for liberalism (Uncle Joe notwithstanding), and Dad was a force for the traditional values of honesty, hard work and fair dealing.

Casting my mind back, I do just remember food parcels full of colourful sticky sweets – atomic pinks and hydrogen blue – from a great-aunt Gertie in New York. Gertie fell in with an obscure religious sect shortly afterwards and was never heard of again. Between her parcels and puberty, there lay long summer days, helping Dad break up lumps of chalk to mark out the grass tennis court with an ancient, wobbly machine, and hurling apples at anyone who ventured into the orchard intent on stealing them. Pimple the pony grazed there until she was despatched by a Mini on the Broad Hinton Road, and the house always had a dog or two, one of which was shot brilliantly, though not fatally, by Fergie with an air rifle from his bedroom window.

Always up for a dare, Fergie would lead Pimple on a halter, accompanied by Polly Smith, daughter of the town's undertaker, down into the town and along Regent Street, Swindon's premier shopping destination, until they reached Woolworths. Blithely sweeping in, Fergie would express surprise at being told to 'Get that horse out of here!' In a wounded tone, he would plead, 'But it only says "No dogs allowed" on the door.' Woolworths was not the only store to be treated to this entertainment.

My dog, a sweet spaniel cross pup called Pitch, died of distemper, which was a bit rich in a house full of vets. In an attempt to assuage my grief, a friend's mother, a Corgi fan, presented me with Ricky, a Carmarthenshire Corgi, and one with a deeply depressed personality. Sigh. A boy of that age would never be impressed with a *Corgi*. I was later able to palm it off onto my brother David.

Picnic expeditions were a popular way to spend summer Sundays, and the weir at Buscot afforded enough danger to make the outing worthwhile. With an elderly kayak on the roof of Mum's car, we would pitch up at the bank of a Thames backwater and five children would slide into the slippery water, holding onto the exposed roots of the riverside willows, just below the roaring weir, while Mum would sit on the bank, her eyes wildly flitting from child to child. Kayaks are not stable at the best of times, and rolling them over in order to encourage motherly shrieks of alarm was always worth the discomfort.

A goat appeared and for a time the fridge was full of goat's milk, destined to become cheese, but Dad, who did the milking, couldn't keep up and the nanny goat disappeared. The clatter of tiny feet could often be heard in the kitchen as yet another orphaned lamb spent a few days being bottle-fed by Annabelle. Stella, ever one for a drama, was witnessed one day as I came home with a pal, lying on her stomach in the hall, her hands and feet drumming the carpet. 'Lord French is dead, he is gone …' she howled. Alarmed, my friend enquired, 'Lord French?' 'Her guinea pig,' I explained. 'A black and tan number, named after the general commanding the British forces at the time of the Easter Rising in 1916.' He looked even more confused and we stepped over Stella and went on our way.

We went through a frantic period of budgie slaughter at one time. We boys would let the bird out of the cage in the kitchen and then compete to bring it down by throwing a tea towel onto its back in flight. These small birds are not designed to withstand that sort of treatment, and we sometimes got through a budgie a week. The main problem was not letting the girls know what had happened to Joey, so all replacement birds had to look identical to the deceased, which could sometimes be tricky.

Those of us with the stomach for such things might spend the day with Dad, moving from a Caesarean on a sheep to a difficult calving. There was always something going on involving birth, pain or death. It was never boring, and he was always encouraging and kindly, or so I reported in my wedding anniversary speech. It was a freewheeling sort of household, but early on the children had to attend Sunday School. Mum had been to see the Catholic bishop and, because we were the product of a mixed Catholic-Anglican marriage and were not attending the local Catholic primary school, the future of our souls was considered to be at risk. Sunday School held no pleasures for me; I was very bored with it all. I recall having an earnest debate with David, standing there in the rockery in front of the house. He claimed that if he hit me on the head with a claw hammer, I could reasonably be excused from Sunday School that week. He had the hammer in his hand, swinging it loosely by his side. Our negotiations got down to exactly where on the skull the blow would strike and how hard it would be, at which point I called the whole thing off.

The bishop's insistence, which my mother chiefly ignored, was because I was attending a non-Catholic pre-prep establishment known as the Poplars, housed in a Nissen hut in Wroughton's high street and run by Miss Chamberlain, her silver hair tied tightly in a bun behind her head, assisted by the broad-beamed Miss Hopkins. Amazingly, given our ages of five and seven respectively, Fergie and I on our own would mount an old-fashioned bus run by The Old Firm, which would take us off to school, where I met many boys and girls who would remain lifelong friends. Chief among them was Robert Humphreys, still my best mate sixty-five years later.

How I hated Robert. The hatred started when parents' day came, which saw my mother seated next to Robert's mother, Enid (who had given me the Corgi). It was a chance for the parents to see what the children had learned, for we each had to recite a piece. Enid sat contentedly, her hands folded under her ample bosom, a small smile of anticipated pleasure playing around her lips. Robert stood in front of the stage curtain, perfectly dressed with a small red clip-on bow tie, his red hair combed carefully in place, and his hands behind him as he delivered a polished performance of W.H. Auden's 'Night Mail'. He bowed to the thunderous applause. I was next up, with 'The Owl and the Pussycat', which I had not bothered to learn. Had it not been for Miss Chamberlain prompting from behind the curtain, I wouldn't have got beyond the first line. It was a very poor do, at the end of which my mother heard me murmur, 'Gosh, I'm really sweating now.' Dragging me by the hand to drive me home, she said, 'I have *never* been so embarrassed.'

Robert and I became firm friends, to such an extent that we embarked on a series of adventures that continue to this day. Perhaps one of the first was the time at the Poplars when we chased one of our classmates, Christine S., up a tree and, breaking off some twigs on the way, proceeded to poke her with them. We knew it was wrong but we didn't know why. A more regular jape for these nine- or ten-year-olds involved a tricycle that towed a four-wheeled cart, on the side of which was emblazoned 'Humphreys & Hewer, fruit farmers'. This ensemble belonged to Robert, which entitled him to pedal the trike, with me in the cart, clutching the side. Robert's particular skill was to pedal the trike with one of the rear wheels well off the ground, while towing the trailer with me as cargo.

Our favourite destination was the Old Town Gardens, a heavily wooded park with a network of narrow, hedged lanes connecting numerous little bowers and hidden nooks where young courting couples would cuddle, and it was through these trysting places that we would swoop, tyres humming on the smooth asphalt, Robert heeling over and pedalling furiously with me trying to stop the rig capsizing, both boys beyond excited with high cries as we slid at speed inches away from startled young lovers.

Meanwhile, David, nearly two years older than me, had already been sent, aged eight, to Douai Preparatory Boarding School, now long closed, somewhere in Berkshire. I so well remember him on the eve of his departure with his trunk packed, saying, 'I have put a small rubber band around my little toe and I will not remove it until I see you again.' I cautioned him, saying, 'I do not think this is a good idea. I have seen Dad put rubber bands around lambs' tails and the tail eventually falls off.' In many ways, his departure was the beginning of the fragmentation of our child world at The Grange. Before long, we were all scattered to different schools.

It was now time for Fergie and me to go as day boys to prep school, a small establishment called Bentham House out in the country north of Swindon. The headmaster was Mr Maltby, an Oxford man, and it was the tradition that the whole school would support Oxford in the boat race, it being the nearer of the two universities. My friend John Harding decided he would support Cambridge, and was poked in the ribs by various boys for doing so. A special assembly was called and Mr Maltby addressed the school. Having beside him some parents who had come to see whether Bentham House was appropriate for their boy, Mr Maltby explained why a special assembly had been called. 'It has come to my notice,' he intoned darkly, 'that John Harding has been the subject of bullying for supporting Cambridge in the boat race. This is a very serious offence, and I would like those boys guilty of bullying Harding to raise their hands.'

Nobody stirred. John Harding was one of my best friends and I had never bullied him, but I thought it only polite and helpful that I should raise my hand, so I did, and this started the bidding, although at the end only about four boys had pleaded guilty. It was at this point that the affair took on a more sinister tone, for Mr Maltby produced from behind his back a cane. 'I had intended to beat the guilty boys,' he said. 'But the presence of our visitors denies me that satisfaction. However, I want each boy now to step forward and to shake John Harding by the hand and apologise.' And so we did. To plead guilty to a crime I hadn't committed and under no duress suggests that I am either very stupid or always willing to help.

Some of these episodes from my childhood I described in my speech: three boys and two girls running circles around their parents, an easy-going type of home, and one which became a magnet for our friends during the holidays. Indeed, the kitchen became a sort of feeding station and communications HQ for other kids seeking to escape their more restrictive homes.

The speech went on to praise my mother – the central figure of our early life. Turning to her, I spoke of her 'open-mindedness, humour, charity and intelligence and hospitality'. Then I moved on to my father, praising his 'realism and strong work ethic', the 'perfect counterbalance to my mother', and how together 'they never ceased to be totally supportive despite us testing them to the limits'.

Bizarrely, I now realise, I chose to end with the famous stanza from Philip Larkin's 'This Be The Verse':

> They fuck you up, your mum and dad.
> They may not mean to, but they do.
> They fill you with the faults they had
> And add some extra, just for you.

Yes, but, I added, we their children were happy to inherit our parents' faults if we could also claim to have just some of their qualities. I cringe slightly at the flattery now – and the slightly ambiguous context in which it was couched – but, of course, a speech delivered on a wedding anniversary, with the subjects present, can never tell the full truth. Now, nearly thirty years later, with them long gone, the tendency to idealise our childhood gives way to some of the shadows that fell over it.

My parents' marriage was not made in heaven. My father, burdened by the expense of a large family, was not often, as I claimed in my speech, 'encouraging and kindly'. Rather, he seemed always to be bored or disappointed by his children, and controlling of his wife, my educated and intelligent mother who was torn from the heart of a capital city (Dublin) and dumped in Swindon into the company of grassland farmers who bored her to death with their talk of heifers and horses.

For us children – or at least for me – this sense of my mother's unhappiness was always vaguely present, and her lack of connection with my father never clearer than in the poem she wrote, entitled 'Going Solo', the opening line of which reads: 'I'm never so alone as when I'm with you'. I found it among her papers after her death.

C

Countdown

Seven years ... and counting

The phone rang. It was Tom Mclaughlin, managing director of JLA, the country's largest speaker agency, which had booked me over the last five years and sent me tramping around the country on the surprisingly lucrative after-dinner circuit.

'*Countdown* have been on the phone, and want to know whether you'd be interested in presenting the show.'

'What do you think?' I asked.

'Well,' he replied, 'it's been running since 1982, very well established, probably Britain's best-known afternoon quiz show, and I think you might like it because *The Apprentice*, or your place in it, will not go on forever.'

'I've never watched the show,' I said. 'Let me have a look and I'll come back to you.'

I had never seen *Countdown* because my chances of watching afternoon television over the last thirty years since it had first gone on air had been absolutely zero. I needed to find out what *Countdown* was all about, so I tuned in that afternoon and asked around and came to the firm conclusion there would be a lot of experienced presenters going for this job, but I might as well throw my hat in the ring. It would be good experience but my chances were, I felt, minimal. To my surprise, a few weeks later, I found myself sitting in the studio gallery at the old Granada studios in Quay Street, Manchester, watching Jeff Stelling silkily present *Countdown* in front of a live audience, with Susie Dent in Dictionary Corner and Rachel Riley handling the numbers and letters board.

I sat at the back of the gallery, as Damian Eadie, the producer, and Derek Hallworth, the director, and all the rest of the production team (there are enough of them to fill the cast of *Gone with the Wind*) steered the mighty *Countdown* ship to the end of yet another recording. Having spent an hour or so in the darkness of the gallery, Damian turned to me and said, 'Do you want a go?' I thought it rude to decline, and next thing I knew I was on the floor of the studio being mic'd up by Denise, who to this day is forever poking her hand down my back, clipping mics to my lapel and applying Vaseline to my right ear before inserting an earpiece. Jay, the floor manager, gave me some words of advice (now forgotten), and finally Denise plugged what felt like an onion in my right ear – the famous earpiece.

Damian came through loud and clear, gave me a few curt instructions, the director Derek took over and told me not to worry, Cindy came on the line and told me she would count me down and then the sound engineer and lighting supervisor were on the line checking on my comfort level and thus, with all these voices dancing around in my head, off we went. If Jeff Stelling was a presenter as smooth as polished marble, then I was a heap of rubble by comparison. After ten minutes of falling masonry, it was called to a halt. I thanked Susie and Rachel and staggered out of the studio.

Three minutes later I was in a taxi on my way to Piccadilly station and home to Rectory Farm, where I gave Catherine a silent shake of the head. I thought no more about it, until, a couple of weeks later, the executive producer, Peter Gwyn, called me to ask how I felt it had all gone. I told him I thought it had been a shocking experience and that I was clearly not cut out for such a role. 'Oh, come on,' he said. 'It wasn't that bad. In fact, we'd like to pursue it a little more. I wonder whether you would agree to setting aside a day, and I will bring the team down to a London studio together with an experienced presenter trainer, and we'll see whether we can't knock off some of those rough edges.'

And that's exactly what happened, and the abiding memory and the best piece of advice that I was given is, when presented with a *Countdown* script, do not read it word for word – unless you have an autocue (which we don't) – but just get the general gist and do it in your own words. Another test, which I passed surprisingly easily, was finishing a piece on time – the director in one's earpiece counts you down so that you hit the pips, as they say in news studios.

A few weeks passed, and the executive producer called again to say that they were very happy and would like to offer me a contract. I referred him back to Tom Mclaughlin who would handle the negotiations. Tom was soon in touch and laid out the elements of the deal. 'This is a good gig,' he said. 'It involves 225 shows a year, with five shows recorded per day in three-day blocks, and I have managed to increase their original offer considerably and I think you should take it.'

'But I'm already doing *The Apprentice*, Tom, so I'm committed to an eight-week shoot and all the other random days and events together with all the after-dinner talks that you conjure up for me, and corporate endorsements, not to mention the Nick 'n' Margaret documentaries, so I've got to be a bit careful.'

'Make hay while the sun shines,' he trilled.

'Let me think about it.'

I was in my dressing room on *The Apprentice* set, being rouged up by Mandy the makeup artist, when Alan strolled in, and I told him I'd been offered the job of presenting *Countdown*. Always one to get to the point, he said, 'What's that?' I gave him an outline. 'How much?' he said. I told him. 'Do it,' was his rapid response as he strolled out again. Suddenly, at the age of sixty-eight, I found myself heavily committed but, to put it bluntly, rather surprised at the level of income and flattered to have been asked to take the helm of the quiz show that can boast of more series than any other, as confirmed in the *Guinness Book of World Records*.

People are always surprised to learn that *Countdown* is an adaptation of the French game show *Des Chiffres et des Lettres*, which has been running for more than fifty years. The creator was Armand Jammot, but the show was brought to these shores by Marcel Stellman, a Belgian living in France during the war who was interned in a camp in the south. A fluent English speaker (his mother was Scottish) and a clever boy, aged sixteen he appointed himself camp interpreter when it was liberated by British troops commanded by Prince Aly Khan, who in civvies was a great playboy, the eldest son of HH the Aga Khan and the father of the current Aga Khan (*see* K: AGA KHAN).

By the early 1980s, Marcel was working in the UK as a senior executive at Decca/Polygram, mixing with the Rolling Stones and the Moody Blues and writing songs for Charles Aznavour and Max Bygraves. He and his wife Jeannie found themselves watching *Des Chiffres et des Lettres* while in Paris on business, and Marcel had one of those lightbulb moments. Before long he was standing in the office of Armand, at the time one of the most powerful men in the French television industry, explaining that his creation would be popular in Britain, and asking how much Armand wanted for the English language rights. 'I'll give you six months to sell the show. If you do, then we'll talk money,' Armand said. It was a short meeting, and the rest is history: Marcel acquired the rights and sold them first to Yorkshire Television, then to ITV, with the show always being broadcast on Channel 4.

For those who've been in a medically induced coma for the last thirty-six years and haven't seen the show, then tune in to Channel 4 any weekday afternoon to find out what it's all about. It's basically live Scrabble with a teapot as a prize. This is, I think, what makes it so charming: there are no money prizes, no free holidays, no sets of stainless-steel saucepans to be won, just a dictionary and a teapot and the glory of being a *Countdown* winner. Indeed, the most frequent cry from a winning contestant is, 'I've got my teapot, that's all I came for.' I was recently asked to acquire a teapot for a friend, who was somewhat irritated to learn that this was absolutely out of the question, as supplies were held in a locked room and carefully audited. Even I don't have one, nor does Susie or Rachel.

I'd like to think *Countdown* is a part of that English tradition where playing is more important than carrying off sacks of gold, much like *Mastermind* or *University Challenge*, both programmes without any attached hysteria or flashes and bangs. On the one occasion when the *Countdown* production crew steered away from this simple format by introducing fake snow, on a Christmas special, the audience and presenters all ended up soaking wet when the snow machine had a coughing fit. And that was that. The secret is, just keep it simple.

People often say that I look very relaxed on screen, which surprises me as in truth I don't feel very confident. Half the time I think, I'm terrible at this, and the other half of the time I'm saying to myself, I'm just about getting away with it. In 2017, following news that Channel 4 wanted to increase the number of shows from 225 to 260 a year and furthermore wanted me to sign a two-year deal, I called in on Jay Hunt, then the de facto boss, to thank her for Channel 4's continued support. 'Don't thank us,' she said. 'We're thanking you and the whole *Countdown* team. We're very happy with the show.' I thanked her again and she quietly said, 'Learn to take a compliment.' I've known Jay since she was controller of BBC1 and therefore in charge of *The Apprentice*. She has a fearsome reputation but somehow has always been kind to me.

I normally arrive in Salford's Media City, where the show is now recorded, the evening before the first day of recording, and I spend the journey in the car marking up my scripts and familiarising myself with the biographies of the Dictionary Corner guests, together with thumbnail sketches of the anecdotes they are due to deliver over the following three days. Remembering the advice I was given on that initial training session six years ago, I try to flesh out the intro scripts, written by assistant producer David Smith, so that I can put in some personal anecdotes.

Most of the BBC newsreaders traipse over from their nearby studio to our studio once a year as Dictionary Corner guests, and they're always amazed that I'm not working from an autocue, and I must admit that an autocue would save me a lot of stress, but budgets are budgets and, it's also claimed, the producers want a slightly haphazard and spontaneous approach. Sometimes, as I sort of wander off-piste, I see Rachel's eyes widening in dread anticipation of what I might say next. In truth, it's anybody's guess because I often don't know myself where I'm heading. In the very early days, I once worked out the word CONIFERS on the board – a creditable score of eight – and, with the clock still ticking, I was so excited I shouted it out. When the clock had finished its sweep, and with the rebuke of the director ringing in my earpiece, I asked each competitor for their word, and was not surprised to find that each had also chosen the word 'conifers'. To my huge embarrassment, we had to do it all over again.

Susie, on the other hand, is the mistress of self-control, and I never cease to be amazed at her professionalism and extraordinary learning as she delivers, over each three-day block of fifteen programmes, fifteen perfectly crafted and executed little essays on her chosen theme – an exceptional talent. And Rachel, an Oxford maths graduate, blazes her way through the most difficult mathematical challenges without a moment's hesitation.

The day starts when I leave the hotel at 9:30 in the morning and head for the studio, into the Dock 10 building at Media City, lift to the first floor and, with my own key fob, I let myself into the *Countdown* corridor. Dropping my stuff off in my rather luxurious dressing room, I head off to the makeup room where we all mill about before and after each show (we record five episodes a day, so it's necessary, after every game, to get a fresh set of clothes to differentiate Monday from Tuesday, etc). Three makeup artists – Lauren, Jessica and Jeanette – are at their stations in front of the mirrors, spray guns at the ready.

Bending over the ironing board is to be found the quietly spoken and quite acerbic Lee Josephs, the wardrobe master and talented actor whom I refer to as Mr Sticky because when he approaches me in the studio with one of those sticky rollers to pick up an errant hair or a piece of fluff from my jacket, I remonstrate with him that all he is doing is rolling sticky bits all over my jacket, which then act as a magnet for any fluff that happens to be floating around the studio. He takes no notice. Lee's dark and brilliant play, *Dead Ground*, detailing the lives of Moors murderers Ian Brady and Myra Hindley, was staged at a pub theatre in Salford, and transfixed the audience. A talented fellow indeed.

Rootling around in the makeup-room biscuit box is Dudley Doolittle, *Countdown*'s warm-up man, who has delighted the studio audience and the *Countdown* team for years. A well-known stand-up comedian and singer in his own right and former warm-up man for the great David Frost, Dudley is the warmest of characters, one of the great Northern comics and a very good tease. In comes Yvonne, who's in charge of looking after the audience on site. Dave, the assistant producer and scriptwriter, trails off to drag another Dictionary Corner guest in – some of whom tend to get nervous by this time.

Jo Lewis and Sarah Woolley, the hugely competent production managers, are at their computers: apart from handling all the important stuff, they give us our daily post, and ask us to sign the *Countdown* photo cards with our pictures on. Rachel and Susie get a lot of mail from young bloods, and I occasionally find myself opening what might be considered fan mail. Two such items caused me to hold my breath, the first being a pair of red nylon mesh knickers of what I believe are known as the crotchless variety, from a woman in Swindon, my home town. Another envelope gave me something of a chill, for it was a congratulations card which had been packed with confetti and on which had been written many, many times, 'Marry me, marry me, marry me,' together with a phone number. This had all the hallmarks of a stalker, and I kept it for a couple of years lest the police were called.

Laura the runner looks after me so well and deftly slides a cup of latte into my ever-outreached hand. Sarah, who also manages the audience, anxiously wonders if too many will turn up for the first show of the day. Damian Eadie, a one-time *Countdown* champion who has produced the show for many years, saunters in looking every inch the biker/rocker. What makes him exceptional is that, for me and Susie and the guests, he can give some helpful advice down our earpieces on words to be found on the board. But what makes him a special genius is that he can, as soon as the letters appear, spill out three or four or five words that each relate to the other. I remain flabbergasted as he pushes down my earpiece the words that lie within that jumble on the board. Not only that, but his wit and very near-the-bone humour keep us amused day after day. He's a very singular character, much loved by all of us and the backbone of the show. No compliment escapes a vicious response.

Damian sits in the gallery next to Derek, the director and disciplinarian of the whole set-up, who barks in a gentle type of way that I've got to hurry up, we all want to go home, there are trains to catch and we're running late. He keeps the show rolling at the right speed. Derek, already in the gallery, links to Laura for the five-minute call and there's a flurry of activity and then we're all in the lift to the studio. Past Tony and Jonny, our studio security men, and into the studio where Dudley is already warming up the audience. A cheery hello to Nurse

Jayne (who checks the wellbeing of the audience and, I like to think, of me too), to the crew in charge of handling the set, to the sound engineers, to the scorers with their bank of computers, to the six cameramen and women who are facing a long day ahead of them, a quick chat with Dudley and the audience, and Jay the floor manager cries, 'Cameras on cans, please!', which is the signal to get to my chair and get wired for sound by Denise, with whom I have a running gag – namely, every time she plunges her hand down my back or under my jacket, I give her a slap on the wrist. It has now become a studio ritual. We have a spill check, which means that the studio is called to silence while Damian speaks to me, Susie and Rachel, and then the floor manager checks that he cannot be heard by the contestants. Derek asks if I'm ready, the *Countdown* intro music rolls, the spinning logo appears on my monitor, Derek murmurs 'action', and I'm on with the opening script.

So, there we all are in Dock 10, plunged into the parallel universe that is a television studio with no natural light – a kind of crepuscular half-world in which, beyond the painfully bright key lights which Taras, the lighting director, deliberately and sadistically insists on pointing straight at me, I can see nothing of the audience that lurks in the darkness beyond.

Most of the Dictionary Corner guests come because they love *Countdown*, none more so than Jo Brand and Gyles Brandreth, who've been in Dictionary Corner since almost the beginning of time. Nothing fazes performers like this, but there are those who come and, while acting in a nonchalant manner, are unable to disguise their nerves as they enter the studio, for there is no place to hide for those who airily wave away an earpiece. It always amuses me to see that same celeb call for an earpiece two games later and be attached to Damian's lifeline.

For me, the success of a show, or certainly the enjoyment, depends on the chemistry I have with the Dictionary Corner guest. That certainly applies to Jo and Gyles, but add to them celebrities like Janet Street-Porter, the remarkable wildlife experts Chris Packham and Steve Backshall, Jimmy Osmond, the hilarious Rufus Hound, Gloria Hunniford, Hugh Dennis, Dr Phil Hammond, Adam Henson, Dan Walker, Michael Whitehall, Jon Culshaw, Richard Madeley, Tim Rice and the twinkling eyes of Louise Minchin, to name just a few.

A recent guest, the great Barry McGuigan, proved to be delightful. It gave me great pleasure to tell him that my mother, who herself was born in Northern Ireland, adored Barry and when watching him fight on television, used to plead, 'Don't you hurt my Barry!' A more unlikely fight fan would be hard to find, but strangely she loved boxing and fell into a long and friendly correspondence with the commentator Harry Carpenter. I was surprised to be told by my sister Annabelle recently that Mum was a daily *Countdown* viewer, slipping away to the television room with a cup of tea, pad and pencil and a cigarette to watch Richard Whiteley. Princess Margaret also revealed in an interview that her sister, the Queen, was a keen *Countdown* viewer, although she failed to say whether HMQ played along.

The pressure on the contestants is intense, for though they've all passed an audition to test their ability in the game and they all play at home (no doubt brilliantly), once they enter the arena, with the big clock behind them and the bright lights in front and a live audience and all the other elements of a television studio, any confidence or overconfidence soon evaporates, particularly for those who are now facing a player who has already accumulated five wins.

My greatest fear, yet to be realised, is for the contestant who hasn't managed to get on the scoreboard while his or her competitor is racking up a massive score. He/she stands at zero, the competitor stands at 55, and I pray that the underdog will score at least something before the final round. He/she starts to panic, I start to panic, praying that the competitor in the lead will just ease off the throttle a little bit to give the other person a chance, but of course this is a very competitive situation. I've yet to preside over a game when one player stays on zero, and I hope that situation never occurs.

While I can have fun with the celebrities sitting next to Susie, I like to gain some rapport with the contestants, not always an easy task given the stress they must be under. There are exceptions, contestants who can relax and enjoy the experience, notably, in recent times, the famous Moose, an ex-copper who charmed us all; and I'll never forget Liam Moloney from Galway who went home to a hero's welcome and free pints of the black stuff for evermore after a successful *Countdown* run.

Fifteen programmes are recorded over each three-day slot, so that's three weeks' worth of output. It's an exhausting schedule, and by the end of it I'm thrown semi-conscious into the back of the car to return to Rectory Farm, where Catherine awaits with the words, 'You must be *sick* with exhaustion. There's duck for dinner.'

Until the next time.

D

Determination

Finding it

By the late summer of 1962, after seven years at the Irish Jesuit boarding school, Clongowes (*see* J: JESUITS), I had my Leaving Certificate and university matriculation certificates neatly rolled up in my pocket, and so was eligible for a place at either University College Dublin or Trinity College. Gone, happily, were the days when Catholic students were forbidden to enter Trinity, though the Jesuits at Clongowes still bristled at any of their boys heading in that direction.

I had gained a place to study law, hopefully at Trinity, where my older brother David had started to read medicine, but who by this time had experienced something of an upset and had returned home to Wiltshire. His early recall prompted my father to consider whether it was wise to propel his second son off to the fun and games that Dublin had to offer in such abundance. Also, I think that having educated two boys privately, with three younger children still away at school, the prospect now of starting them off at university was perhaps a bit too expensive for him. In appearance, he was quite well-to-do – he was senior partner in a successful and modern large animal veterinary practice, which his father had started on returning from the First World War; there was a biggish house with no mortgage, which Grandfather had bought in the thirties, and the pre-war comforts including a full-time gardener and Grandfather's old groom, but there never seemed to be any surplus money, so the thought of ploughing into the costs of a university education in a different country without the grants and student loans of today must surely have weighed on Dad's mind.

One way around this was to get me articled to a local solicitor, for in those days one could take either a law degree with two years' training afterwards, or a five-year articled clerkship. This proposal was a disappointing development. I fretted at not being at university in Dublin, where all my pals were. I'd been in Ireland for the best part of seven years, that was where my life was, and I didn't really have many friends at home anymore. But in those days, you did what you were told, so off I went to be articled to one of the two big firms in Swindon – Lemon, Humphreys and Parker – the senior partner of which was Sidney George Gordon Humphreys, disrespectfully known as 'Sid', a friend of the family and a rather imposing, some would say fearsome, figure.

Unfortunately, they hadn't had an articled clerk for years, and I found myself passed on to one of the junior partners in the firm as a kind of office boy on a salary of £5 a week. There was very little training, so I pottered about the office, housed in those days in two Edwardian red-brick townhouses in Regent Circus, the business hub in downtown Swindon, waiting for the next little task to be handed to me. But it wasn't all boring boundary disputes and County Court judgments, for there were some interesting projects where I proved myself to be really quite mature for my age.

The firm had been appointed to represent a middle-aged man on remand at Bristol's Horfield prison, on a charge of bigamy. With the trial looming, it was felt appropriate to send me, a nineteen-year-old articled clerk, to visit him with the aim of preparing a brief for counsel. Horfield was the quintessentially Victorian penal heap: noisy, smelly and painted in a drab green. I was ushered into an interview room to meet our client and sat opposite him, a steel table between us. I produced a pad and a pen and asked him to tell me of his troubles. All these years later, I can still recall him sizing me up, and the look in his eye told me that I was unlikely to be a problem.

Off he went, regaling me with tales of his conquests and the extraordinary effect he exercised over women. As a decorator and painter, he roamed the housing estates of the town, cutting through the weakening protests of legions of housewives, or so he would have me believe. As I scribbled away, his stories became more elaborate and tragic, as he explained that he was unable to resist the entreaties of his many lovers until, inevitably, he started to marry quite a lot of them in quick succession. On and on he went, the time slid by until, unexpectedly, he started to cry, imploring me to understand how difficult his life had been and now here he was, banged up in Horfield, facing the prospect of a lengthy spell without the benefits of female company. He eyed me carefully. 'Do you know how many times I masturbate every day?' he asked. I told him I didn't wish to hazard a guess on that subject and so he told me that, on average, it was eighteen times, but perhaps more on the weekends, when he had more time to devote himself to himself, so to speak. I looked at my watch and was surprised to discover that I had been taking notes for nearly two hours.

I thanked him for providing such a wealth of information for his statement, and then, with a dramatic flourish, I took my notebook, tore it in half and threw it on the floor and invited him to start again, but this time with a true and accurate account of his life. He crumbled before my eyes and then, in quiet tones, he recounted a rather sad and shabby life and one that just might soften the heart of a judge when offered in mitigation.

I returned to Regent Circus, crafted the statement for counsel and passed it to Chris Sheward, the young partner handling the case. An amusing and portly little man, often affecting a slightly-too-small trilby, he berated me for striking a rather too confident tone to counsel in the statement. 'They are at the Bar!' he seemed to be saying. 'And we are just lowly country solicitors.' I can't remember what became of my bigamist, but I'd like to think that he did not have to keep up his masturbating rate for too long.

It was shortly after my little sortie to Bristol that I ran into a group of top silks at the Winchester assizes. Our client, a bank manager, was a defendant in a fraud case. I seem to recall that he was in cahoots with a number of used-car dealers and between them they were fleecing the bank. The partner in charge was Micky Mather, a kindly, boozy, ruddy-faced solicitor who liked to get home on time. We drove down to Winchester on the opening day of the trial and, from then on, he stayed in the office and I would troop down to Winchester each day and report on the day's proceedings each evening.

There were a number of defendants, each represented by a QC and a junior, and over the course of the trial I was adopted as a sort of mascot by this clutch of top silks, each of whom would tell the group over the lunch break of their great trial successes, glancing at me from time to time to measure how impressed I was. I was far more impressed by the rank of sleek Bentleys parked outside the assize courthouse. Each evening they would sweep off, one after the other, scattering the good citizens of Winchester as they headed to the London road and drinks before dinner in Mayfair.

I recall that our client was represented by an eminent QC, Edgar Fay, who put up a good defence, but the jury was not swayed and our man went down. Unfortunately, Micky Mather had decided to stay at the office that day and the bank manager's family had also failed to show and so it fell to me to take possession of our now-incarcerated client's bag and head back to Swindon to break the bad news to them.

I still recall how nervous I was, standing in the darkened porch of a modest terraced house in Avenue Road, Swindon, as I rang the bell. The door swung open, and crowded in the doorway I saw the family of wife and teenage children, their eyes wide with expectation, but narrowing quickly into slits of fury as they spotted Dad's bag and no Dad. I was dragged into the front room and they sat around me, demanding an explanation, their anger ill-disguised and mounting. After two hours, I had managed to talk them down and they invited me to stay for supper.

The time came for me to go to law school to take the inter-mediates, so I was despatched to the brand-new School of Law in Bristol with my good friend, fellow Swindonian and fellow articled clerk at the rival firm Townsends, Michael Kellas. I'm sorry to say that the Bristol experience was a major farce: nobody had a clue what was going on, including the professors.

Somehow, I managed to pass nearly every exam – contract, tort, criminal law, even the English legal system – but was completely foxed by Cheshire and Fifoot's law of property, elements of which I found complicated because it involved things like 'perpetuities'. Nowadays they don't exist because all land is registered, but in the early sixties you still had to pore through all the documents to see if the title was sound: was it the 'fee simple'? Or a fee something else? Or was there hiding, deep in the sub-clauses, a restrictive covenant? So, I failed, because a pass in all the subjects at the same time was the requirement. Michael failed at Bristol too, though he went on to become a partner at Clifford Chance, one of the great City firms. In fact, I'm not sure anybody got through at Bristol in that, its first year.

It was then decided that I should, the following term, go to the long-established Guildford law school with another friend articled in Swindon, Neil Davidson. There, Neil, life and soul of the party, shared a house and he taught me to play snooker and poker, drink beer and chase girls, and we both did exactly the same thing again, we flunked the intermediates by failing on one paper. At which point there was a general feeling that I wasn't enjoying the law and the Law Society wasn't enjoying me, and what was meant to be a five-year apprenticeship ended in something of a whimper after only three years.

Now what was I going to do? I was twenty-one, and had no idea. I'd been educated in another country, in a very rigidly structured environment, and I didn't really know how to cope with the lack of structure when I got back to England. I remember my father muttering something like, 'Well, you're going to have to find your own thing to do.' I packed a bag. He took me to the station, gave me a fiver and waved me off on a train to London. From that moment, I became rather determined about my future.

I hurried to the flat that some friends of mine from home were sharing, opposite Olympia, and moved in with them until I could establish my own base. The next day, I took myself off to the employment agency Manpower, in nearby Hammersmith, and sat there in the waiting room with all the other people, all sorts of ages and backgrounds, and a chap appeared waving a piece of paper and asked if anybody could drive a lorry. I put my hand up and said I could (I'd never driven a lorry). He gave me the piece of paper, which had an address on it, and when I got there I was given the keys to a lorry which I then drove around the West End of London delivering great bales of fabric to the rag trade. This was my introduction to determination. I never stopped for lunch, and always finished my run earlier than the other drivers because they were all sitting on park benches drinking coffee and studying pornography.

After a few weeks of this, I heard tell of something called public relations, which I understood to be an altruistic sort of occupation whereby you would explain to people, such as the workforce, why the management was actually firing half of them, and it was all very reasonable and if we could just explain it properly they would then readily accept solid management reasons for laying off everybody, or not paying them, or going bust. I liked the idea that people were reasonable and would accept what I had to say, so I did a bit of research and discovered there was something called the Institute of Public Relations, and I went to see them and found out they had a magazine, so I put in a little advertisement: 'KEEN YOUNG MAN SEEKS TRAINEESHIP'.

In those days, PR in Britain was in its infancy and was slightly suspect, even more so than today. When I told my father I was thinking about PR as a career, he gave the impression that I was contemplating a career in burglary. He was very old school, a countryman (for a time he even wandered about in plus-fours) who believed in the old professions and remained snooty about the fact I hadn't qualified in anything. Looking back, I realise that if I had passed my law exams I probably would've ended up being a solicitor in Swindon – a worthy enough ambition, I dare say, but one that would've deprived me of what turned out to be a more amusing and, frankly, remunerative career.

Shortly after I had placed the ad, Michael Joyce – blessed be his name – invited me to an interview. His company, Michael Joyce Consultants (MJC), was in the old Grand Buildings, the first Grand Hotel in London, curving from Northumberland Avenue into Trafalgar Square and then on into the Strand. His offices were on the third floor and looked straight out over the square and the view from here had featured in that great movie, *The Spy Who Came in from the Cold*, starring Richard Burton.

Michael was a charming, gentle man, ex-military, who had somehow stumbled into PR and was very happy to let other people do the work as long as he could take the applause (which was something he readily admitted). He also had a certain lucky streak: he once bought a raffle ticket from the Variety Club and won a Cherokee Sundowner light aircraft. I got the job, and joined his small company, maybe eight of us. I realised that the way to get on there was to make myself really useful. Michael would go to the theatre a lot, and he would often come back very late and find me still in the office, sometimes asleep at my desk. I was keen to make an impression and to get on after the disappointment of failing law school. I worked really long hours. I had a very determined point of view, which was that by the age of thirty, I'd be a shareholder, indeed a parity shareholder in whichever company I toiled, and therefore nobody would be able to fire me. I would be master of my own destiny.

After a couple of years, and still learning, I suggested in a mild voice to Michael that it would be very nice to get some shares. He prevaricated – charmingly – so I decided the only way to achieve my goal was to leave, in the fervent hope that he would come and hook me back when he realised his mistake. Off I went and joined a company called Rea PR, owned by a small, fat, wily man called Bill Rea, operating out of the top floor of a building in Panton Street, near Leicester Square. And I did the same thing at Rea, working long, long hours for Mr Rea and his number two, Gerry Knight, the latter a large-boned, gruff Yorkshireman, lacking Michael's metro-sophistication, but effective in a hard-working, thin-on-charm, honest if uncreative sort of way.

This was the late sixties, and wherever the counter-culture was, it wasn't in Rea PR, or in the boardrooms of any of our clients, who tended to run their businesses in a rather high-handed way. Most business leaders at this time were men, and many of them were ex-military – veterans of one, if not two, world wars. (One of Michael Joyce's big clients was Securicor, which was run by Keith Erskine, a dreadful bully who on more than one occasion took great pleasure in making me feel like a totally idiotic subaltern. He'd fought with General Alexander in Italy, and the Securicor board was full of ex-military and ex-policemen: Sir Freddy Delve, head of the London Fire Brigade during the Blitz, Sir Richard Jackson who was head of Interpol, Sir Philip Margetson of the Met, and so on. They talked as if they were in a black and white war film, and would say things like, 'Ah, yes, Colonel Paine, have you got a moment, please? Major Peat, if you please.')

Oddly enough, Gerry Knight was converted by a member of staff to the Bahá'í Faith, and not long afterwards he found himself in the United Nations in New York as a sort of alternative representative of the Bahá'í Faith – whose beliefs, by the way, include never lying, which of course suits the PR profession very well.

Rea PR's office was in a building with a concierge, and when he did the rounds in the evening and locked up, I would frequently hide in a cupboard and wait until he'd gone so I could go back to my desk and finish what I was doing. We were on the top floor, so the only way out at this point was to pull up a sash window, climb out, and lower myself onto the roof of the Odeon cinema next door, on which was painted a yellow road running all the way across Leicester Square. I would follow the yellow brick road and then clamber down some steep steps which ended with a set of fire exit doors. Pushing open the crash bars, I'd find myself on the street with the rather dishevelled remnants of Leicester Square's nightlife.

I didn't think anything of this rather unusual way of leaving the office. The point was I had finished the work. Brighter people might have said, Sod it, I'll deal with that tomorrow; or they might have done it quicker. But I was dogged – I knew the taste of failure, and I didn't like it. The enduring problem was that I never stopped to eat. Sometimes my first and only meal would be at ten o'clock at night. I was smoking heavily and drinking gallons of coffee, so for years I had terrible migraines. I was also rather diffident and lacking in confidence, maybe born of the fact that I had failed in my first choice of law, and Dad's unconcealed disappointment in me. I wasn't a great schmoozer like Bill Rea, who spent most afternoons in some dark Soho drinking club with his journalist pals, or the more elegant Michael, but what I lacked in confidence I made up for in creativity. I was good with ideas.

I can't remember exactly what happened – I think the company lost an important client – but after a couple of years at Rea PR I was 'let go'. It was all very nicely done, but effectively I'd been made redundant. However, I'd stayed in touch with Michael, and had secretly been engineering a return to his company. I'd told him that I was perfectly happy where I was and that things were going well, but that I missed the good old days at MJC, though of course I could only come back if there was a strict understanding about shareholding. This time, he agreed. I think the deal was that I would have 25 per cent initially, and later, parity. Michael was faithful to his word, and before I was thirty I had a 50 per cent share in the company. Later, I bought him out completely by enabling him to put all the profits of the company into his pension scheme. We agreed that in return for the balance of shares I would not take any dividends over a number of years, so he could fatten up his pension.

Determination seemed to be paying off. It also got me out of a few scrapes (*see* F: FRIGHTS), though not always elegantly. For example, MJC was appointed to handle the publicity for a cultural exhibition of the government of Oman, which was being held somewhere on the South Bank. It was, necessarily, quite a thin exhibition – I remember there were a couple of dhows, a few scale models of camels, some gold bangles and that was about it. I explained to the client that I was unfamiliar with the Middle Eastern press and its representatives in London, but I'd be very happy to draw up a list from various sources, though I'd need them to check it. I sent them the list and they approved it, and the gilt invitations were mailed out. At this point, some bright spark in the Oman Embassy belatedly spotted there was an Israeli newspaper on the list. Huge consternation, and it was no good me reminding them that they had signed off on the list, because by now the horse had bolted. 'This is an absolute disaster. We shall have to call the whole thing off, and there *will* be consequences,' they said ominously, 'unless you cancel and retrieve the invitation to this Israeli paper.'

The paper in question had a one-room office for its London correspondent in a stone corridor of a very old building in Carmelite Street, just off Fleet Street. But the correspondent worked on Middle Eastern time, so he only went into the office at about ten o'clock at night. Night after night I would tramp down to Carmelite Street, and somehow I'd get into the building, up to the third floor, along the unlit stone corridor to Room 23, only to find that, once again, nobody was in. Meanwhile, I'm being asked if I've managed to secure the return of the invitation, and I keep saying, 'No, but I'm going back there tonight.' I didn't want to do anything on the phone because it's always better to deal with these situations face to face. Eventually, I trailed off to Carmelite Street and crept down the dark stone corridor for the umpteenth time, but on this occasion I noticed a sliver of light under the door to Room 23. I knocked. 'Yes?' I opened the door, gingerly, to reveal a figure behind a desk, lit only by an Anglepoise lamp and surrounded by untidy heaps of paper.

'Yes?' he repeated. 'Who are you?'

'I'm so sorry to trouble you,' I answered. 'My name is Nick Hewer, and you will have received from my office an invitation from the government of Oman for a cultural exhibition which opens shortly ...'

'Yes, yes,' he interrupted. 'We were *so* delighted and surprised to receive it. My editors have agreed it must signal some kind of thawing of relations and have encouraged my attendance, so I'm greatly looking forward to it.'

'Unfortunately,' I squeaked, 'I have made a most terrible error. I shouldn't have sent it to you.'

'Oh. So, there is no move to improve relations between the government of Oman and the sovereign state of Israel?'

'Well, I'm not sure about that; all I know is they don't want you to come. It's very embarrassing for me as it's all my fault.'

A long pause.

'All right, all right,' he replied with a forced smile. 'Well, thank you for coming. I recognise how awkward it must have been for you. It's disappointing, but there we are.'

'Er, there's one further thing.'

'What's that?'

'I'm afraid they really would like the invitation back,' I muttered.

The smile had gone, as had the air in the room. I had to sit there, squirming, as, after a long hard stare, he rifled through his wire filing basket. He pulled it out and gave it back to me. I felt utterly ashamed. My doggedness and determination achieved a result, but at a price.

By this time, I was living in a small flat in York Buildings, just off the Strand, with two friends from Swindon, Robert Humphreys and Mike Roworth. I had always liked cars and was very envious of Mike's long-wheelbase, Hooper-bodied Daimler monster limousine, complete with glass partition so that the chauffeur couldn't earwig. One evening from those days is etched on my memory, when we drove back to Swindon for the weekend, he driving and me sitting in the cavernous rear snuggled up to Linda Davidson, my friend Neil's sister. But to top it all, being piped through from the Royal Albert

Hall was Mahler's great Eighth Symphony, the 'Symphony of a Thousand'. What a journey.

By contrast, I was driving around in a rather battered red Austin-Healey 3000. I used to drive it all over the country for meetings – regularly driving to Hull in the morning for a day of meetings before going back to the office, getting there at nine or ten at night, just to clear my desk for the next day. Once, on my way back to London, I was so tired I pulled over on the hard shoulder of the motorway for a nap, and then there was a knock on the window and a policeman writing out a ticket.

By the time Michael Joyce retired, I had long been divorced and found myself in the office seven days a week, till ten o'clock at night, slogging through it on a diet of cigarettes and coffee, having infernal migraines. Nevertheless, I loved the office, all my stuff was there; it was more like home than my rented flat in London. With no family to return to, I would suddenly discover it was Friday night and I was still in the office, and I had no plans at all for the weekend. All my mates were married with children; I couldn't ring them up and say let's go out, so I'd spend Saturday and Sunday in the office. And then Monday came around and the whole thing started all over again. Pathetic, really. Determination had been the spur not to screw up again, to make something of myself. I was never a particularly clever or confident fellow, but I realised that hard graft can compensate for any lack of those qualities. But determination can also become a kind of obsession, to compensate for failure.

Perhaps I am a workaholic? I'm not naturally happy if I haven't got anything to do, and this can get me into trouble. As with all things, it's a question of balance. When I look back on my younger self, I think that if I'd had the self-confidence that I have now, life would've been much easier. And yet, determination, the drive to do a job creatively and finish the task, also opened up the world to me.

Michael Joyce died, aged eighty-eight, in 2011, and I remained close to him till the end. He was a gentleman of the industry and always honourable in his dealings with me, and I'm happy to say that I dealt with him the same way.

On his retirement, we had written to each other and our letters crossed in the post. Each spoke warmly of the other and I nodded in agreement when I read Michael's comment that, in all the years we had known each other, there had never been an argument or unkind word. How many business partners can say that, I wonder?

E

Endoscopy

You done good, meestah

Reflux is common enough in babies, indeed one of my grandsons was engulfed by bile for months on end as an infant, so I was surprised to find myself walking along Pall Mall in my mid-fifties when suddenly and without warning my mouth filled with an acidic backwash. I had recently stopped smoking and put this little unpleasantness down to a slight but sudden increase in weight.

Within a few weeks, this reflux became a regular visitor, particularly at night. I considered whether a few glasses of red wine at dinner might be the culprit, for I had taken up a liking to red wine, after many years of being almost a teetotaller, perhaps as a substitute for the cigarettes.

My GP sent me off to see Dr Silk, an expert in matters of the stomach. We spent quite a long time talking about his race-horses and their chances in some upcoming fixtures before we got down to business. He would undertake a procedure I had been told about, involving an endoscope.

I later learned that this device, the saviour of many an internal organ, had been invented in the 1860s by Sir Francis Cruise, an Old Clongownian whose portrait hangs in the Serpentine Gallery at the college (see J: JESUITS). Researching his achievements, I discovered that he was respected as a careful clinician and an inspiring teacher. Most famous for the construction of the first effective endoscope, enabling the examination of internal organs, including the bladder, rectum, uterus, pharynx and larynx, he exhibited his invention at the British Medical Association in Dublin in 1867.

Not satisfied with that accomplishment, he turned his hand to psychiatry and the use of hypnotism in medical practice, though he soon lost interest in that branch of medicine and started to write a number of books on the medieval Christian monk St Thomas à Kempis. So, I had much to thank Sir Francis for, as Dr Silk applied a modest dose of what I believe was Rohypnol. 'It will relax you,' he murmured as I slid into the arms of Morpheus.

Today, the endoscope has moved on from Sir Francis's prototype and is a flexible tube with a light and camera attached to it, so that the doctor can examine pictures of your digestive tract on a colour monitor. Additionally, if he does not like the look of a particular polyp, he can snip it off with the use of a cute little integrated snipper for closer examination later.

'There,' a voice said soothingly, 'that didn't hurt, did it?' Dr Silk's features swam into view. I nodded in agreement and stumbled to my feet. 'I bear good tidings,' the good doctor said. 'Your oesophagus is in fine condition but you will need to take 20 mg of a wonder drug called omeprazole every morning. That will deal with the acid problem. Come and see me in five years. Now, have a cup of tea and when you've found your legs, you can leave.'

True to his words, the 20 mg omeprazole pill became my steadfast and constant companion. I never travel without that little yellow obloid capsule. Twenty years passed, and I noticed that from time to time, two of my little yellow friends were needed, particularly after a heavy dinner. I consulted my doctor and he suggested that it was time for me to swallow another camera crew to check on the situation.

I was recommended to another prominent gastroenterologist and an appointment was made at his clinic. After a cursory chat, he enquired as to whom I had brought along to take me home afterwards. 'I am alone. I came by train, having left my car at the station,' I replied, not sensing anything alarming about that.

'Alone?' he gasped. 'You'll need to be sedated and you certainly can't drive after I have finished with you.' I detected a hint of acidic irritation in his voice, perhaps prompted by the possibility of a cancelled procedure and a yawning gap in the day's income.

'Well, it is possible to receive the procedure without the normal calming sedation,' he said. 'Though, to be frank, not many choose that option. Would you like to try it that way?' It seemed only decent to help out, to go commando style, as it was obviously my fault for not reading the notes for guidance.

'I can give you a little spray on the back of the throat which will help the tube go down. Please lie on your side. My nurses will guide you.'

With that, two almost identical Chinese nurses appeared, their faces obscured by medical masks, and took station, one on either shoulder. The spray was applied and what appeared to be a long, thick black python approached my clenched mouth. 'Open wide, please,' came the command. 'You can watch on the television screen. You can see the screen, can't you?' I nodded furiously as the python filled my mouth and had a tentative attempt at my throat. I felt the four-handed grip of the nurses tighten as, in unison, they cried, 'You done good, meestah.'

Down went the python, each yard, or so it felt, being greeted by a murmur of approval by the python operator and another synchronised cry of 'You done really good, meestah!' by my captors, who by now were almost sitting on my heaving shoulders. Each descending inch was matched by an equal and opposite effort on my part to reverse the descent. As I gagged and choked, I could feel the snake moving slowly about below my chest, probing here and there in search of something to snip.

'Very well done!' the doctor cried. 'Very good effort all round.' I felt a moment of pride but it was short-lived as the ascent, the recovery of the python, commenced; going down was bad enough, but hauling him out was a whole lot worse, for it must not be rushed and I was doing all I could to expel the intruder. 'You brave, meestah,' the nurses continued to chant. Finally, just when I thought I would never be separated from the python, the patting on the back started as their iron grip relaxed. I lay slumped as Mr Gastro declared a clean bill of health. 'See you in five years, old chap. Keep taking the tablets.'

Some months later, having got the hang of it, I decided to go for the other end, the colonoscopy, reasoning that to do so would be a bit like the British and French diggers meeting halfway in the Eurotunnel – I'd have covered all the ground between intake and outgoing. With the benefit of a sedative this time, the anal intruder was hardly felt. It was a breeze and revealed my gut to be clear as a whistle with a bit of diverticulitis thrown in, about which the professor manipulating the apparatus seemed indifferent.

A few days later, I received the full report of the colonoscopy, which opened with the triumphant news, 'The anus is normal.'

F

Frights

Out of my depths in the Thames

Product launches are fraught with danger. The client normally requests some ideas as to how their precious new product can be launched to the public with the maximum publicity at a reasonable cost. Those charged with the task are confronted with a number of possible problems. Will anyone be interested? Will the product demonstration, surely a requirement in any product launch, work? The key to a successful launch is creativity, which is shorthand for pushing your luck.

One client we had at MJC for more than twenty years was Holt Lloyd, a Cheshire-based international chemicals company that manufactured or imported all sorts of products for cars – to stop rust, polish your windscreen, seal a hole in your exhaust pipe, and so on. We launched all sorts of products for them – Tyreweld, an aerosol used to seal a puncture at the roadside, being one.

We hired the Woolwich-based army motorcycle display team, a sort of two-wheeled Red Arrows, invited the press

71

along to admire their breathtakingly dangerous routine, then casually drilled a hole in several of the team's front tyres, sealed them up with Tyreweld, and asked them to repeat their high-speed, death-defying antics. But this time, in order to prove the faith we had in the product, the company marketing manager Martin Grant and I would lie down on the tarmac alongside a lot of squaddies while the team would take turns to jump over us. So, there we were, laid out at the end of the squaddie line, with the motorbikes landing heavily just inches from our ears. All very safe, really.

Holt Lloyd had bought from America the rights to a product called LPS, which claimed to chase water off surfaces – apparently developed by the US Navy to keep saltwater off their battleships – and which would be marketed in the UK as a 'damp start' spray for car engines in Britain's cold and wet winters. Holt Lloyd's boss, Tom Haywood, having laid out lots of money on the acquisition, wanted a splashy PR launch.

So, the first thing he did was go to one of the biggest, finest advertising agencies in the country, J. Walter Thompson, who mocked up an ad showing a big Perspex tank into which they had lowered a car until it was completely submerged but all the lights were on and the windscreen wipers were working and the engine was running, which proved that even if it was immersed in water, once you'd sprayed all the components with LPS, everything would work as normal. Simple.

Next thing I know, Martin Grant, ever the fearless marketing man and a long-term pal ever since, asks me to do it live, for real, at a press launch: drive a car underwater. The words 'out of my depth' started to form in my brain, but my mouth intervened and I found myself saying, 'Sure, fine. We'll drive a car under the Thames.'

I picked up the phone and traced the British Army amphibious warfare unit down in Barnstaple, Devon, and explained that what I wanted to do was buy a Ford Escort and then I wanted one of their boffins to come up and deal with the mechanical side of things like sealing the clutch and we were going to spray all the electrics with LPS, and then take the exhaust pipe up above the water level, and do the same with the air intake into the carburettor, and then we were going to have a frogman drive it under the Thames. Right? A short pause, and then, 'Yes, I think we can do that. We'll send you up a squaddie.' I bought a brand-new Daytona Yellow Ford Escort from a nervous Ford marketing department and the squaddie arrived and set up camp outside the London Rowing Club on the Thames slipway in Putney.

Meanwhile, I arranged for *Tomorrow's World*, a hugely popular BBC science and technology programme, to preview this in their studio in two days' time by putting it in a tank of water under an enormous industrial showerhead. There were no mobile phones at this time, so the squaddie and I communicated through a phone on the bar in a nearby pub against which he was no doubt propped for much of the time. I got the firm impression that everything was going well, until he called late in the afternoon of day two. 'Okay, boss, I've got to go back to Barnstaple now. I've left the keys to the car behind the bar.'

'Uh, right, so have you done it? Does it work?'

'Nah, I don't get it, boss, can't figure it out. Anyway, I'm off to Barnstaple now, good luck.'

And with that he put the phone down. This was something of a hammer blow. My natural inclination is always to take a bit of a gamble, but this one was blowing up in my face, and I risked losing an important long-term client.

It was now six o'clock in the evening, and I was meant to get the Ford into the *Tomorrow's World* studio in west London by ten o'clock the following morning. But when I got down to Putney from my office in Covent Garden and retrieved the keys, I couldn't even start the car. It didn't work as a Ford Escort, let alone as an amphibian Ford Escort. If a client smells danger, everyone runs a mile, so I knew I had to sort this out on my own. I called a recovery service to collect a rather forlorn Escort, and within the hour a low-loader truck loomed into view. As we were putting it on the truck, I said to the driver, 'I don't suppose you know anybody who could, overnight, do x, y and z to this car? What we need is welding to take that pipe from there to here, and that one from here to there, and we need to seal this, and this, and spray that, and that.'

'And why would you want to do that?' he asked.

'Because we want to drive it under the Thames, stupid,' was my reply.

To my amazement he replied, 'Yeah, I know someone who can do that.' I climbed up into the passenger seat: 'TAKE ME TO HIM.'

We drove through the London rush hour to Hanger Lane, a notorious bottleneck for northbound traffic, and it was already nine o'clock by the time we pulled into a really dodgy-looking, unlit industrial estate, now shut for the night but in which, during daylight hours, many sins were no doubt committed. Light was seeping from under a big wooden garage door which had 'PETER KEEGAN MOTOR ENGINEER' splashed across it in paint that had dripped down under each letter. We knocked on the door and all you could hear was the sound of scurrying feet as the occupants furiously covered up whatever they were doing (they were, I assumed, busy filing the numbers off engines). Eventually the door opened with a kind of gothic creak, and the recovery driver, whom they all seemed to know, asked, 'Is Peter in?' They nodded and gestured silently towards a car hoisted way up on a ramp. The back door opened slowly and a pair of stockinged feet came out and it was Keegan, who'd been sleeping in the back seat. He dropped to the ground and said, in an Irish accent so thick you could lean on it, 'What's de trouble now?' I explained it all to him breathlessly and he said, 'Ah sure, dat's no problem, let's have a look den.'

Short and stocky, Keegan was just the sort of chap I like, an enthusiast who is always up for a mission and won't give up. He stayed up with his team all night and I stayed up all night, running out onto Hanger Lane to get sandwiches and coffee. I must have left at about 9:30 in the morning to get to the TV studio in Shepherd's Bush. They were still working on the car. 'Lads, don't let me down, will you? No hanging around and smoking and larking about.' 'Ah sure, don't worry,' Keegan answered. 'Oi've got everyting completely onder control.'

We waited and waited in the studio, pacifying the client, the men from Ford and the floor manager, and I was thinking, Right, this is where I get exposed as a total fraud, when suddenly I heard all manner of banging and clanging, followed by a motley crew of oil-stained men with wide grins who sprayed LPS all over the electronics and the exposed engine bay, drove the car (complete with the legend 'Conversion by Peter Keegan expert engineers' painted wonkily on the boot lid) into a water-filled tank, and lo!, the wipers moved from side to side, the lights all blazed, the engine ran. It worked!

The team from the client murmured relief and the team

from Ford melted away, their jobs secure. But this was Boy Scout stuff. We now had to drive it under the Thames. Keegan took the car back to his garage and tinkered a bit, and then one evening we took it down to the river at Putney for a test run. Our friend with the low-loader, who was now part of the team, attached a cable from his truck to the back of the Ford, and trained the headlights on it as Keegan drove it into the water. And there he was, 100 feet out with the engine still running, bobbing about midstream on the strong currents of the Thames.

It was dark, it was raining, and Keegan started to shout, 'Nick, it's going down!' We hadn't, at this stage, finessed the plan for how to submerge the car. 'Stand on the roof, Pete!' I yelled. 'Oi am on de roof, Nick!' At this point, the police arrived in a motor launch with all the lights on and Tannoys blaring. 'What's going on here? Get that man ashore!' Trouble was, our friend with the low-loader had unreeled the total length of his cable, and it was grinding so slowly that it was taking forever to winch Keegan in, who was by now halfway to Hammersmith. The police came ashore and I could see they were seriously concerned. They waited till we got Keegan and the car out of the water and gave us a thorough scolding for being so foolish.

It's true, we must've been mad: Keegan was within an inch of drowning. But he was undeterred. 'We got it working,' he said triumphantly. 'This is moy project now, Nick, and oi'll be droiving it for de press launch.'

'Pete,' I asked, 'can you swim?'

'Sure, I can't, no, but don't you worry, Nick, oi've gone and got a wetsuit and an oxygen tank and oi've bin practising in de bath.'

'Absolutely not,' I protested. 'Unless you agree to having a professional frogman sitting next to you.'

He agreed.

Come the day, I had all the press down there on the banks of the Thames right outside the London Rowing Club, and Keegan's Irish contingent – who had clanked onto the bridge in their cars and stopped all the traffic – were shouting and whooping ('Up the Republic!' 'Go on now, Pete, you can do it!'). As they arrived, a police inspector turned to me and said archly, 'That's quite a lot of faces known to the Met you've got there, sir.' 'A fine body of men, officer,' I answered.

Keegan was standing there in his wetsuit, and I was standing there thinking this was all going to go horribly wrong. It was high tide, and the plan was to go down the slipway of the London Rowing Club until the car was fully submerged and then drive it parallel to the shore for about 300 feet. Keegan drove in, and slowly disappeared under the water on the slipway until only the LPS flags attached to the exhaust pipe and air intake were visible, and then he reversed it back again, surfacing to great cheers from the hundreds of onlookers who had gathered along the bank. It was a huge success: we were all over the evening TV news, and made the front page of every national newspaper the next morning, by which time Keegan and his mates were nursing a terrible hangover, having got hammered in the local pub.

Shortly after, Keegan took the car to Ireland and drove it under the Shannon to show off to all his family and friends (he didn't actually mention this to me beforehand, but by now it had been tacitly agreed the car was his). About six months later, I read in the *Evening Standard* that he'd been found dead in his caravan in the industrial estate. Shot in the head. Awful, such a sorry tale; he was such a good bloke, game for anything, but I guess he took a risk with the wrong sort of people and I imagine that's what got him killed. RIP Peter Keegan, thanks for saving my scalp.

G

Gee-Gees

Runners and riders

Although there were five looseboxes at The Grange, there was barely sight nor sound of a horse when I was growing up there. We had little Pimple, a New Forest pony who grazed in the orchard but was stabled at night, and it was on her felt saddle that Dad taught us to ride. Why the name Pimple? The story goes that she arrived with some hifalutin Italian name which my younger brother Fergus found difficult to pronounce – he could only manage 'Pimple' and that was that. She lasted a long time but like pretty much all Hewer pets she came to a sticky end before her time (*see* B: BOYHOOD).

Pimple was a pretty little thing but she must have mixed with the mules at some stage in her life as she had acquired a nasty stubborn streak, added to which she enjoyed a bit of cruelty. Her stubbornness showed itself in throwing you off and then standing with one hoof on your clothing as you lay stunned, putting all her weight on that leg so that it sometimes took an age to free yourself. Her cruelty always emerged during a favourite game, which was to race bareback, slalom fashion, between the apple trees. You could keep your head down to avoid the branches, but Pimple loved a near-miss and liked to graze the tree trunk itself as she passed, which necessitated you lifting a leg out of the way followed by a fall and the inevitable hoof on the jacket.

Mum would lead one or other of us out of the gates and across the adjoining fields – in those days, we really were on the outskirts of Swindon Old Town, and Betjeman's sprawling 'brick-built breeding boxes' were yet to eat up the fields. I remember one occasion when by some foolishness we let ourselves into a field which contained three or maybe four enormous shire horses, animals of unimaginable height, weight and strength. They set off in a thunderous circular canter and to our horror Pimple broke free and joined them. We watched aghast, terrified lest Pimple, minute by comparison, should get mown down. We didn't know how to stop the madness but mercifully the big boys eventually got bored and Pimple returned to a barrage of admonishments.

Grandpa was an excellent horseman – indeed he was so described in his First World War record – and he hunted twice a week with the Vale of the White Horse (VWH) hunt. Looking back, it seems extraordinary that he could afford to spend so much time on the hunting field, but he was riding with his clients, never a bad idea. Dad too was a keen rider, and once told me that riding boots must be very tight-fitting, and the secret for getting them on and off was to wear women's stockings with a liberal sprinkling of talcum powder. At the age of nineteen, while hunting with his father with the VWH at Highworth, he came a cropper and smashed up part of his back. 'I was travelling too fast, all hands and heels, and came off on Ding-Dong Bell's land [Ding-Dong being the nickname of the farmer], and had to be carried away on a gate,' he told me. He spent a year recuperating in a convalescent home called Glenwood, which years later my pal Robert Humphrey's father bought as a family home, so I got to know it well.

I only ever saw Dad on a horse once, when a friend brought a difficult horse for him to look at, and I remember Dad, who was always a quiet man, mounting the recalcitrant steed in the yard and effortlessly putting it through its paces – moving it forwards and backwards, side to side, with barely a movement of wrist or heel. 'Nothing wrong with this horse,' he said, and our friend led it away not really knowing what to do next. Pamela Enderby, a lifelong friend, told me of the time she was riding along the road near her home in Lydiard Millicent, a village near Swindon, when she came across my father in his car, confronted by a flooded road. 'Ah, Pam, lend me your horse,' he said. 'There's a nasty case of milk fever up the road. Be back in twenty minutes.' He sprang onto her rather surprised horse and charged off, calcium drip at the ready and, true to his word, returned at the trot half an hour later.

As an eleven-year-old at Clongowes school (*see* J: JESUITS), sitting on the hot heating pipes one March day, I was approached by two senior boys, Caiman Flannery and Raphael Emmanuel, who both later qualified as doctors, went to America, and made millions with a chain of varicose vein clinics, or so the story goes. 'We want you to take out a book,' said Caiman. I said, 'You have your own library, why can't you get your own book out?' 'Stupid boy, a book on the National. Your job is to run the book among the junior school. Each day, you'll meet me and I will give you the odds and your job is to release as much money as possible from your lot. You will share the dividend, if there is any.'

The most lucrative time for this operation was in the dormitories at bedtime, as I would move from bed to bed and push the book to the boys there or those lining up for the lavatories. Sixpences rolled in, and each morning the cash and the book would be handed over to Caiman and Raphael and the odds would be adjusted accordingly. Brendan, who had a portfolio of college jobs but undertook freelance work such as altering our trousers to become drainpipes, acted as the runner between school and the bookies in Clane, the local village. Each morning the new odds were passed to me.

The Aintree Grand National is run on the Saturday afternoon, which meant it clashed with the numerous school rugby matches. I ensured that a pal of mine with a transistor radio moved up and down the touchline, keeping pace with the action, so that he could relay the progress of the race as it ran. An Irish-trained horse called E.S.B. (which, as everybody in Ireland knew, stood for Electricity Supply Board) came through, but I had no idea what that meant in terms of profit or loss. That only became clear the next day when Caiman and Raphael presented me with £11.10s.6d., which astonished me on two counts: firstly, I'd never seen so much money before (about £250 in today's value), and secondly, the senior boys had clearly given me a fair share.

My brush with racing encouraged me to ever greater daring when riding a horse. In the village of Hinton Parva, just underneath the Ridgeway, was a stable yard owned by a rather eccentric couple who would generously lend Robert and me a couple of ex-racehorses if we asked nicely. One day in late August, when we were about eighteen, we rode out of the yard, feeling rather cocky, to go for a canter up on the Ridgeway. 'You will notice that The House of Usher has only one eye,' the owner told me. 'But it's safe as houses.' Robert and I, Jack-the-lads, decided that we'd ride with short stirrups and off we blazed up the hill and across the stubbled fields. I don't know what spooked my one-eyed mare – maybe it was a rabbit that caused her to veer sharply to the right. Sadly, I failed to follow that trajectory and hit the stubble at high speed, each blade of cut straw like a razor made by Mr Gillette. As I skidded across the surface at 30 miles per hour, it was like death by a thousand cuts.

Robert, with an air of supreme superiority, led my horse back to where I lay on the ground and simply said, 'Longer stirrups for you, old chap.' I remounted the horse and walked her back to the yard, my forearms torn to shreds. The moral of the story? Always inspect your vehicle for missing parts before setting out (*see* P: PROOF OF LIFE).

H

Hewer

Who do you think you are?

In her last will and testament, my great-granny Elizabeth Tuckey Hewer kindly left me her cylinder music box (which I later sold, shamefully, to buy an airline ticket to New York), some very old hunting prints still with the dimpled glass in their frames, and a dented, dome-lidded tin deed box. This came in handy when the production team of *Who Do You Think You Are?* came a-calling. In it were no end of old letters, probate documents, wills, land deeds and photographs, all jam-packed. Most of this referred to the Hewer family, but there were also various references to the Frampton family, the Tuckeys and the Badcocks.

The producer was impressed with this cache but warned me that at this stage they hadn't yet confirmed who the subjects of the next series would be. They needed to do a bit of preliminary research, she explained, because it was often the case that an interesting family story would only go back as far as the 1840s, beyond which everybody, it seemed, was a farm labourer. Three months passed before I got the call to tell me that they wished to proceed with both sides of my family's story, so I knew they must have dug something up worth investigating. Part of the deal with *WDYTYA?* is that they do not reveal what they have found out at the outset; each part of your history will be unveiled as the film progresses. The date was set for filming and off we went on an eight-day jaunt through Dublin, Belfast and to the area around Swindon where I was brought up.

I was well aware of my mother's family, an unremarkable lot until my grandfather, Oswald Jamison, took to politics as a young man. A Catholic, he married a young Presbyterian Belfast woman in 1912, the year of the Covenant, when the Protestant majority signed a declaration of allegiance to the British Crown. Not great timing, added to which he was now in politics, as well as running his family's business. Although a Home Ruler, in contrast to his own beliefs he represented the Falls Road, a deeply Republican Sinn Féin constituency, and he continued to do so for many years. He rapidly rose in the city's political ranks, becoming in turn an alderman, the first Catholic High Sheriff, then Deputy Lord Lieutenant for Belfast and, amazingly for those deeply partisan days, one of the twelve commissioners of the Belfast Harbour Board, the pinnacle of the city's business community. Not long before he died, I met in Derry the Sinn Féin firebrand-turned-peacemaker, the late Martin McGuinness. Telling him of my grandfather Ossie, I asked him whether his story of social and political advancement made him a 'Castle Catholic' (essentially, from the Republican viewpoint, not one to rely on politically). 'Possibly so,' McGuinness said. 'But thankfully we've all moved on from those days.'

On the Hewer side, the team of genealogists had indeed unearthed a family line about which I knew nothing, leading back on my father's side, via Great-granny through the Frampton and Badcock families, to the 1550s. The family crest, drawn in pencil, is in one of the great ledgers at the College of Arms, dated 1587. Great-granny, it turned out, was descended from the Nott family. Edward Nott (my great-grandfather x 12) had been a Royalist cavalry colonel and fought at the battles of Lansdowne, near Bath, and Roundway, near Devizes, before being captured at the siege of Lacock Abbey towards the end of the Civil War. He narrowly escaped the fate of many Royalists and kept his head but was stripped of his property and 3,000-acre estate, and had a miserable time of it thereafter.

The family didn't stagger back to its feet until Charles II regained the throne, at which time the tables were turned. I was very excited by this swashbuckling Civil War story of riches to rags and back again. The final scene of the film saw me standing at the front door of the beautiful red-brick family home of the Notts, Red Lodge, built in 1620 in Braydon Forest, north of Swindon, much of which the Nott family had received as a gift from Charles I. I wish my father had lived to see this film, because as a boy he and his father would have known Red Lodge well, as the VWH meets would have taken place there in their hunting days (*see* G: GEE-GEES).

Clearly, the researchers on *WDYTYA?* couldn't sniff out any other interesting stories in the Hewer line, and this should've been no surprise to me – we were simple farming people, taking tenancies of farms in Wiltshire, Oxfordshire and Gloucestershire. In the 1880s, my great-grandfather farmed Bradenstoke Priory, where his sons were born. This Augustinian priory and its tithe barn, dating back to the twelfth century, was snapped up in the 1920s by the American media tycoon William Randolph Hearst, who was rampaging through Europe buying up artefacts, and indeed entire buildings, to add to his collection. The barn was dismantled, stone by stone, packed into wooden boxes and shipped to the West Coast of the United States, where Hearst planned to rebuild it at San Simeon, his Californian retreat. But first, he dropped off the great fireplace, the windows and the hammer-beam roof at St Donat's Castle in Wales, where he had recently installed a mistress. At least those elements of the building remain, for the numbered stones shipped to California are still stored in a warehouse, much to the fury of the villagers of Bradenstoke. Last I heard, they were demanding them back.

My great-grandfather's last farm was at Appleton, just outside Oxford, which he sold before retiring to nearby Cumnor. He had no sons to hand the farm on to, as his eldest boy, Richard, had been killed in the battle for Jerusalem in the First World War, and his second son, John – my father's father – had taken himself off to university where he'd qualified as a veterinary surgeon.

Appleton Farm and its contents were auctioned in September 1917, and in the deed box there is a printed brochure listing farm equipment and livestock to be sold which includes the entry: 'Handsome Bay Gelding, 16 hands, 6 years old, grand hunter, and good-mannered officer's charger, the property of Lieut. Hewer, who is now serving in Palestine.' Two months later, on 21 November 1917, Richard (my great-uncle Dickie) fell to a Turkish bullet in General Allenby's advance on Jerusalem. At the outbreak of the First World War, Palestine was part of the Turkish empire and until December 1916 had not been entered by British forces. By the time of his death, the British Expeditionary Force was advancing fast on the Holy City.

I know about Richard's miserable end because Great-granny's deed box contains two letters written to his parents: one from his regiment, the Berkshire Yeomanry, and another from a fellow trooper called Syd, who describes how Richard, a young second lieutenant, fell some 8 miles north of the Holy City. 'He and I were taking observation for artillery,' Syd explains. 'His wound was at the back of his head, and he soon became insensible and oblivious of all pain.' Syd held his fallen friend and 'nursed his poor head' from early morning until evening, unable to move him as 'the show was too hot to shift from in daytime'. Richard's body was buried 'in a deep valley amid the fig trees', the spot marked by 'a neat little heap of stones arranged very artistically'. Later, a rudimentary cross marked the spot, before Richard was eventually re-buried in the British military cemetery in Jerusalem. In 2007, while attending a wedding in Jerusalem, I took the opportunity to lay a flower on his grave. Closer to home, Richard's name is inscribed on the village war memorial in Appleton.

Tragically, there was nothing much exceptional about Richard's story. How many other simple farming folk after the war found themselves short of heirs to take over the work? I'm not surprised that the producers of *Who Do You Think You Are?* were more drawn by the other, more historically glamorous, line of the family. But perhaps they blinked and missed a claim to fame that the Hewers could reasonably be proud of.

Very recently, I received a small parcel in the post from one of my father's old practice partners which contained a book, *History of Hereford Cattle*, published in 1909. But for an accompanying note that insisted that I would find much of interest in it, I would not have put it to the top of my bedside reading pile. Flicking through it, I was immediately intrigued. It talks at length of William Hewer, whom I believe could be my great-great-grandfather, who lies buried in a roomy tomb in the churchyard of Sevenhampton – I visited the church-yard twenty-five years ago, with a view to securing a tenancy in that same tomb after my death (*see* X: 'XX'). William, the book explains, is counted among the great pioneers of cattle-breeding not only in this country, but indeed across the world. If I've understood correctly, the Hewers were almost single-handedly responsible for the introduction of the Hereford, the first English cattle to be recognised as a distinct breed.

The Hereford is descended from the small red cattle of Roman Britain and the large Welsh breed found along the Welsh Hereford border. It's essentially a beef breed, and today it has been edged out of popularity, certainly in the UK, by the massive beef cattle imported originally from France, such as the Charolais. But in its day, the Hereford was the mainstay of our domestic beef produc-tion, and there are still more than five million pedigree Hereford cattle chewing the cud in over fifty countries.

Many strains of the Hereford have used other cattle breeds to import desired characteristics, and this has led to changes in the breed as a whole. But some breeds have been kept sep-arate, and these have retained characteristics – 'hardiness and thriftiness', for example – of the earlier breeds. The tradi-tional, pure pedigree Hereford, as bred by my neighbour in Northamptonshire, Bob Borwick, has long been treated as a minority breed, of value only for genetic conservation.

However, when I popped over to see Bob recently, he was feeling very positive about the comeback of the Hereford. Now seventy-six, but still arm-deep in farming, Bob explained his affection for his white-faced Herefords, which he has been breeding for almost half a century. In the late 1960s, he took over a small herd from a friend who had bought a nucleus of five heifers but had lost two cows and three calves almost immediately and decided that, not knowing anything about it, the remaining heifers would be in safer hands with Bob. At one point, Bob was managing a herd of over seventy head.

The demise of the Hereford occurred in the 1960s, after a famous breeder called Captain de Quincey bred them very small in order, Bob explained, 'to captivate the South American market which at the time was after these fancy small animals'. The domestic market was interested in larger cuts, so the Hereford's popularity waned. Now, however, the pendulum is beginning to swing in their favour again. 'They are old-fashioned,' Bob conceded, 'but they don't need the input of concentrates that some of the continental breeds do. Herefords will finish off on grass; you don't need to give them concen-trates, so they're a lot cheaper to keep. Plus, you don't want a huge carcass nowadays because the modern family doesn't want a big joint; it wants a small joint, so the carcass size of beef cattle in general is coming down. Also, the taste is beautiful because it's reared on grass and it has good internal marbling fat as well as external fat – you can't cook meat unless it's got fat in it because it would just be leathery. So, the Hereford gives very good value for money.' He pointed out that the Hereford, which is being vigorously promoted by the Hereford Breed Society, is once again finding its place on the supermarket shelves next to the more familiar cuts of Aberdeen Angus.

History of Hereford Cattle is a penny short on how exactly the Hewers first built up their white-faced herd – as there's no evidence they ever farmed in Hereford, it was most likely a cross-county affair, with a few cattle wandering over the border into Gloucestershire or Oxfordshire, where the Hewers were certainly already set up. But the book does record that the best of the Hewer Herefords could be traced back to the bull called Silver 540 (calved in 1797), which greatly impressed its owner 'with the red and white face character, and also with that massive heavy flesh and full eye'.

Wait, it gets better. Here's the opening of Chapter Four:

The student of the herd book will find that nearly every valuable strain of Herefords at the present day is full of Hewer blood. The influence of the Hewer cattle has indeed been remarkable. It is not merely that a few families that have become exceedingly valuable are of this line of descent, but that the modern character of the entire breed has to a large extent been determined by this variety, not alone as regards colour marking, on which the Hewer impress has been very powerful, but on the more essential matters of shape and quality.

Every Hereford in existence can be traced back to the Hewer stock. These cattle 'were beautiful to look at and good rent-paying animals of great scale and splendid quality', and the bulls among them were immense, often weighing in at between a ton and a ton-and-a-half. In 1822, one Hewer bull, Wellington (no doubt a popular name at the time), demonstrated just how enormous these beasts were: 'Length from the setting on of the tail to the end of the nose, 11 feet 4 inches; girth, 11 feet 3 inches; across the hips, 3 feet 2 inches'; and just for good measure, the length of the tail is given as '3 feet 2 inches' (good for a hearty oxtail soup, perhaps?).

In the early nineteenth century, my forebears and their relatives let these bulls run with the herd for the sum of £80–100 per season (roughly £6,000–8,000 in today's money). One bull, Defiance 416, was let for an astronomical £200 (£16,000). The big money came from cattle auctions, where Hewer bulls attracted much interest from international buyers: one was sold to Australia for a thousand guineas (nearly £100,000), and yet another prize specimen was exhibited at the Great Fair of Chicago in 1893.

I have not delved into the exact ancestry, but I'd like to think this exhibition bull was one of the two whose portraits used to hang in the breakfast room at The Grange, my childhood home. These nineteenth-century paintings, one of which was said to have been shown at the Royal Academy, drew very little interest from any of us, and yet they represent perhaps the only noteworthy thing about the Hewer family. It's made me quite proud of the Hewer bloodline – 'heavily fleshed, of nice quality, with great aptitude to fatten'.

Bob Borwick is close to retirement and without an heir willing to take over the farm (his children aren't interested). He has just nine Herefords left, but they are very dear to him. 'It's my reason to get up in the morning,' he told me. 'They're lovely animals. When you can trust your wife in with them and be quite sure she's safe, what better advertisement is there for the breed? They've always been docile, though you do get an odd one which is a bit naughty, but that's an exception.' Quite so.

I

India

The lotus flower and a Hovis loaf

Although I spent nearly all my career at one PR company, Michael Joyce Consultants, there was a little bit of an interruption in the early 1970s when I left, hoping to pressure Michael Joyce into appointing me a director of the company and putting a share deal on the table. I went off to a company called Rea PR, run by Bill Rea and his number two, Gerry Knight (*see* D: DETERMINATION).

Gerry, a bluff, business-like character, surprised us all by becoming very enamoured of the Bahá'í Faith, which originated in Shiite Islam in Iran in the mid-nineteenth century but is essentially a non-denominational world religion which emphasises 'the oneness of God, oneness of religions and oneness of mankind'. In other words, all are welcome, including gruff Yorkshiremen, and indeed it wasn't long before Gerry had left the commercial PR business and moved with his wife to New York, where they were involved in some kind of institutional PR/lobbying role representing the interests of the Bahá'í at the UN, no less.

Time passed, I was back at MJC as a director, and I learned from some key members of the British Bahá'í community, whom I had got to know through Gerry, that there was to be a big bash in Delhi to celebrate the opening of an extraordinary new Bahá'í House of Worship, a temple which took the form of an opening lotus flower – in India, a cherished symbol of purity and peace, and a manifestation of God. Almost fully funded by a man of the Bahá'í Faith from Hyderabad, who donated his entire life savings, and designed by an Italian architect, the project had drawn the attention of the world's construction industry for its complex geometric structure. There were virtually no straight lines, and the framework and construction, in poured concrete of complex double-curved surfaces (the petals of the lotus flower) and their intersections, was a miracle of alignment. The task was being carried out entirely by a team of 700 local labourers, including 400 carpenters, using traditional techniques and equipment. Concrete was carried up the staging by women bearing fifty-pound loads in baskets balanced on their heads. Once the petals were poured in concrete (a continuous operation for forty-eight hours, to avoid construction joints), they were reinforced with steel and clad with marble.

This was to be a House of Worship unlike any other, an embodiment on a massively ambitious scale of the Bahá'í principle of unity in diversity. I fancied a trip to India, so I welcomed an invitation from a leading member of the Bahá'í hierarchy to join them in Delhi, where I would deal with an aspect of the press management. My plan was to create stories about the British Bahá'í who were going to India for the celebrations: we would coordinate their photographs at the opening and give them a pro forma press release which, on their return to Britain, they could then give to their local papers, and that way a little sprinkling of news stories promoting the Bahá'í would appear all over the UK.

I arrived in Delhi in late December 1986 with a photographer, an adventurous soul called Peter (actually, he wasn't called Peter, but turns out he was a bit of a hash man so I'll spare him any embarrassment). Together, we went to see the temple, which was extraordinary if far from finished – the marble cladding had yet to go up, so I remember only the greyness of the concrete; the 26 acres of garden surrounding it, intended to be a recreation of Eden, was a bit of a muddle, but there was furious hacking and mowing as lots of Indians were racing to complete the landscaping.

Before leaving London, I had spoken to the *Observer* magazine about getting some coverage and, in the hallowed tradition of the PR man, I bloviated: this building was a world-first, I told them; in fact, surely the Ninth Wonder of the World. Bearing in mind the relative obscurity of the Bahá'í Faith, my pitch depended entirely on the visual impact of the Lotus Temple. Perhaps this was the reason the *Observer* people said they might run it but only if we gave them an aerial shot. 'You'll need a helicopter,' they said. 'No problem,' I blustered.

I was fully confident that somebody in Delhi would be happy to show off their city and in particular this new, world-beating building, but on arrival I learned that the only people who had a helicopter were the military. So, I talked my way into a local military airfield to speak to the colonel who was in charge of these things, and he was brilliant – the Indian army, when their boots are parade-ground polished, look just wonderful; the pleats in their trousers are as sharp as knives, and their moustaches are works of art. I explained to the colonel what I had come for and he said that they did indeed have a helicopter but I couldn't have it. I pleaded – such a shame to miss this opportunity to showcase Delhi at its best – to which he replied, 'I don't care about that. We are on high alert since the assassination of our prime minister.' (Indira Gandhi had been killed by Sikh nationalists in 1984, and a series of violent reprisals had rocked the country.) There would be no aerial picture, a great disappointment.

One of the highlights of the trip was seeing my old school friend Michael Courtney, with whom I'd spent holidays sailing at Lough Derg, near Nenagh in County Tipperary, where his family had a summer house. After leaving school, Michael had become not, as might have been expected of him, one of those rather classy and aloof Jesuits, but a local parish priest. This route, for an ambitious and intelligent chap, would get him to Rome fairly quickly, and soon enough he had joined the Vatican diplomatic service and was progressing at an impressively fast rate. He'd been stationed in Cuba and in the Balkans; in fact, wherever there was a bit of awkwardness for the Holy Roman Catholic Apostolic Church, Michael was to be found busying himself in the service of the Vatican.

Now here he was in Delhi, a monsignor and number two at the Apostolic Nunciature, fresh from handling the visit of Pope John Paul II to India earlier in the year. He invited me to lunch at the nuncio's splendid residence, where the gold and white flags of the Papacy were flying and the lawns had obviously been cut by a great number of people each carrying nail scissors as it was absolute perfection. A guard at the gate let Peter and me in and Michael introduced us to the Italian papal nuncio, who was dressed in pure cashmere – a suave, quiet grey, nothing too colourful. We had a wonderful lunch, served by white-gloved waiters. I ventured, and was not contradicted, that maybe the delicious food was being flown in from Rome a couple of times a week on an Alitalia flight.

Michael asked me what exactly I was doing here, and I explained about the Bahá'í temple and he said, 'Well, I'm not doing anything on Thursday, would you like me to come along?' I knew they'd be tickled pink to have a monsignor present, so I eagerly accepted. He duly turned up wearing one of those long cassocks with thousands of red buttons all the way down to his ankles and red lining to the collar. Good old Michael, our Bahá'í hosts loved it. The ceremony went off terribly well, and the enormous space for the congregation was packed with members of the international Bahá'í Faith, complete with a marvellous choir. Everybody was very pleased. Peter took the photographs and these were distributed to the British guests, although I assumed they had run out of photographic paper in Delhi because the shots were printed on what appeared to be soggy cardboard.

It was now a couple of days short of Christmas. I hadn't organised my return flight because I didn't know how long I would be there so I was stuck in Delhi. It was an unusually harsh winter, cold as charity. The local newspaper was reporting the number of people found dead in the street in the morning following the freezing temperatures during the night. I hadn't thought to bring any warm clothes, and the hotel too was caught unawares, so at night I shivered under a single blanket as thin as a Kleenex. The hotel was not in the centre of Delhi, and I remember going out one evening in the hopes of buying a warm jersey or a jacket, but here there were no street lights and when I eventually stumbled across a couple of stalls, each with a single, dull, yellow flickering paraffin lamp, I actually couldn't see anything other than a Nehru-style hat which they said was tiger skin, though it certainly wasn't, but I thought it would be warm and plonked it on my head (I later gave it to my daughter Katie).

Peter, sensibly, had booked his return flight and come his departure he suggested that I move into his room as it was bigger than mine. I accepted, and shortly before he was due to leave for the airport late that night, I took the elevator up to his floor. Just as the elevator door opened he began to get in, and, holding the door open with his foot, said, 'Here, this is for you,' and handed me what looked like a small Hovis loaf. It was at that moment I noticed that the corridor had a very strong smell of cannabis. I looked at this thing and realised I'd just been given half a pound of the stuff. 'Oh my God,' I stuttered.

Peter's parting words were 'Have fun', and with that he pressed the down button and disappeared out of my life, leaving me with the cannabis resin and the key to a room which I saw, as I approached it, had a light on inside that illuminated a thick carpet of cannabis smoke curling into the corridor from under the door. Peter had obviously been caning it the whole time we were in Delhi. I opened the door, thinking I was going to end up doing five years for this, apprehended with a huge lump of cannabis that was obviously not for my personal use (it was enough to keep the whole of Enfield going for two years). I spent the next couple of hours with the windows open to the cold wind outside, chopping the lump up and flushing it piece by piece down the lavatory.

Michael had mentioned that there was a party at the British Embassy on Christmas Eve – I knew some of the people at the embassy, including the cultural attaché who had come to the opening of the Lotus Temple with his very exotic Brazilian wife. We arranged that I meet Michael at the Nunciature, and when I got there he emerged sporting a white polo-neck sweater over which he had a grey V-neck sweater, so he looked a little bit like Arnold Palmer going off for a round of golf. We set out in the papal nuncio's Ambassador car, based on the Morris Cowley, and joined a colourful diplomatic crowd, demob happy and swirling around the embassy.

The Brazilian wife of the cultural attaché had taken an enormous liking to Michael. I'm told that in the southern hemisphere, water goes down the plughole in the opposite direction to the northern hemisphere; similarly, a vine will go around a column in the opposite way. Thus, the Brazilian was twisting around Michael in the southern hemisphere way. I caught his eye, and raised one eyebrow in silent enquiry. 'Nick,' he said, giving me a slightly funny look and pointing up to the ceiling, 'there's only one Numero Uno.' He then waltzed off with the clambering Brazilian. He was, after all, in the diplomatic service, and sometimes one has to go along with things that one might prefer to avoid. Poor Michael, he made it to archbishop and would easily have gone higher had he not met a violent end, aged fifty-eight, in Burundi (*see* J: JESUITS).

I kept checking for return flights to London, but they were all booked. Knowing that I would have to spend Christmas Day on my own in Delhi, I had asked the hotel manager to book me a seat on a tour bus that would be leaving at 8:00 a.m. on Christmas Day to go to the Taj Mahal. I placed an alarm call for 7:30. At 8:30 there was furious hammering on the door and I sprang out of bed to find the manager outside. 'The bus is here,' he said. 'They've been waiting for half an hour. You must hurry, they're very upset.' With that, I struggled into my clothes and, with no time for a coffee or even a glass of water, I floundered onto the bus and was met with a loud hissing noise from a coachload of German tourists who were obviously 'doing' India and were furious with me for breaking the German law of punctuality. I sat there in absolute misery for the hour-and-a-half journey to Agra. There, still craving a coffee, I looked around the Taj Mahal, which was rather smaller than I had imagined, although the nearby Red Fort was fantastic.

Inevitably, being a tour bus, the next stop was to the local marble-carving workshops selling overpriced, hideous souvenir trinkets. In these dust-filled workshops they use foot pedals to drive emery wheels upon which they shape and carve the marble souvenirs, and I was fascinated to note that the people working on these wheels all had incredibly sharp fingers because it only takes a second of the wheel as it flies around to knock a corner off a finger, and in time they had lost all the corners of their fingers and they were pointy like sharp nails. Awful.

I managed to get a flight a few days later, and though I was relieved to be home, I had fallen in love with India and determined to get back as soon as possible. Incidentally, I wasn't such a bloviator after all. I was right about the Lotus Temple: it is now one of the most visited attractions in the world, beating both the Taj Mahal and the Eiffel Tower.

It was more than ten years later, in late December 1999, that I found myself flying into Kolkata – or Calcutta, as we called it then – this time with my partner Catherine, a recently rediscovered flame of twenty-five years earlier (*see* V: VEUVE-VERVE). We were non-playing members of the Fleet Street XI Cricket Tour, masterminded by my old pal Mihir Bose, sports journalist and prolific author. The group, almost entirely made up of journalists, their wives, girlfriends and hangers-on like us, would start off in Kolkata then travel westwards, stopping off here and there for a prearranged match.

It was a lively group, with much discussion and debate fuelled by such Fleet Street luminaries as Philip Webster and Michael Evans of *The Times*, the wonderful Brian Scovell of the *Mail* and Michael Cockerell, whose BBC television profiles of prime ministers and prominent politicians go way back to Roy Jenkins and Barbara Castle. His efforts are always eagerly awaited, none more so than his successful effort in unzipping the character of Boris Johnson, much to the latter's embarrassment. Others on the trip included Richard Heller, then of the *Mail* and the MP Alan Simpson, whose presence required us to have a security detail as we edged towards Kashmir.

Kolkata was simply marvellous, and a highlight was being invited to the Bengal Club for their New Year's Eve party. Passing into the club, a destination for the snooty denizens of that great city, we tiptoed past the carefully painted hammer and sickle signs of this communist-run city. Each provided with a party hat, our group joined in the swing of things. There was a dancing competition and I was whisked onto the floor by an altogether too pretty girl. Rather like *Strictly Come Dancing*, it was an elimination affair and to our amazement, my pretty girl and I won. Our prize? A tin of toffees to share. The following morning was a day at the races, for the Eveready Calcutta Cup. What a blast.

We left Kolkata's magnificent central station on the Rajdhani Express and settled down in our first-class carriages for the eighteen-hour journey. Each coach had a cook stationed at either end, and Phil Webster devised a quiz to keep us occupied. I so clearly remember the first question: 'Who wrote: "Once upon a time and a very good time it was there was a moocow coming down along the road and this moocow that was coming down along the road met a nicens little boy named baby tuckoo"?' Nobody got it though I certainly should have done, as it's the opening to James Joyce's *A Portrait of the Artist as a Young Man*, which I had read and reread at Clongowes school in Ireland, of which Joyce was an alumnus (*see* J: JESUITS).

Sadly, the Rajdhani Express did not live up to its name. Not its fault, actually: the fact it took twenty-eight hours was blamed on 'dacoits on the line'. Southern Rail moans about leaves on the line, but dacoits, fast hit-and-run bandits, are another cause for alarm and delay entirely.

Delhi came and went, as did Jaipur, where I persuaded a very reluctant Catherine to pose beside the curious trunk of an elephant; then Udaipur, then north for the last match at Chandigarh, India's first planned city, dreamt up by Le Corbusier and Maxwell Fry in the 1960s and, by the time we saw it, already showing signs of decay. It was at a reception there held in our honour that I committed a faux pas I shrink from even to this day. It was the social event of the week and the town had turned out – it was endless, with hours of chatter and small talk that I found mind-numbingly boring. I told Catherine that I had had quite enough and suggested that we break away quietly and head back to the hotel. She was having none of it. 'You go if you want to, but I'm not prepared to be so rude to our hosts as to push off before the appropriate time.'

I approached our host, holding my temple, feigning a migraine and begging him to excuse me, and asking whether he could organise a taxi to ferry me gently to our hotel. 'My dear fellow,' cried our host, clearly a big cheese in the Punjab state, 'you will take my driver, and he will bear you to your lodgings.

Please wait here.' Within minutes, a turbaned military type pitched up and led me to a dark-green Morris Ambassador, which sported a government flag flying from the bonnet. The interior was completely swathed in red velvet, the seats and the headlining too, and the windows were swooshed in red velvet curtains. I entered what felt like a warm haemorrhage.

The turban had just taken the wheel when the front passenger door opened and in stepped an extremely tall, lean gentleman dressed in black military fatigues with shoulder patches emblazoned with a tiger's head. On his lap, he cradled a machine gun, and we were off at speed. Commandeering the centre of the road, lights on, horn tooting, its pennant now stiff as the wind roared past, the Ambassador sped the fraudulent invalid, moaning gently on the back seat, towards the centre of town. Oncoming traffic swerved to avoid us and many a car moved over swiftly to let us pass.

On reaching the hotel, my gun-toting bodyguard, a member of India's crack special services, turned to me and bared his teeth in a deadly grin which asked, 'How did we do?' I indicated that I wanted to tip the turban but this gesture was waved away as distinctly unnecessary. The bodyguard opened the door for me and on the pavement I made to shake his hand. He stiffened and a look of horror crossed his face, and as I was contemplating where I had gone wrong, I was surprised to see him bending down, half-kneeling, tugging at my trousers just below one knee. I lurched forward, not sure what to do, when he straightened himself, crashed me a salute, got back in the car and disappeared into the traffic. I tottered into the hotel and went straight to bed, by now nursing the onset of a genuine headache.

When Catherine eventually returned to the hotel, she airily

enquired after my health, before being engulfed in a coughing fit. She had stayed too long at the reception and had contracted a nasty chest infection to thank for it, poor thing. This lasted for the rest of the trip. When Sarah, Catherine's sister, met us at Heathrow, she was horrified to discover that the tiny, hunched figure accompanying me into the arrivals hall was, in fact, her sibling.

'What have you done to her?' she asked, eyes narrowed, in a tone that suggested I had put her through some terrible initiation rite on our very first overseas trip together. Needless to say, I've never managed to coax Catherine back to India.

J

Jesuits

Give me a boy at seven and he's mine for life

I first realised something momentous was in the offing when I strolled into the breakfast room, which had been renamed the television room after a TV had finally been installed, to meet the sight of my mother stifling her sobs as she sewed name tags onto a strange purple school blazer with a badge of four spread eagles. There was also the sound of muffled hammering from Poole's potting shed, where my father had taken himself with a small box of brass nails, a hammer and a pair of black school shoes. When I enquired, he showed me that on the arch of my shoes he had hammered in the school number 329. That number would stay with me for the rest of my life.

In early September 1955, as an eleven-year-old, I found myself staring into my maternal grandfather Oswald Jamison's bedroom at 4 Aylesbury Road, Ballsbridge, Dublin, to see him in only a blurred outline. He was in an oxygen tent and I was forbidden to cross the threshold. My mother was sitting next to him and her sobs drowned out his quiet farewell. It would be the last time I would ever see my grandfather because this was September 3rd and he died on the 11th, by which time I had been introduced, in a state of some anxiety, to Clongowes Wood College, out in the lush pasturelands of County Kildare.

One arrives at Clongowes through a castellated gateway and down a long, arrow-straight avenue with twin lines of towering ancient limes on either side. At the end of the avenue one crosses a ditch, known to generations of boys as the Gollymocky, before being confronted by the Castle, originally a thirteenth-century Norman castle, one of the garrisons that stood guard on the Pale, a medieval rampart and ditch that ran for many miles from the garrison town of Dundalk, north of Dublin on the coast, to the south of Dublin. This fortified border was built by the English to keep the 'barbarous' Irish out, hence the expression, 'beyond the Pale'. The Castle was the seat of the Wogan-Browne family until the Jesuits at Stonyhurst lent the Irish Jesuits the money in 1814 to buy it, making it the first Catholic boarding school in Ireland, and one that is often referred to as the Eton of Ireland, always by those who clearly don't know much about Eton.

It no longer looks anything like a Norman castle because it was later modernised and prettified and has lost the visual authority it once commanded. I remember so clearly entering the hall, which had on the right a marble statue of St Ignatius Loyola with a broken sword, the Spanish nobleman and soldier who founded the Society of Jesus in 1534.

My brother David, eighteen months my senior, who had left Douai, his Benedictine prep school in Berkshire, for Clongowes (my younger brother Fergus would follow on a couple of years later) was nowhere to be seen as I trailed my parents up to the first floor and through a massive door, before fighting our way through a heavy, dark-blue velvet curtain on the other side. Castles can be draughty, and these curtains were a feature of every room occupied by officialdom. There stood an enormous raven which introduced itself as Rector Baggott, SJ. This was my first introduction to seven years at Clongowes, alma mater of James Joyce and as disparate a group as any school anywhere could manage. As my parents disappeared back down the avenue, I was hurried out of the Castle and down to the boys' quarters through the Serpentine Gallery. As I trotted along this long curving corridor I marvelled, through my tears, at the number of ancient portraits on its walls celebrating those Clongownians who had made a name for themselves.

Very recently the military historian Dr Harman Murtagh, another man from my year, was commissioned to research and write a guide to all those in the Serpentine collection, and it's a pretty eclectic bunch – a surprising number of them were international revolutionaries, starting with A for Alfred Aylward, wounded fighting with Garibaldi in Sicily, and then moving to the battlefields of the American Civil War before leading a rebellion in South Africa, then switching to fight the British in the first Boer War before causing trouble in Sweden and becoming an advisor to the Mahdi in the Sudan.

B is for Frederick Boland, President of the UN General Assembly, where he broke his gavel trying to bring Nikita Khrushchev to heel when the USSR premier took off his shoe and used it to beat his lectern. C is for Michael Courtney (*see* I: INDIA), a good friend in my year who became a Vatican diplomat in various hotspots around the world and, when archbishop and papal nuncio in Burundi, was assassinated in a rebel-orchestrated machine-gun ambush.

Perhaps my favourite is The O'Rahilly, a nationalist and gunrunner in the years leading up to the 1916 uprising. He thought the Easter Monday rising premature but joined the men he had trained at the barricades anyway, declaring the event to be 'madness, but glorious madness', adding, 'I helped wind the clock, so I might as well hear it strike.' So many 'men of arms'. Maybe it's because Harman is a military historian, but all the VC holders are there, more than any other school outside Britain.

So, down the steps from the Serpentine to be, in some terror, engulfed by the size of the school buildings and the cries and shouts of the boys returning, dragging their trunks and tuck-boxes, crashing down the marble steps from the school door, past the Boys' Chapel and into the heart of Clongowes Wood College. A foreign land indeed.

The Jesuits, the great educators of Europe since the sixteenth century, have always observed the same educational structure, known as the *Studio Rudiorum*, wherever they teach in the world. Each year had a name: the first year, which I was about to enter, was *Preparatorium*, or Preparatory, from which you progressed to Elements, then Rudiments, Grammar, Syntax, Poetry and finally to Rhetoric.

However, classes for the new boys would not start for three days because at the beginning of each academic year there would be a silent retreat for all the boys from Rudiments and up – these boys you would see walking alone in the grounds, heads bowed, venturing into the heavily wooded Pleasure Grounds, normally the preserve of the Jesuit community, reading holy tracts, attending lectures and talks, going to chapel and generally contemplating. Meanwhile, the new boys, or 'new Scuts', were fighting a brave rearguard action against the 'old Scuts' – confined to the gym, both groups were in the business of shaking out the pecking order. This consisted almost entirely of fighting it out. Looking back, it was an ugly, brutal exercise in which you had to stand up for yourself and forge important alliances.

Sensing danger, I cleverly tagged onto an old Scut who'd already been through this, Mark Conroy, who remains a great friend to this day; a wit, raconteur, scholar and artist who went on, as a brigadier doctor, to run the General Medical Practice of the British Army. (Interestingly, another Clongownian, Thomas Bouchier Hayes, ran the surgical branch of the Royal Army Medical Corps, so two Irishmen had the control of the health of the British Army at a time when Anglo-British relations were tricky, to say the least.) Mark kept an eye on me, and, with my native cunning, I managed to keep on the right side of the maul.

However, Niall MacDonagh was not all right, and for no particular reason. In a scene reminiscent of *Lord of the Flies*, he was immediately picked on and it never really stopped for the whole of that year, and maybe beyond. It was dreadful; to this day our year hang our heads in shame for the indignities we submitted him and others to: head down the lavatory, again and again and again. His mother, a well-known actress and accomplished singer, had knitted him a red sweater and that too was pushed down the lavatory.

Niall's father was a renowned judge and playwright, and his grandfather, also a man of letters, was one of the signatories to the Declaration of Independence in the 1916 uprising, who met his end facing a British firing squad in Kilmainham Gaol – a great Irish hero. So, a serious Republican intellectual family, and here we were, a baying mob, holding its youngest member upside down over a lavatory. Terrible, but sadly common behaviour at the time in any boarding school.

I never knew what happened to Niall until recently, when I spotted a reference to him on Facebook. He seems, heroically, to have overcome the trauma of his Clongowes initiation: he read for the Bar and ended up in California, where he writes the most entertaining and observant Facebook entries and seems enthralled by traditional Irish music, as he appears to spend every waking minute playing the bodhran, an Irish drum, in various ceilidh bands.

There was another chap who was teased heavily, and he had only one functioning eye. When threatened, he would remove his thick-lensed spectacles, take his glass eye out and put it on the table, as a kind of defensive opening gambit, which inevitably proved ineffectual. Then there was J.J., also bullied, who during the first term made a couple of bids for freedom. He would auction off all his worldly possessions such as pens, penknives, magnifying glasses and all the usual schoolboy paraphernalia, which we were happy to buy on the cheap, but he would only ever get as far as the local village before being swooped upon and dragged back, Colditz-style. (As it happens, another Clongownian, Major Pat Reid, who wrote *The Colditz Story*, had better luck when on the run: he was the only Colditz prisoner to make a 'home run', crossing the Pyrenees into Spain.) When J.J. asked for his stuff back, we would remind him of the change of ownership and would regretfully inform him that he'd have to pay heavily for its return.

The three days of unlegislated argy-bargy in the gym gave way to the more conventional setting of the *Preparatorium* schoolroom. Each class had a boy who was known as the *Imperator*, or Emperor, who had a special desk in a special place and was supposed to keep order. In Preparatory, it was Gerry Wilkinson, then and later a great friend who ended up as a senior *homme d'affaires* at the Aga Khan's Secretariat at Chantilly, outside Paris. Our schoolroom was entered by one door and at the other end of the room, beyond a sea of desks, there was another door which opened into the People's Chapel (as opposed to the Boy's Chapel), which was for the local farm labourers and their families. As an acolyte serving Mass there, I remember the sodden, warm smell rising from the congregation in the winter months. Ireland was very, very poor in the 1950s, and these people came not from the grand avenue at the front, but from the back avenue, along which there were tiny cottages with stable doors and barefoot children.

Every Sunday morning saw an exam for the entire school in one single subject, held in the Great Study Hall. After about three weeks came the Irish language exam. The Gaelic alphabet and language were being heavily promoted in Irish schools out of a determined effort to forge the Irish identity and to differentiate it from English, the language of the occupier. Irish has many complications, not least the long accent called the *'fada'*, and unusual gender choices. I never quite came to terms with the fact that *'cailín'*, Irish for 'girl', is in fact masculine in gender (fitting for a country that has taken to LBGT and gender fluidity with such aplomb). Nevertheless, I set to manfully with my inky Osmiroid pen, with its mandatory oblique italic nib, to sit the examination.

The results were delivered by the Prefect of Studies, a Jesuit, and at that time it was a small, fiercely intelligent man with a very shiny head and blazing eyes called Skivvy Lawton. It was his function to gather all the results from all the different classes, and he would then deliver them by bursting into each classroom. He was from Skibbereen, County Cork, so he spoke quickly in the singsong way of the Corkman. He would read out the results, starting by calling out the name of the boy who came top. 'O'Reardon! 87 per cent', and O'Reardon would then stand up looking very pleased with himself, go to Father Lawton, shake his hand and receive what was known as a 'place card'. These were awarded for first, second and third place, and came in white, gold and blue, beautifully printed with Latin script – highly desirable and something to send home with the weekly letter.

Those three heroes having returned to their seats, Lawton would then read out the rest of the results, finishing with the lowest. Unbeknown to me, there was a break point at 40 per cent, below which was a fail. I got 17 per cent, which I thought was remarkable, bearing in mind that I was unaware that the Irish language even existed three weeks beforehand, so you can imagine my surprise when I was invited to step outside, at which point Skivvy dived into his floor-length soutane and produced a leather object about 15 inches long. This, I quickly understood, was a pandybat, a spatula-shaped whalebone encased in leather, apparently manufactured in Scotland. Certain Jesuit masters carried them, together with a cheque book printed in Latin: *Pueri nomen* (name of boy), *Poena* (punishments), *Quam ob causam* (description of offence), *Datum* (date), topped by a crest and then signed with a flourish. For a more detailed account of this bizarre currency of pain, please see James Joyce's *A Portrait of the Artist as a Young Man*.

For any misdemeanour, you would be issued with a cheque which you were then obliged to redeem for a pandying. You would hunt for the Jesuit least likely to give you a hard pandying. You held your hand out, palm up, while the Jesuit gripped the tips of your fingers to steady the target, because there'd be a temptation to try to remove it from the path of an incoming pandybat travelling at what seemed like 80 miles per hour. You'd get four, two on each hand, for failing an exam. Two to four blows were the norm. Six was a little bit heavy. The other version was to be 'cockered', in which case the pandybat would be directed at the backside. To be cockered was considered very bad form due to the indignity.

One might be forgiven for thinking that the Jesuit priests and scholastics administering such punishments were in some way brutish, but the opposite is true, and while there was for some a low cloud of fear (and I certainly was fearful at times), ask most boys taught by the Js and you will meet, in the main, a stout and proud defender of the order. I doubt there's a more arduous journey taken by a religious order, for it takes a full fifteen years from being a novice, three years of First Studies, the three-year Regency period, three years of Theology, then Ordination followed by the Tertianship followed by final vows. This training follows the *Spiritual Exercises* of the founder, St Ignatius, the purpose of which is 'to conquer oneself and regulate one's life in such a way that no decision is made under the influence of any inordinate attachment'. The idea is to 'find God in all things' – including, by this logic, the pandybat.

Looking back all these years later, it seems that each member of the Jesuit community at Clongowes was an island to himself, for I cannot ever recall any banter or comradeship between them, no noise or laughter, and maybe the discipline they imposed upon us was as nothing compared to the discipline they imposed upon themselves.

We mixed with the scholastics, who were in the Regency stage of training, and mostly in their mid- to late twenties. I remember Jem Healey, a very kind man; and The Beam (because whenever you looked at him he was beaming); and a wonderful, kind young scholastic from Malta, Mr Azzopardi, who taught us Latin. I loved my Latin lessons with him. I also liked Frankie Frewen, an ordained Jesuit known as The Frew, who looked like a Roman emperor and was a very good golfer. While all the others were to be seen flitting between the trees in the Pleasure Gardens, head bowed to their breviaries, The Frew was there with a golf club in one hand and the breviary in the other, practising his swing.

I was pretty smart in Prep and having got the hang of things I took my foot off the accelerator a bit and cruised right through. I was never top flight, but I rarely got pandied for handing in poor schoolwork. Which isn't to say I escaped the pandybat for general misdemeanours. As the classes were all down one long corridor, you could hear this rolling thunder coming ever nearer, a slam of a door and then the crash of pandybats followed by silence, and then the slam of another door and the next victims being hauled out. As it came nearer and nearer, it was a bit like sitting in a German trench during the opening barrage of the Somme: you'd be thinking, Oh God, they're going to get the range right in a minute, and then suddenly the door bursts open and in skips Skivvy.

True to the principles of St Ignatius, discipline was applied in many ways. I soon grasped the drill: always walk in a line along the wall into chapel, always walk in a line along the wall to the refectory. All rather odd when you think about it, but at the time it was just what you did. The Jesuits themselves had a particular way of walking: they wore rubber-soled shoes and glided silently. If they wanted to announce their impending presence, they would do so by rattling their keys.

There was no roustabouting with the teachers at all. There was no affection, no emotional connection: we were their charges and they were supreme beings. There was fun, though. One of the great traditions was a game called 'gravel ball', so-named because it was played outside the 1929 building, which gave onto a large, grey gravelled area imaginatively called Gravel. The game consisted of a small rugby ball being kicked high into the air, and then everybody descended on it – fifty to a hundred boys, divided into two teams by age, in a total mêlée. The team in possession when the whistle sounded had to get the ball through the doorway by the infirmary. The clever ones used the smaller boys to smuggle the ball through the scrum, but the doorway could be five-boys high. It was the best fun; there we were in our school clothes, completely covered in gravel and mud and blood. I suppose the official thinking was that this incredibly rough game toughened us up, but it must also have acted as a vast release on the pressure valve.

The door through which the ball was thrown connected to the infirmary, a very pretty little building with an iron railing around it and a beautiful cherry tree. This was the home of the Drak, the school nurse, who dressed in full nursing rig. Shortened from Dracula, she was the only woman in the school. (When I was older, there was briefly another woman who was brought in to teach us to dance. She didn't last very long. We all signed up enthusiastically for her class, but, disappointed at the lack of the close physical contact we had dreamed of, it was a very short cha-cha-cha. Within three weeks nobody turned up and the class was cancelled.) Ahead of difficult exams there'd be a queue of boys moaning and groaning and trying to gain access to the small infirmary ward – oh, to be put to bed for a few days – but the Drak wasn't having any of it.

Tragically, the Drak was unable to save the life of poor little Philip Shanahan, who'd come all the way from Khartoum, where his father was in the embassy, only to die in the first few weeks from meningitis. He was buried in the school cemetery, which is at the very top of the great avenue, shrouded by yew trees – in this dark, damp and dripping place lie all the Clongowes Jesuits, as well as my good friend Michael Rosenstock, who died in the sixth year, Poetry. He and his brother Pascal were the sons of a German medical student based in wartime Jersey and a Galway girl working there. Michael was a delightful fellow: tall, with high cheekbones and long, lank, jet-black hair. He was a good artist, a very sophisticated boy for his age, but above all a strongly opinionated rebel. He somehow got hold of a copy of *Lady Chatterley's Lover*, and he would lead a phalanx of followers around Gravel reading this book, which was banned in Ireland, all of us following and begging him for more: 'Michael, what was that bit about the curly hairs? Read it again.'

There was an outing for a small group of boys belonging to the Academy, a small and rather elite club of scholars, to Glendalough, an inky-black lake with an old Celtic tower in the Wicklow Mountains. Michael ate lunch and then he began to swim across the lake but disappeared before reaching the far shore. He was seventeen years old. My classmate, John Kelleher, also an Academician, remembers the journey back to college, one Academician short, and how the Jesuit in charge, Father Ray Lawlor, never recovered from that terrible outing on 1 June 1961. They found the body several days later and there followed a Requiem Mass in the Boys' Chapel. The awful moment came when his poor parents and Pascal, who sat in the front pew, had to follow the coffin of their boy down the long aisle in front of the whole school. It was terribly shocking for us all.

An important part of life at Clongowes was eating. The whole school, then of about 360 boys, ate in a huge refectory. Each table of eighteen places was split in half, with those at the top of the table taking what they wanted first and then pushing it down to the less fortunate ones at the other end. Steps in a wooden tower in the middle of the refectory led up to the Minister, a Jesuit, who sat with an open field of fire, and people would be summoned to him for talking during grace or other infringements. I seem to remember he would blow a whistle and then suddenly out of a black tunnel in the wall, the Johnnies, or servers, would come roaring out in their dirty aprons carrying great battered deep aluminium trays full of potatoes and slops and slices of this and that.

Breakfast was porridge, delivered in the same trays. On Sundays we had boiled eggs for breakfast and I was particularly fond of them. My standard offer price was sixpence per egg, and I would normally attract a small clutch. In the middle of the afternoon there was *Frustulum*, in Latin 'a small parcel of food to be taken on a journey' – huge aluminium pots of tea, milk, bread and jam. We were always hungry but there was a tuckbox room, though I didn't have a tuckbox for some reason, nor did a lot of other boys, and therefore a culture of scrounging was in full play. 'Can I have a scrounge?' you'd ask a boy, and he'd say, 'No, fuck off.'

If you looked up, you could see circular butter stains on the ceiling of the refectory. The trick was to lay your knife on the table, hold the handle down firmly, put a pat of butter on the tip of the blade, bend it down and then release with a satisfying 'boing', and if you were good at it you could get it to adhere to the ceiling. It was a question of getting the angles right (think moon landings). I heard a wonderful account of a

South American contingent who had been sent to Clongowes in the 1860s to get them the hell out of some revolution or other. As the legend goes, somebody had released a chicken into the refectory and the Minister stood up in his tower and bellowed, 'Will a boy kindly catch that chicken!' – a wonderful invitation for everybody to get up and chase this chicken around. Finally, the chicken flapped up onto a rafter, at which point one of the South American boys produced a revolver from his waistband and shot it dead.

Despite the disciplinary atmosphere, I think we were happy overall. Scholastically, the work was undertaken seriously, and it was quite a rigorous regime. We had a wonderful English master called Tom MacIntyre, a lay teacher, a writer and playwright, and it was his personal function in life to introduce us to the Great American Novel – Steinbeck, Faulkner, Hemingway, Scott Fitzgerald – and he was terrific and enthused us. My friend Gerry Wilkinson was leaning against a wall one summer afternoon reading *For Whom the Bell Tolls* when he was approached by Father Spillane, our Line Prefect, who said, 'What's that book you're reading, Wilkinson?'

'Oh, *For Whom the Bell Tolls*, Father.'

To which Spillane answered, 'It's a dirty book.'

'But Hemingway won the Nobel Prize for Literature, Father.'

'It's still a dirty book. Give it to me!'

With that, Spillane snatched it and marched off. Clearly Tom MacIntyre was operating slightly outside of the approved curriculum.

School visits were on Sundays. Mothers and fathers would meet at the Castle with their little darlings and the occasional priest would glide through making the right noises as we were having tea and cakes. That was the only touch of the outside

▲ A rowdy dinner after launching the first Amstrad computer.

▲ A gaunt PR man attends Alan Sugar at an impromptu press conference at the height of Amstrad's success.

▲ The original *Apprentice* team with Alan and the bowler, which featured in one famous episode. Pictured at the dinner I hosted to mark my retirement from the show.

A Margaret and I always tussled to be in charge. Here, once again, we wrestle over the wheel, this time at the 'funfair' put on for the *Comic Relief Does The Apprentice*.

A Lord Sugar saddling up for his early morning 30-mile spin while I contemplate a leisurely breakfast somewhere in the south of France.

B Mum and Dad at a university 'Tramps Ball', Dublin 1940.

B Sisters Annabelle and Stella, cuddling the ill-fated Lord French on the infamous mounting block at The Grange.

B Brother David, me and Cousin Patrick holding my
doomed pup Pitch on the 'Dinky' weekend. Mum,
unaware of our exploits, looks on.

B My parents' fiftieth wedding anniversary with their brood. From left: Nick, Stella,
David, Annabelle and Fergus.

C Denise, the studio sound recordist who looks after me, gets another slap for delving.

C Damian Eadie, *Countdown* producer, with the world's only golden *Countdown* teapot – presented after twenty-one years in the job.

C Dictionary Corner guest Griff Rhys Jones is mic'd up. Susie Dent in attendance.

F An anxious moment as a military motorcyclist flies overhead.

G My pensive young father at a local point-to-point with Grandpa in his 'Coker' talking to a Colonel Burley.

G My father (right) and his older brother, Tom, rode to school every day under the watchful eye of Grandpa's groom Clark.

H My great-grandfather and great-granny, who I remember looking like a sprightly walnut (when she was ninety-nine years old), with her mother and daughter, great-aunt Nora and, I believe, son Dickie, killed in the assault on Jerusalem in 1917.

H Richard Tuckey Hewer, a young lieutenant in the Berkshire Yeomanry, destined for a grave in Jerusalem.

H The oil painting of two white-faced Herefords from The Grange. © Janet French

H Outside the Red Lodge in Braydon Forest, Wiltshire, which my grandfather x12 built in 1620.

H Grandchildren on their first skiing holiday. Freddie, Raif, Katie-Grace, Theo and little Clara.

world for three months. Sometimes uncles and aunts (on my mother's side) would come and see me, or friends of my parents. Otherwise, there were no connections to the outside world, and leaving the school grounds without permission was an absolute no-no, which of course made the idea very attractive. The bit of the Pale that ran through the grounds was a rampart with a deep ditch, rather like a tunnel, overgrown with trees and bushes and sometimes there'd be a dead sheep in it, swollen up and distended with methane, and you'd run down the Pale to Clane, the local village a mile or so away, to go to the shop and buy something and then get back in the full knowledge that the shopkeeper was ringing the school to say he'd got some of the boys there. You had to get it and go and see if you could actually make it back. Great fun.

At the end of the great avenue, as you turned right, there was a pub called the Royal Oak, a place of thrilling danger. To be caught with alcohol! No punishment had been devised for such a terrible event. On one infamous Union Day, the big summer parents' day, a group in blazers and whites and others in the uniforms of the army cadet force, went to the Royal Oak and got a bit squiffy. On the way back across the fields, they came upon the tomb of the Wogan-Browne family. I think I might have been there. On entering the building, and descending the tomb proper, the lid of the sarcophagus was gently slid to one side, a skull was lifted clear and a running game of touch rugby ensued. Unfortunately, some of the perpetrators were members of the FCA, the officer cadet corps, who would be on parade shortly afterwards, taking the salute from a general whose son, Dick Callanan, was in our year. High on the battlements of the Castle stood a bugler whose job it was to sound an order but he was also pissed. A shrill screech was all he could manage.

Worse was to come. The platoon came marching down to orders given in Irish, carrying their Lee Enfield rifles, and the story goes that a 'turn left' order was issued and obeyed. At which point the entire platoon was consumed by the deep ditch which lay to its left, as the school, community and parents – including the general – watched on in disbelief. Some budding soldiers were given their marching orders for that little exercise.

We had a Spiritual Father who was a very kindly man, a little bit less aloof than the rest of the teaching staff and community, and when I was about fifteen, I was told to go and see him. Come the day, I'm standing outside his room with others in my class and suddenly it's my turn. I knock on the door. 'Enter!' I open the door, go through the velvet curtain, and there's his bed and a turf fire lit in the grate with a chair on either side, all very cosy, and Father McDowell offers me a cigarette. 'Thank you very much,' I say, and take a few puffs. 'Well, yes,' he says, 'I've been wanting to talk to you.' Short pause. 'The Lord has given you mystical powers which, well, frankly, mustn't be abused. Now, will you send in the next boy?' That was it. Sex education at Clongowes.

Somehow, we filled in the gaps ourselves, but it does remind me of my viciously curtailed rugby career brought about by the dreaded Father Spillane. Rugby was very, very important and when I was picked as the inside centre in the Senior Cup team, my prestige soared gratifyingly. I played in that position for the whole season until the cup competition started, at which point I was summarily dropped, as was my fellow centre. It was some years later that I read in the 'Rugby Notes' in the Clongownian magazine of that year that 'the two centres had been replaced due to lack of penetrative thrust'. That hurt.

Certainly, by the time I was fifteen I had a mind of my own

and had long been quite independent. As young as twelve, I was already making my own way to and from Clongowes from home. I vividly recall dragging my school trunk onto the steam train at Swindon Town to Fishguard or Holyhead, the window open all the way with the smoke trailing past. From there, I'd take an overnight ferry to Rosslare. Sometimes I'd be given money for a berth, but I'd put that in my pocket and unhook the tarpaulin over one of the lifeboats slung outside the ship and sleep in there. Completely mad, but what bliss to wake up in Rosslare early in the morning to the smell of bacon being cooked in the galley, and the sound of whistles blowing as cars were unloaded onto the dock. (This was before drive-on–drive-off: the cars were driven one by one onto a big net and then the net would be hoisted on board, and the operation repeated in reverse at the other end.)

I'd haul my trunk to Rosslare Station and get on the train that wound up through the beautiful Avoca Valley to Dublin; then I'd cross the city to another station to catch the school train to the little station of Sallins, about 5 miles away. With the other boys, I used to smoke long cigarettes called Joysticks, puffing away and feeling sick. At Sallins, there were horse-drawn carts waiting at the station into which all our trunks were put while we climbed into buses which took us the last few miles, on a warm, early September evening, to Clongowes.

I can see them now, my classmates. Dick Butler, whom I once wrestled to the ground and suddenly he froze and a look of alarm crossed his face. He put his hands in his pocket and, producing the body of a dead white mouse, said, matter-of-factly, 'That's one and six you owe me.' And then he suddenly left the school and nobody knew why he went. Brian Arkins, quiet, shy and clever, whose obsession lay in cricket. We were all slightly suspicious at the lengths he took to rub and polish the ball on his white cricket whites; somehow, we transferred the name Brian to Groin. He ended up as Professor of Classics at Galway, and at school reunions he used to sing famous Irish ballads in Latin. Some said that he had published a book called *Oral Sex in Catullus*, although none of us ever managed to get our hands on a copy. Other stand-out characters included John Kelleher and Dick Callanan, both of whom carved out successful careers in the theatre and filmmaking, and the Deeny cousins Michael and James, from that fiercely competitive clan.

Michael, refusing to be 'cockered' for stalking out of a heavily edited, indeed butchered film (all kissing scenes removed Cinema Paradiso style) just weeks before his finals, was invited to pack his bags. He went up to Oxford, and later emerged as the leader of the fight to recover the losses sustained by ordinary 'names' at Lloyd's in the scandalous Gooda Walker fiasco. I seem to recall that £500 million was recovered and that Michael, putting his occasional stutter to magnificent effect, addressed a packed and enthralled Great Room at the Grosvenor House Hotel on the progress of the good fight. It was Michael who smuggled a portrait of James Joyce into the school's Serpentine gallery at a time when Joyce's name would never be uttered (considered subversive to public morality, all Joyce's work was still, in effect, banned in Ireland).

Most of Michael's escapades were undertaken on matters of principle, perhaps none more so than his London kidnapping of the Springbok team when he was in his mid-twenties and the anti-apartheid movement was at its height. After Oxford, where his high spirits were well known, he trained to become a chartered accountant, but took the afternoon off one day to inveigle his way into the Springbok team headquarters at the Park Lane Hotel in London's Piccadilly. Nobody took any notice of the quiet, well-dressed young man in a tightly buttoned overcoat, hands firmly plunged in the pockets. Closer inspection could have perhaps detected a chain wound around his chest, with each end, complete with a padlock, descending through the sleeves, now nestling in each of his pockets.

With about half of the Springbok team already on board their coach outside the hotel, Michael approached the driver in his cab, urging him to report immediately to the team manager, who was inside, to discuss a change of route, given the increasingly loud anti-Springbok demonstrations now raging around the hotel. As the driver jumped out, Michael clambered into his seat and was surprised to find that the engine was still running. It had been his intention to merely chain himself to the steering wheel in the hope that the match would be delayed, bringing much-needed publicity to the anti-apartheid cause, but here was a more exciting opportunity. Chaining himself to the steering wheel and ramming the coach into first gear, he and his Springboks pulled away unsteadily from the kerb, swiping a Post Office van as it progressed jerkily down Piccadilly, pursued on foot by policemen and the furious driver.

Realising what had happened, some of the more alert team members proceeded to batter the defenceless kidnapper about the head until the coach was brought to a halt and the police arrived, breathless and feeling rather silly. Bolt cutters were called for, but by the time they arrived, the delayed Springboks were on their way to Twickenham, while our bloodied kidnapper was on his way to West End Central and an eventual meeting with a Westminster magistrate. All very worthwhile for a man committed to standing up for what is right.

Michael's cousin James took himself off to Yale and became a banker, while his younger brother Sir Donnell, with whom in recent years I have become friendly, is a glorious wit and has recently been appointed a Lord Justice of Appeal in Belfast.

These were at the more studious end of things. At the other end of the spectrum there were those who weren't of an academic bent, though they had certain other, often commercial attributes. One such person was Lily (Peter) Lawlor, from a family of wealthy farmers who also owned a hotel in Naas and a very successful outside catering company – so successful, indeed, it was said that Granny Lawlor had actually bought the Irish state silver from the government which she then hired back for state banquets. It was also said that as soon as the horse-racing season was over, Granny Lawlor would sit up in bed and start making the sandwiches for the following season.

Peter was a good-looking boy, very tall, played in the second row. We were all very jealous of him for two reasons: firstly, because he was given an MG sports car as a gift from his father for his seventeenth birthday, which he kept garaged quietly behind the school infirmary, and we were all goggled-eyed at such opulence and good fortune; secondly, there had been a strong suspicion that Lawlor had been the first to lose his virginity, which made him something of a hero to the rest of us. He embarked on a career as a pop star but sadly he didn't quite catch on.

One of the more exciting boys in our year was Donal Cussen. Donal was from the south country, I think Limerick way, and he was essentially a rebel. There was a time known as the bomb-making period, where we would pinch chemicals from the chemistry lab and, using the barrel of a biro, we would remove the ink tube and cram the plastic casing with explosives (in very small amounts, obviously). There was a tremendous science about how long fuses would burn for: a rugby lace would burn for x minutes per inch, a shoelace for y minutes, a simple piece of string for considerably less. These biro bombs would be slotted into trees around the school and surreptitiously lit, and then a number of cracks would be heard, at which point there would be a general whispered warning that Cussen was on the move.

Somebody had let lie in the shadow of an old building a length of heavy lead piping, 2 or 3 feet long, and this caught the eye of various groups who were in the bomb-making business until eventually one day it had gone: it had been lifted. There was a rumour that Cussen had taken it, and then there was the distant sound of hammering over several days in the boot room. Word got out that tomorrow was D-Day, or B-Day, the rumour mill suggesting that something would be taking place after lunch.

Come the morrow, small groups of boys drifted nonchalantly towards the areas overlooking the cricket crease, towards a very attractive, late Victorian cricket pavilion surrounded by a low iron railing and a pretty gate. I remember stationing myself on a seat underneath an oak tree on the edge of the cricket field – they say, the best in Ireland – and a number of us gathered there as Cussen was seen to march purposefully from the main building towards the pavilion carrying a bundle. He then disappeared inside. Eager anticipation, crowd murmuring. Suddenly all went quiet and heads turned to look behind, to find that on the steps of the main building stood the Higher Line Prefect Gerry Spillane SJ, a very hard man.

Spillane stood there gazing out, wondering why everybody was standing around looking at the pavilion, when, rather like the election of a pope, a puff of white smoke rose above the pavilion. Cussen had rammed his bomb up a drainpipe, which acted like a chimney, and then there was the most terrible CRACK, and Spillane stormed into action, leapt down the steps and poor Cussen was pretty much nailed at that moment. I don't think he saw another dawn at Clongowes. I later learned that he fathered eleven children, so he had clearly paid attention to the little lecture from the Spiritual Father on the mystical powers that God had given us.

When I think of these old friends, I'm reminded of John Updike's wonderful poem, 'Peggy Lutz, Fred Muth':

> *Dear friends of childhood, classmates, thank you,*
> *scant hundred of you, for providing a*
> *sufficiency of human types: beauty,*
> *bully, hanger-on, natural,*
> *twin, and fatso ...*
> *To think of you brings tears less caustic*
> *than those the thought of death brings. Perhaps*
> *we meet our heaven at the start and not*
> *the end of life.*

Over the years, we've met up for dinner at least once a decade and nothing has changed, except that the numbers, as we reach our mid-seventies, are beginning to dwindle. There are always wonderful moments and I remember with amusement a dinner in the 1970s, a time of some considerable Anglo-Irish awkwardness, when the table placements had been switched by some wag, putting Colonel Michael Lucey of the Irish army opposite Surgeon Captain Morgan O'Connell of the Royal Navy. It took five minutes for the mutual wariness to turn to warmth.

When I meet my classmates now, I'm humbled by their decency. I think particularly of Peter McVerry, who became a Jesuit and on ordination promptly started to build a large and now very effective charity for the homeless, remarking: 'The homeless in Ireland are not a problem, they are simply people who have come upon difficult times and circumstances.'

I think there was a tremendously strong sense of justice that came from the Clongowes education, from the Jesuit theme of 'a man for others'. True, we were institutionalised and the austere regime made us at times anxious: the rough justice (a pandying for missing a Sunday examination when I was playing rugby away for the school, for example), the general absence of compassion. But the other Jesuit saying, 'Give me a boy at seven and he's mine for life', may explain why, like most of the other young men who walked down the grand avenue of Clongowes for the last time, I was in tears.

PS: As I finish, my thoughts turn to Niall MacDonagh, clearly an intelligent and well-read man, proud of his heritage, and it's for him that I include this beautiful elegy, composed by Francis Ledwidge, shortly after Niall's grandfather faced and fell to a British firing squad. The Dark Cow refers to Ireland, whose departure from the moor and its poor pasture (British rule) was surely hastened by Thomas MacDonagh's death one hundred years ago.

'Lament for Thomas MacDonagh'

He shall not hear the bittern cry
In the wild sky where he is lain,
Nor voices of the sweeter birds,
Above the wailing of the rain.

Nor shall he know when loud March blows
Thro' slanting snows her fanfare shrill,
Blowing to flame the golden cup
Of many an upset daffodil.

But when the Dark Cow leaves the moor,
And pastures poor with greedy weeds,
Perhaps he'll hear her low at morn,
Lifting her horn in pleasant meads.

K

Aga Khan

Prince Karim Aga Khan and the magic carpet

In the summer of 1985, I fell hopelessly in love with an old Afghan rug in a lock-up shed deep in the bowels of the market in Karachi, Pakistan, perhaps one of the most threatening places I have encountered. The rug was not so expensive, but I had been brought up in that rather ugly Western way of feeling that one had to drive the price down and I was having a hard time making a dent in the seller's price. He was unmovable, and I was pressed for time, so I said I'd think about it. 'I will be here till seven tonight,' he said, with studied insouciance. 'And then I will lock up and I will go home.' I started to walk away, fully expecting him to call me back. He didn't. I fumbled my way out of the dizzying labyrinth of the ancient market and took a taxi back to my hotel.

I had come to Karachi for the opening of the Aga Khan University Hospital, the centrepiece of a 65-acre medical complex dedicated to an international programme of promoting modern healthcare in societies in which Muslims have a significant presence. The Aga Khan, who studied architecture at Harvard for a time, remains passionate about maintaining and evolving the great architectural heritage of Islamic civilisation (think Samarkand or Bukhara), and has funded schools, hospitals and development projects in virtually every corner of the globe, from Canada to Yemen, Burkina Faso to Kabul.

A serious man, Imam of the Ismaili branch of Islam, His Highness Prince Karim Aga Khan certainly comes from a colourful line. His father, Prince Aly Aga Khan, was a darling of the 1930s international set, a familiar figure wherever the 'season' had moved to, though in the summer months it centred on the Côte d'Azur at the magnificent Château d'Horizon, that Art Deco extravagance which featured a water shoot from the terrace into the limpid waters of the Mediterranean. I believe the Saudi royal family now owns the château, and I'll bet they don't have nearly as much fun.

Aly married Rita Hayworth (his second wife, her third husband), and was old enough to see his father pass him over in favour of the current Aga before fatally ramming his speeding Ferrari into a lamppost on the Champs-Élysées.

Aly's father, Muhammed Shah, who was once weighed in precious stones on the racecourse at Calcutta by the Ismaili community, was another charismatic character. Larger than life, he was once held up by a gang while being driven, I think in an open car, along the Croisette in Cannes. The party in the car having been stripped of their valuables, the thieves then waved them on. The magnificent old man threw a handful of coins at them, shouting 'Pour boire!' Such style.

Speaking of which, a year or so ago I lunched with Simon Berry, the seventh-generation family member to run Berry

Bros. & Rudd, the great wine company in St James's. Simon showed me the jockeys' scales in the front of the shop and pointed out in the record book the number of times the portly old Aga would weigh himself in the morning before embarking on a day of feasting. He would put up at the Ritz nearby but he had a habit, Simon told me, of spending the night at a Turkish bath establishment in Jermyn Street, where he would lose all the weight gained during the day before returning to the jockey scales to make sure. And so the routine would roll around again. A hugely popular figure, not least on Britain's racecourses – he founded the family's huge thoroughbred breeding and racing dynasty – he also inspired the advertising slogan 'Cadbury's, as dark and rich as the Aga Khan', which for a time was carried on London buses.

Through the introduction of Gerry Wilkinson, at the time a senior member of the current Aga Khan's management team, and a great friend of mine since our schooldays (we were in the same class at Clongowes), my company had been appointed as the London end of the Information Office of the Secretariat of His Royal Highness the Aga Khan, based in a magnificent château called Aiglemont, in Chantilly. So, my job in Karachi was not to buy rugs, but to help organise press coverage of the new hospital, designed by the Boston architecture firm of Payette.

Their brief, consistent with the Aga Khan's vision of using indigenous Islamic styles and construction methods, was brilliantly achieved in an award-winning series of buildings connected by internal courtyards with fountains and aromatic trees and shrubs, and covered walkways with fenestrated jali (screened) walls designed to take advantage of natural through-ventilation. The external walls were finished with 'weeping' plaster, which forms a ribbed surface to create shadow: an ingenious method for cooling the walls by deflecting the midday sun. It's a hugely successful hospital, reporting in 2015 alone that it had treated 80,000 patients, a record that put most equivalent large hospitals in Canada and USA in the shade.

The Aga Khan was also insistent, as he is with all his projects, that men and women be treated equally. In mid-1980s Pakistan, nursing was not considered a respectable occupation for young women (because they had to touch men's bodies), but in the new Karachi hospital, these perceptions were challenged: medical students, mostly male, and female nurses were all mixed together, treated with equal respect and paid the same during training. As the walls of the hospital were being constructed, other, invisible, walls were quietly being taken down. Wherever there are Ismaili Muslims – the small branch of Shiite Islam of which the Aga Khan is the head – you find the same phenomenon.

So here I am, dashing from my hotel to one of the events organised around the opening of the hospital – this one a reception in the former British Regent's magnificent mansion. Our host is the President of Pakistan, no less, General Zia-ul-Haq (assassinated on his Hercules plane a few years later when a bomb timed to explode when the plane reached a certain altitude detonated). We're all skulking around in a vast, regal room on the ground floor, about a hundred officials and journalists, sipping soft drinks, and all I can think about is my beloved rug. It would be bad form to mention this to Gerry Wilkinson, not least because at school he had been imperator – 'emperor' – of our class, and I don't want to risk the imperial veto.

I sidle up to a journalist from the Maghreb press called Mo, and whisper in his ear. 'Mo, earlier today I found myself deep in some godforsaken part of the souk, I can't quite describe where but I've got the card, and I saw a carpet I really liked, so could you spend some time with me when this is all over? I could use your help with negotiating and language.'

'Sure, no problem,' Mo says.

We knock back another soft drink and I look around and think, Dear God, this is going to go on forever. 'Mo,' I persist, 'the thing is, the rug man said he'd only wait till seven o'clock and it's now six-thirty and it's getting dark.' 'Okay, don't worry,' Mo replies, 'follow me'.

And, with that, we slip between the heavy velvet folds of the kind of curtains you'd find onstage in an opera house, slide open a window, and drop down silently onto the floodlit lawn. All around us, the presidential guard is glinting: the chromed wheel nuts of the jeeps, chiming nicely with the chromed ceremonial helmets and the not-at-all-ceremonial automatic rifles, and there we are, strolling casually across the floodlit lawn with no obvious reason for being there.

My chest tightens a little as we approach one of the gates, guarded by a soldier with a gun strapped across his front. 'Hello there!' I say, with forced heartiness. 'Do you mind letting us out?'

'No sir, I can't do that.'

'No, no, it's fine, we've been to the reception with the president – lovely man – and we're just popping out now because we need to go shopping.' With this, I look urgently at my watch. 'Actually, if you don't mind, we're in a bit of a hurry because the man in the souk says he's closing shop at seven.'

At this point, another soldier appears and we're marched to the guardhouse. There, the captain of the guard is caught unawares with his boots off: massive loss of dignity in a Muslim country, like being caught with your trousers down.

Addressing the soldier, he barks, 'What are you doing here? Who are these people?' Mo throws his shoulders back and says, in a voice straight out of the Raj, 'Now look here, we are guests of the government of Pakistan!'

'You will sit down and be quiet,' booms the captain of the guard, who is now lacing up his boots.

'Mo,' I say between clenched teeth, 'calm down.' Nothing doing.

'This is appalling!' Mo continues, but addressing me this time. 'We Muslims are famous for our hospitality, and now in front of you, an honoured guest from England, this frightful man is letting us all down.'

It's now five to seven, and the countdown to a diplomatic incident is ticking. But somehow, all parties find a way of standing down, and we are released into the dark streets beyond, teeming with tuk-tuks and motorcycles, each carrying three generations of the same family, and taxis, one of which we leap into, waving the card of the rug man in the driver's face. Next thing I know is we're hurtling on foot deep, deep down into the souk which is now plunged into darkness and an atmosphere of nefarious doings. I have the distinct feeling that I am going to end up as the first patient in the Aga Khan's new hospital.

Miraculously, we find the shop just as its owner is locking up. 'No, wait! We're here!' I gasp. He ushers us in. I introduce my friend, 'An important journalist from Morocco.' The vendor is suitably unimpressed. He rolls out the carpet, my carpet, with a flourish and turns on a battery of high-intensity bulbs, the better to dazzle us. Mo asks, 'How much are you asking my friend from London for this carpet?'

'One thousand American dollars.'

To which Mo replies, after a thoughtful pause, 'I spit on your carpet! I offer you thirty-five dollars. You talk to my friend who has come all the way from London and you insult him with this horrible carpet? I spit on it!'

My eyes are now popping out of my head. And with that the vendor ushers us out wordlessly, switches off the lights, locks up, gets on his bicycle and heads off into the night. 'Don't worry,' Mo says, 'it's a negotiating tactic. He'll be back.'

So, we're standing there in the dark and all I can see are the glowing tips of lit cigarettes. 'Mo, he's not coming back,' I squeak. I could swear I hear a sort of grumble of assent coming from behind the burning cigarette tips. We wait. For what feels like ages. Someone, and it's not Mo, says, 'Pssst, are you looking for carpets?' I've almost got lockjaw by this point, but I manage to whimper, 'Yes.'

'Follow me,' comes the voice, and without actually seeing his face, off we go, up ladders, across roofs, up and down and around until eventually we get to a little shed where, under a single, swaying lightbulb, he produces the most beautiful, old Afghan rug, of far better quality than my former love-object, and for a quarter of the price. It's under my feet now as I write this. I will be buried rolled up in it.

L

Lacroix

Life at the crossroads

'It is the destiny of the divorced man to lose his family,' writes Martin Amis in his autobiography *Experience*. The risk of losing my children, James and Katie, following my divorce was a constant worry. That risk, when allied with all the financial pressures that divorce inevitably brings – alimony, maintenance for the children, school fees and all the ancillary family expenses, combined with my own housing expenses in London – put tremendous strains on me. The possibility of ever buying my own house – for the family home quite reasonably had gone to the family – was extremely remote, certainly in London. Rental was the only option.

Where, then, could I afford a home that the children could visit during holiday times? My thoughts turned to rural France, particularly the deep south-west, with which I was familiar from visiting Michael Joyce, my boss at the time, at his house near the ancient city of Moissac, in the Tarn-et-Garonne *département*. I determined to see whether I could afford a small property in that area and set off to find one. And so it was, in 1989, when the children were fourteen and ten years old respectively, that I found a run-down farmhouse with a barn and a *pigeonnier*, perched on top of a hill between two villages, in a hamlet of five houses called Lacroix.

My plan to provide a holiday home for the children did not, in all honesty, work out. Their Christmas holidays saw them whisked away to relatives in America, as indeed, in the main, did their summer holidays, so the house at Lacroix saw little of them. I had long come to accept that they would inevitably spend most if not all of the major holidays with their mother and her family, which meant that I would find myself on Christmas Day placing a call to them in the US from Lacroix. The conversations were painfully brief; the children had presents to open and other distractions.

However, while there were periods of sadness and loneliness, I set about turning Lacroix into a home and there was much to be done. I'd bought the property, with a couple of acres, from Claude, the son of Etienne, the old farmer who had survived German forced labour in Poland during the war and had walked home in 1945. Etienne and his wife looked out for me in my first years at Lacroix, and it was from her that I used to buy eggs which she wrapped in a cone of newspaper. Whenever I needed wood, Etienne would appear atop his huge old tractor, drawing a trailer full of hefty oak logs, covering, one soon realised, a multitude of very spindly ones, but I always believed that I was a visitor in their country and should pay for that privilege by occasionally being duped.

Etienne also became my advisor on country matters. Returning home one day I was surprised to find a large snake

137

in the kitchen. Reaching for a stick, I approached and rather cleverly feinted a blow and caught him unawares on the other side. Two blows saw him dead. Lowering the lengthy carcass gingerly into a black plastic sack, I trotted off to show it to Etienne, expecting a round of applause, instead of which I was roundly rebuked as a stupid Englishman, for I had killed the one snake that would keep the mouse population in the house to a minimum.

'You were very lucky to have such a snake, and now you will be overrun,' Etienne said with doom in his voice.

'Where can I find another?' I said sheepishly.

'You must pray.'

The field mice brought their extended families into the house and for a period I was overrun. Then things quietened down, but recently I noticed a surge. This seemed to be related to the failure of the hot water system. I was away when Patrick the plumber called by to deal with the immersion heater, only to discover the scorched corpse of another large snake which had slithered into the base of the tank and blown the electrics. Hence the mice. More prayers required.

Gradually, I began to make friends with people in the local village. Baptiste, the gravedigger, would come and plant my trees and I would buy him Pernod in the Relais bar in the centre of the village. Baptiste was a stranger to the bathroom but no stranger to the bar: he lived there, and was the centre of jollity. The trouble with the Relais was that it bore some kind of domestic curse: it changed hands from one couple to the next with alarming frequency, each change being occasioned by some dread story of adultery (part and parcel of French life, this activity has its own euphemism, the *'cinq à sept'*, or 'five till seven', referring to the time of day when infidelity peaks).

The sad news is that the Relais has closed now, ripping the heart out of the village, although for a time there was also another bar-restaurant called the Café des Amis, run by a Moroccan and his rather haughty Parisian wife. He drank quite a lot and pinched girls' bottoms and was generally an unpopular face in the village. His eldest daughter worked for Eurotunnel; there was a younger daughter, a pretty girl with whom my son Jim used to play table football, his eyes locked on her increasingly curvy features; and the youngest, a boy, who was noted locally as an excellent footballer. The Café des Amis closed suddenly amid much gossip, the reasons for which I discovered on my return the following summer.

The younger daughter, Jim's teenage dream, who had by now turned eighteen and was a student at the local university, had been groomed by a much older man and toured with him around France to those ultra-chic but dark corners of large city society, as part of a sado-masochist sex troupe. None of this was known to her parents until shortly after her death in a car crash in Montpellier. It was only when her book, *Le Lien* (The Leash), was published posthumously – presumably a deal arranged by her dissolute partner – that the sordid facts emerged. Twenty years later, Café des Amis is still closed, the shutters now sagging, the terrace a mass of weeds, its unfortunate family long scattered in different directions.

In addition to Etienne and his wife, my little hamlet included a very beautiful and artistic woman in her eighties who lived across the lane. She'd had many children and one son, Jean, had stayed on living at home with her, through lack of ambition mainly, and became a pal of mine. He desperately wanted to be considered an artist, whereas in fact he was a brilliant artisan, and it was into his hands that I placed the renovation of the house. He was also an excellent gardener and cultivated a particularly fine species of cannabis, hence many a long summer evening spent gazing at the stars with the benefit of heightened perception.

Jean's cannabis was of a gentler variety to that of Luc, a neighbour from the next valley, an Italian who despised regular employment but who, as the owner of a tractor and a mower, could be seen cutting fields and paddocks in the area. He agreed to mow my grass. I remember leaning out of an upstairs window, watching his arrival on his tractor – he gave me a cheery wave and set about his task. I was surprised when I next looked out of the window to see him driving in ever-decreasing circles, dragging the mower behind him. Normally, one mows in straight lines, but not Luc. Round and round he went, and I suddenly realised that the cigarette attached to his lips was a very special one. He too was in the cultivating business, but at the very strong end compared to Jean's less powerful mix.

Before long, friends were turning up at Lacroix and furniture was being moved in. I bought a little bit more land and some sort of order was being established. Carpenters and roofers arrived to restore the beautiful *toit celtique* on the *pigeonnier*; I bought my own little grey Fergie tractor with a topper on the back; a motorbike arrived; a Renault 4L took up station in the barn. Jean re-tiled the ground floor of the house and turned the upstairs *grenier*, or granary, into two bedrooms and a bathroom. The old wood-burning furnace that ran the central heating was changed to oil, and I spent a whole summer building bookshelves in my study and replacing all the rotten external shutters with my own homemade, heavy Norwegian pine version. The newly planted apple trees started to produce a decent crop, as did the walnut and the cherries, figs and pears. Occasionally, the house benefited from a womanly touch.

During all this time, work still dominated everything. If I wasn't working late at night and at weekends in the office in Covent Garden, I was drinking coffee in my small rented flat in Dolphin Square. Life didn't extend much beyond either, so my spiritual home was now firmly at Lacroix, where I came as often as possible, though even when I was there the fax machine, phone and computer were rarely at rest. I remember standing in the doorway of the house one Saturday morning, looking out across through the trees, the sun beating down, and fearing to go into the garden in case the landline would ring (these were the early days of mobile phones and the signal had not quite reached Lacroix). I realised I was addicted to work, a prisoner of its demands. I didn't *have* to do this, but I couldn't tear myself away. This fear of not being available to clients or press was of my own making – I was a captive only of myself. Years later, when I sold my company, I suddenly understood that I had undervalued myself, that clients were astounded that I had felt it necessary to be always on duty.

At Lacroix, when I wanted to witness other people hard at work, I had only to drive to the Relais for morning coffee and pass the Zambonini family toiling on their small farm. Paolo, who had brought his three sisters with him from Italy just before the war, had a small milking herd and some beef cattle, and a few acres of cereal crops. Together they lived a medieval farming life. One winter I called by to find them all sitting in a row in the chimney breast, a gentle fire at their feet and bowls of milky coffee at their lips. Their love was concentrated on their 1-acre vegetable strip, which contained three rows of vines and a mishmash of artichokes, broad beans, potatoes, tomatoes, peas and carrots. These the ageing sisters tended, bent double in the searing heat, their heads covered by wide-brimmed sun hats, until they died in their nineties (although one was killed by their bull: on being brought under cover in a thunderstorm, it panicked and crushed her). Today only Paolo remains, bare-chested at ninety-one, still driving the little Honda cultivator to break up the soil or pushing a wheelbarrow laden with firewood up the steep incline of the field in front of his house. I always stop to say hello when I'm driving past, and he shells a pea or two for me.

Etienne and his faithful dog Tango had their little vegetable garden just below my house and I would stop by there, too. But then he left the big house and moved into the nearby village, so our meetings became less frequent. Last time I saw him, I greeted him and enquired after his wife. As soon as I spoke I knew there was a great sadness about him. He fumbled for a handkerchief, slumped slightly and told me tearfully that she had gone. She was buried in the village, he said, gesturing towards the little walled cemetery. He started to cry, this old man in his nineties, and I started to cry too as I gave him a hug. Tango was no longer there either, and before the autumn leaves had fallen, Etienne had rejoined his wife and is now in the family tomb.

And so, life is changing down by Lacroix. The old genera-tion has almost all gone, but what remains is the beauty of this extraordinary country. It always surprises me that the British take such delight in loathing the French. I find them to have made a great success of their lifestyle; they even invented an expression for it, 'to be happy in one's skin'. They love their countryside, their food, their wine, their leisure time. Who should blame them for closing their shops on Sundays and not opening till Monday afternoon? Or for the quietness that descends on every village between two and four o'clock every afternoon?

It's taken me decades, but I've finally learned from my French friends how to let go, drop my shoulders and fully embrace the pleasure of driving from Lacroix for Sunday lunch at a restaurant in a medieval *bastide* high in the hills forty minutes away without passing a single other car; or the boyish pleasure I get from clambering into my beautiful wartime Willys Jeep and trickling through the woods and valleys off-road without seeing another soul. As I write this, I mourn the loss of Jasmine, my lovely black Labrador bitch, whose presence on the seat beside me used to heighten the enjoyment of these rambles. I suppose it all boils down to this: there simply aren't many people here, and those that are I find invariably kindly and quiet. It's a simple life, uncomplicated by the rush and push elsewhere.

It's only taken nearly thirty years to bring the house up to scratch, though there's still much to do. To put it mildly, even after all this time, the house is pretty rudimentary. Suddenly, faced with my advancing years, I've decided to get a bit of a push on. And that's where Reg the Master comes in. From time to time, one runs into a person of really great value. I have met two such people and both have worked here in Lacroix. The first is Daniel (*see* M: MONGOLIA), from Görlitz on the Neisse River in Poland. I met him through a friend who lived deep in the wild Ariège, the empty quarter of France lying beside the Pyrenees Oriental, and he came to work at Lacroix. Daniel has golden hands, he can do absolutely everything: electrician, builder, plumber, car mechanic. Over several years he worked here and would then return to Poland. He didn't speak any

English and I speak no Polish, but somehow we understood each other perfectly. I would telephone him in Poland and the conversation would go like this:

'Daniel?'

'Neeek.'

'Daniel: Toulouse, Monday-Tuesday-Wednesday-THURSDAY,' I'd say, slowly running through the days of the week before landing with emphasis on the day in question.

'Okay,' he would reply. 'Toorshtay.'

End of conversation. On the Thursday, I would drive to Toulouse bus station to meet the Eurolines bus from Poland, and Daniel would be on it. It never failed.

All I had to do to satisfy Daniel was to cook gargantuan helpings of food – potatoes, cabbages, sausages. The trick of retaining him was feeding him, paying him and then putting him back on the bus to Poland. On a few occasions, he came to England to do some work at our home Rectory Farm, staying for a couple of months at a time and progressing his English until we were able to sustain a conversation. Sadly, he developed a heart condition which necessitated a stent or two and, while we continue to exchange cordial phone calls, his return to Lacroix or Rectory Farm is still on hold.

Fortunately for me, I was introduced to the magnificent Reg, an Englishman living in the Dordogne, and every bit Daniel's equal. A man of few words, massive in physique, with the strength of Hercules, and always accompanied by his Old English sheepdog, Blue, Reg is one of the most intelligent men I have ever met. Not only does he have golden hands, but he is an artist and an engineer of extraordinary ability. As I write this, in my study at Lacroix, he is outside on the terrace hoisting a massive oak beam, weighing every bit of three-quarters of a ton, with a crane apparatus he has constructed out of some timber spars, and, with an ancient block and tackle, he's lowering the beam into position, allowing the weight of the timber to work in his favour. His artistry comes from the way he has fashioned the beams so that one slides into another and locks together without the use of screws or nails. I now have an almost-completed veranda built to a specification and with the same skills as the carpenters who put the roof on this house more than 250 years ago.

The swimming pool is yet to come. When that arrives, then I have hopes that the children and grandchildren will descend, and Lacroix will finally fulfil the purpose for which it was bought all those years ago, albeit a generation apart. The pool may also prove an attraction for Catherine, who tells me time and again that such a thing would provide a focus for guests and for her too.

Catherine enjoys comfort and security. Indeed, we laugh at home about her position as a health and safety officer. Her interest in these matters may well have been sparked by an incident at Lacroix some fifteen years ago. An English friend in Paris told me that she was moving back to the UK, and would I like her perfectly serviceable though elderly Renault 19. I jumped at the chance, and drove it from Paris to Lacroix, where it languished in the barn for some years. Catherine was on one of her fleeting visits, and we decided to have lunch in Pujols, an exceptionally pretty ancient *bastide*. I told her we should take the Renault for a little run. She looked downcast, as the barn owl had taken a fancy to voiding itself on the white roof and bonnet. Catherine pointed out that one of the tyres seemed flatter than the others, but I waved away her concerns and we set off to Pujols.

As we climbed the steep and winding road up to the *bastide*,

Catherine asked whether I could turn the heating off. I said that the heating was turned off, but she insisted it was very hot. A few moments later, I too sensed that the floor of the car felt a little warm, at which point, as we crested the hill, wisps of smoke were rising from the opening of the bonnet near the windscreen. I said nothing, but Catherine is a sharp-witted and observant woman, and within seconds she said, 'I think this car is on fire.'

I was in a tricky position, for I had a precipice on one side and a stone wall on the other. There was nowhere to stop. 'Don't worry,' I murmured nervously. 'I know there's a car park in front of the *Mairie* – it's just around the corner.' 'Well, hurry,' she said. The smoke was thickening and streaming over the windscreen as we turned the bend to find ourselves facing the town hall, where I'd already mentally taken the decision to pull the car into the forecourt immediately in front of the main entrance.

Panicking, I failed to appreciate the significance of a man with a red, white and blue sash who was tensioning a microphone on the front step. Either side of him there were lots of people. I then noticed that behind me, by the war memorial, what appeared to be the entire village school had assembled as a choir and was warming up. But my course was set, and I drew up to a sudden halt, the bonnet just nudging the microphone stand. I told Catherine to get out. She needed no encouragement. She's agile, a one-time captain of her school lacrosse team, and in one movement she shot out of the car. I watched her go, concerned for her, but was surprised to see her enter the crowd and immediately turn towards the scene of the drama, arms folded, as though she had been a member of the crowd all along.

The mayor was now knocking furiously at my window. I had one leg out when he asked me to produce my car documents. I re-entered the car and as I bent to search for the papers underneath the dashboard I was alarmed to see flames licking at the windscreen. I fumbled for the documents, found them and was guided by the mayor away from the fast-developing catastrophe.

And then it dawned: it was eleven o'clock on the eleventh day of the eleventh month, and I had unwittingly disrupted a precious Armistice ceremony, held in the heart of every French town, to commemorate the loss of 1.7 million French lives in the First World War alone. The crowd was restless as they watched *les Anglais* disappear into the *Mairie* (Catherine had now joined me, her head held low), at which point the fire brigade and the police, both of whom were present in their official capacities at the ceremony, converged on the car. As one fireman lifted the bonnet, flames erupted but were rapidly doused with a surprisingly bright blue foam from a hose held by his colleague. Belt and braces is clearly a French motto, for he was not satisfied with just flooding the engine compartment but set to with a will to cover the whole vehicle and indeed under the vehicle with the foam.

The community had every right to be upset with this appalling intrusion, but in truth the mayor and the authorities were kindness itself, and as the poor Renault was dragged in due course onto the back of a breakdown vehicle, and Catherine and I stepped into a taxi to return to Lacroix, we agreed that my stupidity had been met only with grace. Even the bill, for 250 euros, which arrived sometime later, seemed a small price to pay.

M

Mongolia

Diary of the Mongol Rally

How I decided to take part in the Mongol Rally remains something of a mystery to me. In July 2007, there was a boozy night at some shabby nightclub in a Covent Garden backstreet during which I think it was mentioned, then a meeting shortly after with the amiable and entrepreneurial Tom Morgan, founder of the League of Adventurists, who explained that the rally involved driving eastwards for 10,000 miles in a suitably old, sub-1,000cc car, across 25 per cent of the world's surface, over five mountain ranges and across three deserts with Ulaanbaatar, capital of Mongolia, as the finishing line. Before I knew it, I had registered to take part.

There were forms to fill out, visas to be obtained, supplies to be ordered. I was lucky enough to dine with the ambassador of Mongolia, who was very kind and full of good advice, one strand of which was always to travel across Mongolia in a small convoy. 'It is a vast and beautiful country,' the ambassador said, 'but it's very easy to get lost. We Mongolians have an inbuilt compass, developed over thousands of years. At night, we have only to lie on our backs and look at the stars to know exactly where we are.'

I reported back to Margaret, my fellow sidekick to Sir Alan on *The Apprentice*. 'Very simple,' she said. 'Get a Mongolian, lie him on his back and get him to tell you where you are.' That's Maggie for you.

There we were, me and Hortense, a 1989 Renault 4L (with *'faible kilométrage'*) bought from a bloke called Boris in Angers for 2,000 euros. When I told him of my intentions, Boris fitted Hortense with an internal tubular steel cage, and a visit to a firm of steel fabricators in Buckingham saw her suspension beefed up, a larger radiator with auxiliary fans fitted and, most beautifully, a bespoke spare-wheel carrier mounted on the back. They also added a shining aluminium pipe, mirroring the slope of the windscreen and running from the air intake to the roof, with a filter on top, designed to keep the motor running whether crossing a river or, more probably, driving through a sandstorm. Desert tyres were sourced and fitted, as were a figure-hugging rally seat and a reclining one too, for those nights to be spent curled up with Hortense. Finally, I tracked down a leather-clad steering wheel from a racy Renault Gordini. I stocked her to the gills with everything including a case of claret to sustain me in times of despair. We were ready to roll.

The rally – 300 other old bangers manned by young blokes and girls – was due to set off in the third week of July 2008, but I slipped quietly out of England, alone, nineteen days ahead of the pack. I wanted to take it gently, stopping off here and there while the thundering herd relentlessly closed in on me. With a bit of luck, they'd be swarming all around me by the time I hit the sand roads of Mongolia.

Dover came and went and after a stopover in Le Touquet, Hortense lifted her skirts and with her little engine purring away, we headed for Paris where I had arranged to meet Benjamin Darras, who with his brother had driven to Mongolia in a Renault 4 the previous year. Arriving at Place de la Bastille, I drove around the great monument, erected by Napoleon, for about an hour, along with the rest of Paris, looking for a parking space. Eventually I stuck Hortense on a pavement. Benjamin arrived and talked enthusiastically of how he and his brother had made the finishing line in fifty-one days after fifty-eight breakdowns. Clearly, he had found the Mongol Rally a life-enhancing experience, but having listened to his advice and guidance for an hour, I wasn't altogether sure I wanted my life to be further enhanced.

'How many spare wheel rims are you taking?' he asked.

'Just the spare,' I offered. Not the right answer.

'You will need several more, maybe four; get them in France, they're impossible to find elsewhere because they have only three bolt holes.'

Benjamin scrutinised Hortense. 'Your exhaust system will not last a day in Kazakhstan,' he concluded jauntily. 'It must be changed to the shorter van type – do you have a saw for cutting it out? You think you can imagine how bad the roads are going to be? Imagine the worst, and then multiply it by ten. Sometimes our car would be completely swallowed up by a hole. We tried travelling at high speed to even out the lateral ridges, but after a couple of days the bonnet fell off and one of the suspension arms snapped and catapulted us into the air, flipping the car on its side. We were lucky not to be seriously injured.'

I didn't like the sound of this. There was worse to come.

'When you enter Mongolia, the road simply stops. Pah! No road. So you just drive where you want and sleep in the car at night. You hear strange sounds, animals prowling outside. But the most frightening thing is that from the Russian border to Mongolia, everyone is drunk. Mainly friendly, but they are bored. They want to drink with you and smoke with you, and then they move on.'

'I gave up smoking years ago,' I said.

'You might have to take it up again, they can get offended.'

I left Paris in the morning rush hour, moving in a slow stream of angry syrup around the *Périphérique*, peeling off towards Roissy and the airport. Eventually we reached Hortense's maximum cruising speed of 60 miles per hour and slipped through the lush countryside. The forest of Compiègne ambled past, then we were in Belgium, then Luxembourg and before you could say 'Himmel', we had reached Germany. I kept away from the autobahns, but every minor road in Germany is a three-lane highway thundering with fat Mercedes. As Hortense made her stately progress in the slow lane, they thwacked past at 140 miles per hour, their occupants pointing their fingers at us in derision. They'd be in Latvia by lunchtime.

One summer, when we were kids, my brother David and I, not yet teenagers, were handed two elderly cast-iron bicycles with lever brakes and baskets on the front and told to cycle from Swindon to Hope Cove in Devon, where our parents would meet us. We were to stay in youth hostels. Armed with pakamacs, fifteen shillings and soggy sandwiches, we set off, not entirely sure what we had done to deserve this, and far from convinced that we would ever see home and family again.

Struggling up a hill near Devizes, not far from Swindon,

I lurched to the centre of the road and came crashing to the ground as I was hit from the rear by a racing cyclist. He was furious, and picked up his gleaming, lightweight twenty-gear Rudge, mouthing obscenities and general loathing. Seeking to defuse the situation, I asked politely where he had started that morning. 'Birmingham,' he snarled, and with a whirring of derailleur gears he was gone. I guess he drives a fat Mercedes now.

Two days later, Hortense and I had reached the town of Zgorzelec in Poland, home to my old friend Daniel – builder, pianist, ex-Polish special services sniper and parachutist (*see* L: LACROIX). As a member of the UN forces supervising the withdrawal of Russian troops from Afghanistan, Daniel found himself in the middle of winter doing guard duty on top of a high pole with a sniper rifle. 'It was so cold, I was shaking so much, I could not shoot anything, not even the sky,' he once told me. No matter how cold it is, when push comes to shove, what better to put on a high pole than another Pole?

I had come to see Daniel to pick his brains on what, if any, security precautions I should take before easing myself across the Russian border. His first action on seeing Hortense was to plonk a Polish sticker on her rear quarters: 'Best to travel with old Warsaw Pact identification when you're travelling through the old Soviet Union.' He then lectured me on the folly of venturing into Russia alone. Although lots of friends at home had questioned the wisdom of setting off on this epic journey at all, and certainly cautioned me against doing it solo, I had brushed off their warnings as Home Counties caution.

Here, however, was a bloke who knew what he was talking about. Daniel can clearly look after himself, but he has a healthy respect for the lengths some Russians will go to for a dollar. So have I, having been rather elegantly mugged in St Petersburg a few years ago, when I was relieved of my cameras in broad daylight in Nevsky Prospekt, in total silence.

Daniel told me about his friend who was hauling a truck through Russia when he was stopped, dragged out of the cab, and thrown under the wheels so that the bandits could drive over his legs, presumably to stop him running after them. They were right in that assessment, because both legs were broken and he was left in the ditch to be discovered some hours later by a passing Good Samaritan.

A day or two later I steered back onto the planned Mongol route, driving south along the mighty Danube and stopping overnight at Brno. Next morning, bypassing Bratislava, it was on to Budapest and the great *fin de siècle* Gellert Hotel, hunched on the banks of the Danube. I had stayed here a few years back on the homeward stretch of a swing through Eastern Europe with my black Labrador, Jasmine.

One of the great pleasures of the Gellert is the two enormous hot mineral baths in the cavernous basement with vaulted ceilings painted deep blue with golden stars. As a guest, one is given free access to this wonder and explicit instructions are provided in one's room: 'Please wear your modesty apron and bathrobe. Proceed to the iron lift where you will be given a voucher and taken down to the baths.' Modesty apron? That'll be the little square of cloth, no bigger than a handkerchief, dangling in the bathroom. Oh dear. Still, when in Rome. On with the apron, then the bathrobe, thence to the lift.

I enter the vestibule of the baths, to be greeted by an enormous Hungarian masseur dressed as a gymnast, proudly displaying a moustache the size of a yard broom. He demands my bathrobe and I do not argue. I then pass through into the enormous bath area; there are two baths, one hot and the other really *quite* hot, each almost circular and far larger than a swimming pool, with great baroque fountains and marble pillars and sweeping staircases down into the depths.

None of this registers with me. I'm far more focused on the fact that everybody else – and it's fairly crowded – is wearing Speedos and I'm the only bloke wearing a very thin, very small piece of cloth. I slink into the shallows and sit on the long underwater bench lining the wall, at which point my modesty apron loses interest in its job and floats to the surface. I stand up in shock. I sit down hurriedly, and, clinging to bench, I marinate into a prune until closing time, only getting out once everybody has left.

Next day, it was foot hard down towards Romania, where I stopped overnight at Cluj. I regretted having to speed through this lovely county – it deserved a longer stay. The same cannot be said of Moldova. Having passed through a lengthy immigration process, I entered Moldova only to find myself within a few hours confronted with the Ukraine border. More messing about, and then I was spat out into the Ukraine. I was no sooner there than I was once again confronted by the Moldovan frontier, where I was forced to go through the same rigmarole again. To cut a long story short, it takes eight frontier crossings before you are well and truly back into the former USSR.

I headed for Odessa and stayed at the Black Sea Hotel. Having buried Hortense deep in the secured garage, I walked the six blocks to the swinging centre of this great old city and had dinner on a balmy evening watching the boy racers in their 1978 Ladas with blacked-out windows cruise the boulevard. I strolled back to the hotel and popped into the adjoining casino to watch the tables for an hour. From my very poor American guidebook to Eastern Europe, I learned that 'Odessa has taken to crime like a duck to water'. Scanning the faces at the tables, it was clear that I was among people from Odessa's demimonde. Everybody's nose had been badly smashed at one time or another, including the one belonging to a Chinese woman gambler on the blackjack table. Her companion, another Chinese woman, had escaped the same fate but was so extraordinarily ugly that, strange to tell, a broken nose might actually have improved things.

A quick visit to the Potemkin Steps the next morning, then Hortense and I were off through Ukraine's great corn belt, miles and miles of golden crops combed by a light breeze. At Melitopol, we stopped at the world's worst hotel, the Melitopol Hotel, a Soviet-style dump with a surfeit of nylon and filth, ringed by menacing youths and broken concrete. I paid the security drunk $10 to sleep on Hortense's bonnet, and next morning I fled to Mariupol on the Black Sea coast, my last stop before entering the dreaded Mother Russia.

I reached the border crossing just south of Rostov, where I was relieved of $114 for car insurance and then directed to another blockhouse to fill in forms in Russian with the help of kindly Ukrainians who didn't speak English, before finally arriving at the desk of the big Russian cheese, sporting star-studded epaulettes that appeared to be made of thick cardboard. He was a pleasant man and all went swimmingly. At the end of the interview, he produced his wallet, rifled through the contents, and, clearly irritated, summoned his lieutenant who produced a 500-rouble note, which the big cheese waved at me. I also found a 500-rouble note in my wallet, and we waved our notes at each other. He took mine gently from my fingers, and with a flourish popped it into a drawer in his desk.

And so, with one bound, Hortense and I enter Russia. Half a mile down the road, I am pulled in by the cops. Having been accused of all manner of things, I am presented to a magnificent officer, dressed in a white uniform and wearing one of those peculiarly Russian caps, where the crown has the diameter of a flying saucer. He is all smiles as he slides into the passenger seat. 'What are we to do?' his laughing eyes seem to ask. 'Forty dollars,' he suggests. I demure. We end up agreeing that $25 is a very fair price for my serious, non-existent, crimes. I produce the notes and smooth them out on the dashboard. Roaring with laughter, he indicates that fines such as these must be placed 'under the counter'. We part the best of friends.

My trip through Russia was punctuated by police patrols needing to see my papers on an hourly basis, but I experienced only kindness and generosity from them and from all the Russians I met. Notwithstanding the dire warnings of Benjamin and Daniel, I was never menaced, found everybody quite sober, and enjoyed my trip through to Volgograd, a great city, and was sorry to leave Russia. Maybe I was just plain lucky.

I stopped off at Astrakhan, a city I had high hopes for, which proved dull, before moving on towards the border, crossing and running alongside the most beautiful rivers and the most fertile land, irrigated by the nearby Caspian. It really did look like the Garden of Eden. Then to the border with Kazakhstan. Usual wrangle, hour after hour of messing about, being pushed from pillar to post, until eventually I was ushered into Kazakhstan where, ten minutes later, I fell into the arms of the local traffic cops, when the whole palaver was played out again.

Then the big drama. I think I might have been dozing slightly; all I remember is a loud explosion on the passenger side of the car, which sagged down and we slewed at speed off the road. Hortense and I had been introduced to perhaps the single most memorable aspect of life in this enormous country – the Kazakhstan pothole, a wonder to behold. Grey with terror, I clambered out to discover to my very real horror that two steel wheels were bent out of shape and two tyres blown.

I walked back to the pothole and then looked to where the car had stopped at least 200 feet further on. I turned my attention to the pothole, which had been perfectly positioned to catch the nearside wheels, and beautifully shaped; deep and with a clean cut to it. There was nothing gradual about this specimen – perhaps 3 feet square and 1 foot deep?

The early afternoon sun was the size of a saucepan and it was as though somebody was hitting me on the head with it. I stood by the side of the car with a towel on my head for what seemed an eternity, and then in the distance I spotted a plume of dust on the long, dead-straight road. An old Russian van clattered past and I waved feebly at the driver. No reaction as he maintained speed and went on his way. I was still in a bit of shock and dully recognised that I'd have to start *doing* something, when I looked up to see the old van slow and then swing around. Help was on the way.

Two young boys jumped out and immediately inspected the damage. The driver, a burly and wispily bearded Kazak, climbed slowly out, came towards me, shook my hand solemnly and thoughtfully inspected Hortense. From then on it was a blur of activity in which I had no part to play. The car was jacked up, wheels were removed and an almighty steel hammer (even the shaft was steel, probably made when the Revolution was young) was produced.

Ali, for that was his name, walked around the wheel several times, gauging it. He was an artist: he hefted the mighty hammer and with three exquisite blows, each carefully weighted, returned the rim to its original shape. He repeated the process, the tyres were replaced, blown up, refitted, and the car lowered. Wiping his hands on an old towel, he formed a cross with his fingers and said: 'You Chritian? Me Musselman.' My thanks could not have been more profoundly genuine and I shall never forget his generous act. I wrapped up some dollar notes in my hand and passed them into his fist as we shook hands farewell. 'Thanks you, thanks you,' he exclaimed, his broad shoulders heaving with excitement and gratitude. We got into a 'No, thank *you*' competition, which I eventually insisted I had won, and so we parted company, each not believing his luck.

I pulled back onto the road to Atyrau and reached the city late that night. It looked like a two-storey sort of place and I scanned the cityscape for lights. I headed towards some neon and sure enough it was a hotel. Clambering out, I was greeted by two young bloods and their girls. Young Blood 1 spoke English and Young Blood 2 was pleasantly tipsy. The girls were serious. YB1 told me he had studied English in Margate, which I thought deserved a beer at the best of times and I invited them to join me for a drink.

YB1 told me the road ahead to the next big oil town, Aqtobe, was really bad, 'like swimming the big waves'. A delightful young guy, the following morning he took me all around Atyrau, which in daylight turned out to be a high-rise oil town enjoying the boom. We found a tyre depot and they checked all the wheels and I was on my way. YB1 looked to me like the future of Kazakhstan: bright, smart, educated and most of all enthusiastic and energetic. Added to which his brother was in the Kazak KGB. 'Helpful,' he remarked casually.

I hit the big waves not long after leaving Atyrau. I couldn't believe my eyes, they were Atlantic rollers, coming at Hortense one after the other, the hollows big enough to swallow her whole. I slowed to walking pace, climbing crablike from side to side up the road. It took time to work out that the best form of attack was the headlong approach. Slowly. Hortense's bonnet would sink down, the sump guard would grind along the bottom, her bonnet would climb out, and her petrol tank guard would scrape along and we'd be back on the road for another 15 feet before the next chasm appeared.

One must avoid putting the nearside or offside wheels in these potholes because to do so means the sump and petrol tank crash onto the tarmac with shuddering force. But it's impossible to avoid and so every two or three minutes there'd be a sickening crash as yet again I miscalculated the angle of attack. The 6 mm aluminium plate I had installed in England to protect the sump and tank took a terrible beating and I couldn't believe we would survive; every crash sounded terminal. The tow points welded either side of the sump guard were bent as though made of butter. Poor Hortense, *ma belle*, it was not meant to be like this.

Very often the road would become totally impassable. As the density of the great potholes increased it became hopeless, and I would simply dive off down into the desert and drive parallel to the road. This can be pleasant. Driving on soft sand is silent and there are no jolts and bangs, just a huge plume of dust following you and being sucked into the car through every little crack. The cabin is soon caked in dust and it swirls around you as you choke. But it's better than driving on lateral-ridged, iron-hard sand. At low speeds, the car shakes itself to bits, the teeth chatter and you know that only the big 4×4s and the trucks with enormous wheels can manage this. They say it's possible to increase the speed until you find the right frequency, at which time the shuddering stops. Trouble is, there are hard central ridges that can tear your suspension and sump apart at speed and steering becomes impossible.

My blood turns to ice every time I realise that should Hortense stutter and fail, I really am alone. Every hour or so a truck comes lumbering down the road, twisting this way and that, or a 4×4 can be spotted on one of the distant desert roads, a huge billowing trail of dust in its wake. Otherwise, there is no sign of life.

It took three days to creep towards Aqtobe, 370 miles to the north. There are no towns in between, just scrappy villages, so no hotels. But I discovered the places where the truckers sleep, and I liked them. For the equivalent of £2 you'd get a space on the floor or a sort of cubicle, plus supper. With a wonderfully welcome cold beer, cheery truckers and a bowl of potatoes with greasy grey mutton, life was a whole lot better than on the road. The truckers would swarm around Hortense, always with the same questions: Diesel? Make of 'machina'? Where to? Where from? Youfromlunnon? Alone? Me see motor? We would all peer into the engine bay and much discussion would ensue.

How everybody loved Hortense! All the way, other motorists, truck drivers, pedestrians, bystanders, pretty girls as well as men, irrespective of age or nationality, greeted her with affec-tionate laughter, thumbs-up, cries of 'good/great car', taking photos with their mobiles. She drew crowds wherever she went.

After Aqtobe, on the road to Khromtau, I picked up Mukhtar,

a crutch-assisted Kazak. I had pulled off one of the few reasonable sections of the road in the hope of getting a coffee at a clump of huts on the roadside. A woman shook her head and as I was about to rejoin the road, Mukhtar came hobbling and hurrying out of a hut, clasping a ragged knapsack and urging me to give him a lift to the next village.

Mukhtar was with me for three smelly, exasperating days. We stayed in truck stops and ate together. Soon he had appointed himself as my spokesman. He would chat with the truckers and I would pick up snippets such as 'Mongolia', 'Benzine', 'London'. Long John Silver had become my Man Friday, and would consult the menu and order for me, hobbling around on his crutch and inspecting my quarters to ensure they were suitable, taking those interested on a little external tour of Hortense, talking knowledgeably about her, and nodding wisely all the while.

All over the world there are people who persuade you that they know what they're talking about when in fact they know no better than you. Mukhtar falls into that irritating group. The road degenerates into another nightmare. Mukhtar knows best. 'Desert road,' he commands, pointing a grubby finger. I descend into the desert. 'Road,' he barks, and I climb back onto the tarmac. The sky is darkening; raindrops start to splash on the windscreen. We're back on a soft sand. I feel uneasy and say I want to go back to the tarmac, but Mukhtar knows better. 'Sand road,' he insists. It is now dusk and we sweep down into a hollow and are immediately grounded in soft wet sand. I could murder him. Three hours later, during which I maintain an icy silence, a passing Audi Quattro tows us out.

It happens again the next day. Hortense gets stuck at noon on the desert sand. We try to dig ourselves out but the sand is too soft, so I send Mukhtar off to patrol a distant sand road which appears to have some traffic. Turns out the high dust trails are in fact mini-whirlwinds of sand. The chastened Mukhtar, still scalded from the previous day, stoically stands in the blazing sun for two hours. Again, we are eventually towed out, but I realise what a dangerous place this is, especially as the sand-coloured Hortense is pretty much invisible in the heat haze.

Late the next day, we finally get to Aral, which was the main harbour for the Aral Sea until it receded by 40 miles, due to a madcap Soviet irrigation scheme in the 1960s. It's now sadly just a forgotten community with some rusty fishing boats lying in what used to be the quayside. It's an unfriendly, flyblown wreck of a town, which I remember only because it is here that I lie to Mukhtar by telling him how grateful I was for his company and pay him off.

The next day broke cloudless and hot, and that's when I met my first Mongol Rally team, the Three Wise Monkeys: Jamie Story, James McCoy and Tom Morris. Great guys and kind enough to allow me to track them for the next few days. We agreed to meet up that evening for dinner in Qyzylorda, 300 miles to the south. Breaching the steel police cordon that encircles Qyzylorda (pronounced kissy-lorda, for those who are interested) is dead easy: you just pay the cops.

The first encounter was on the outskirts of town where a speed trap had been set up. In common with all policemen in these parts, my speed cop had a baton painted red and white, which he brandished at me, indicating that I should pull onto the hard shoulder. His speed gun was produced so that I could have no wriggle room. I was clearly travelling at 44 miles per hour when the limit was 30 miles per hour. How was I to know, given there were no roadside signs? Taking me gently by the elbow, the cop steered me to the passenger door of a police car and invited me to take a seat next to the police captain, who was lazily scratching himself and rearranging the contents of his trousers. He shook his head wearily at me and sighed. I sighed too, and we both slumped in our seats, gazing sadly out of the windscreen.

At last, the captain stirred himself and, reaching for a pen, scrawled $200 on a police form. I sat bolt upright and affected a look of pained helplessness. I countered with a $25 offer, to which he gave me a look of stern indignation blended with a suggestion that he could get nasty if pushed. We settled on $50 and he indicated that the greenbacks should be placed in the glove compartment. He clearly did not want to touch the notes himself.

I was stopped twice more on my way to the hotel, the second time by a police Jeep bursting with uniformed cops and, rather more worryingly, a plain-clothes type smoking a cigarette. All the papers were produced again and again, but with nothing to go on I was released, though not before the big cop with all the stars on his epaulettes, who had initially been threatening, rather pleadingly asked, 'Present? You have little present for meee?' I shook his hand warmly, gave him a salute, hopped back into Hortense and headed for safety, his sad gaze receding in my rear-view mirror.

At the hotel, I had a beer with the Three Wise Monkeys, who then excused themselves as they had to make a few adjustments to their Fiat Panda. I strolled out later to see what was going on, only to find that they were busy stripping down the gearbox. I felt a sense of panic overcome me. Should I be doing something like this? I had only checked the oil once and it seemed okay.

On to Shymkent, then into Kyrgyzstan, a beautiful mountainous country, lush and fresh. After a stopover in Bishkek,
the capital (where I ran into some obvious CIA female analyst
types), I was back into Kazakhstan, heading for the former
capital, Almaty (so hot I called it God Almaty). I checked into
the Intercontinental, solely because it had high-speed Wi-Fi. I
was feeling a bit lonely. Over the next few days I was able to
catch up with my friends back home.

Catherine: 'Are you carrying enough water? I'm very wor-
ried. You know what happened to me on the M1 that hot
summer. What is your laundry situation? Why have you have
deviated from your planned route?'

My cousin Stephen, irritated that my email from Odessa
failed to mention Mr Beshoff, last known survivor of the battle-
ship *Potemkin*, writes with the following information: 'Beshoff
settled in Dublin, where he founded a fish and chip shop chain
which continues to trade even to this day. Before he found commercial success, he drove into and killed a donkey in Tipperary.
The outraged owner, a farmer, demanded payment, to which
Beshoff airily suggested that the bill should be sent straight to
the Kremlin.'

My friend, the writer Frances Stonor Saunders, sends a text:
'Where are you?' What does she mean by this? She's so terribly clever, it could be anything. Does she mean politically,
emotionally, geographically? I opt for the geographical answer
and reply, rather obliquely, 'Never come to Aral City.' A pause.
Texted reply is, 'Worse than Luton?'

Shortly after this I lost my mobile, had to buy another, swore
a lot and headed north towards Semey, or Semipalatinsk as the
Russians call it. For forty years, the Soviets used an area 100
miles to the west, known as the Polygon, as their nuclear test

site, and in that period detonated some 450 atom and hydrogen bombs. Small wonder that the city's people eventually decided enough was enough and staged a massive and prolonged demonstration that proved so effective that the Russians called a halt. Small wonder also that the health of the citizens of Semey continues to reflect the radiation blowing in from the Polygon steppe.

From here, I began to scent Mongolia and, for the first time, over forty days into the adventure, I thought I might just make the finish line. I stopped over in Barnaul, a city some 450 miles from the border at Tashanta, which boasted a Renault dealership. I was determined that Hortense should have an overhaul before we pressed on. That she had made it thus far without any mechanical or structural damage was a miracle.

I wanted an oil change for the engine and gearbox and asked for a quote. They said it would be 1,850 roubles (about £35), which sounded reasonable. A squad of about six mechanics began to pore all over Hortense. Soon filters were being changed, the suspension and steering were dismantled, plugs renewed and new parts fitted, including, at my request, two spotlights that I had brought with me. They had never seen a Renault 4L before so cameras were produced, office workers summoned, wives and girlfriends phoned and soon there was a little crowd witnessing Hortense being stripped down. Then a camera crew arrived from the Barnaul TV station, followed by a photographer from the local paper. Five hours later, the circus had moved on and I nervously asked for the bill. Andrei, the Russian giant in charge, puffed out his chest: 'No money. It is our present to you.' I was stunned. That's the thing about the Russian Bear – its hug can squeeze the life out of you or it can warm you right through.

I left Barnaul in high spirits, secure in the knowledge that Hortense had suffered no major damage in her encounter with Kazak roads, and, even better, she had just received some deluxe treatment from Renault Russia. It had been a pleasant stopover in this Siberian city, where everybody seemed determined to get as much sunshine as possible before winter settled in again. I was also struck by the cultural diet the young Russians were gobbling up. It seemed that every television was tuned to a Russian version of MTV, showing trite rubbish and featuring young girls who were all aping the Californian 'valley-girl' look, complete with the super-cool mien of indifference. How the young Russians love America; it must drive the old establishment bonkers. Having been pretty much bankrupted by the West, they are now losing a whole generation to the MTV version of the American Dream (though I suspect Putin is trying to redirect their gaze).

Between Barnaul and the Russian–Mongolian border at Tashanta, one passes through the Altai Republic, a quite unspoiled, scenically beautiful mountainous area of pastures, roaring mountain rivers, bubbling streams and enormous lakes. There's no cultivation, so the pastureland stretches from the road up to the tree line. I thought the place a paradise. The grazing cattle and sheep are watched over and herded by Altai on horseback. I watched a lone horseman traverse a pasture of wild flowers and thought he must be a most contented soul in such a peaceful place.

I was climbing steadily uphill when my attention was caught by a rapid movement out of my right eye. It was an Altai horseman galloping parallel to me, all hands and heels and going like the wind. They say they're the best horsemen in the region, and this one would have to be, because when he galloped alongside me, on the tarmac, it was clear that he was dead drunk. I pulled over, fearing an accident. He dismounted, or rather fell off, and came charging up to the window, stuck his whole head through it and started shouting. I thought that my taking his photograph might steady things a little. Not a bit of it. He had me mount his horse so that he could take *my* picture. The saddle was loose, it was a big mare and I was on the road, on a *hill*, with no hospital for 100 miles.

He used the Russian gesture to signal that he needed a drink – that of pointing the index finger at the side of one's neck. I lied and said I had no alcohol on board. Would an apple suffice? He looked doubtful, but took the proffered apple, my last, and then helped himself to an orange he had spotted on the passenger seat. With no sign of him pulling away, I thrust a $5 bill into his hand and waved him farewell. The last I saw, he was tearing across a field on his chestnut mare, no doubt en route to the local off-licence.

I stopped in a small town and enquired about a hotel. This is accomplished by cocking your head to one side and placing one's hands, as though praying, under one's ear. I tried this on a chap who happened to be the local police chief, having a cigarette outside his office. Clearly, not many foreigners pass through his manor, and he was keen for a little chat with one, so he steered me into his office inside the police station and switched on his computer. He logged onto a translation site, and so started a marathon in Anglo-Altai relations.

The hotel was called but the owner was out. Being a policeman in a small town, he knew where to find her. She would be back at the hotel, a very scrappy building, at 10:30 p.m., so that would give us plenty of time to exchange views, he seemed to be saying. It was going to be a long night. With the help of his computer he told me all about Altai, how marvellous the people are, how there would be no police patrols, as in Russia (this, typed with a sniff). Furthermore, should I encounter any problems of any nature, I should telephone him and he would sort it out. 'My name is Karasov,' he typed with a flourish.

I do not know how the vodka subject came up, but I think he said we should drink a little and I foolishly declared that I had a bottle stowed away, a present from Daniel in Poland at the start of this voyage. To cut a long and confused story short, we went to the hotel, drank the bottle of vodka, a fruit-enhanced variety as I recall, together with some bottled Russian beer, and ate slices of cheese and salami. At some stage, he declared his love for Hortense, and said that he would buy her, there would be no argument. I urged him to accept the fact that she was bearing me to Mongolia. This he viewed as unimportant and waved the objection away. All this was conducted by diagram and illustration on a piece of polystyrene foam produced by the hotelkeeper. At last we agreed that the negotiation would continue the next morning at ten o'clock, on the computer in his office, when the deal would be signed and sealed. He had it in his head that $1,000 would do the trick.

We parted best friends, and four sheets to the wind. The next day, unsure whether or not I would pass a breathalyser test, I headed out of town without delay, terrified that Karasov would ambush me, or even phone ahead and denounce me to the border guards as a welcher on the agreed sale of Hortense. Would I be pulled over on the way to the border? I kept a wary eye on the rear-view mirror, fearing an enraged Karasov heaving into sight astride a galloping Altai mare, one fist raised in fury as he closed in on me. Oh, my head.

I arrived unhindered at Tashanta early the following evening, ready to cross when the border opened the following day. There were already a few cars and Jeeps waiting, and so I took my place in the queue. Shortly after, Jools, a seasoned and archetypal traveller, complete with half a ton of silver bangles on his wrist and wearing a cowboy hat, rolled up to inform a small group of us that the Russian border officers had spent the day drinking. Russians never have just a few beers, they drink with deliberation and the drunker they get, the more insistent and belligerent they become. We had to hang around until 5:00 p.m. the following day to pass through the very hung-over Russian border post. And then we were at the Mongolian checkpoint, a rather smart new building with friendly officials who actually welcomed us all to their country.

I teamed up with a French group and three Asian Scots from Edinburgh in a red four-wheel drive Subaru, and off we went into Mongolia. Before you could say 'I wish I had a Subaru', we were confronted by a mountain over which we had to pass on a very steep, long, wide, twisting, heavily rutted track. The gods were getting an early kick in, that's for sure. The Subaru managed it fairly well; the French van, smoking like a locomotive, ground its way up in first gear, and I went at it as fast as I could, and got to within 1,000 feet of the summit before Hortense lost revs and petered out. I tried reversing up but that didn't get us any further. Perhaps an oblique run? No good, and so it was that the Subaru pulled me to safety with my marvellous fifteen-foot tow rope. More of this to come, I thought to myself.

The great debate that had been raging since meeting up at the border concerned the best route to take through Mongolia – the northern, central or southern? I had taken soundings from everyone I met as to the best route and everybody had different advice, although it was generally accepted that the northern route was impassable to all but heavy 4×4 Jeeps.

That night we all stayed at a hotel in Ölgiy, and the debate continued. I rather liked the French group, but they were firm about the central route and so I teamed up with a group of four Mongol Rally drivers, one of whom, an Italian, was driving a battered Renault 4L. Nice company for Hortense, I thought. We set off in a convoy into the middle of nowhere, heading in the general direction of Hovd. Under the benign leadership of Dave, clearly an engineering whiz, we spent the day meandering around the Bayan-Ölgiy province, fording rivers, racing across the steppe with plumes of dust in our wake, until it was agreed that we were lost, and we would camp for the night and have a 6:00 a.m. start.

Delirious with dread, I prepared my campsite, the first since I was a boy (and I hated camping then). I unzipped my circular tent bag, extracted the tent, which I then threw up in the air and to my delight it was a fully formed tent by the time it landed on the sand. All my gear was new, including the inflatable mattress. I searched my kit for the pump and then had a sinking feeling as I remembered I had been offered a pump by the salesman but, feeling an awkward sod at the time, had waved him away. The next morning, I struggled to put the tent back in the bag. I called in Dave, who always seemed keen to help, and he had the thing tamed and bagged in seconds. I knew I had fallen in with a technical genius and determined to stick close.

The next day was a blend of misery, terror and madness as our convoy shot off: Hortense, Dave and his fellow teacher in their Subaru, the Italian in his Renault 4L (with his sister slumped grumpily in the passenger seat), two lads in a green

Polo and a white 4×4 Fiat Panda. We eventually spotted the 'road' – in reality no more than a track, or a series of tracks more or less running parallel that had eluded us the previous day – headed across the steppe and clambered up onto it, and from then on, in a state of collective madness, we were racing.

Trying to hang onto the group, I was foot to the floor for the whole day as this crazed carousel careered across Mongolia towards Hovd, some 150 miles away. The roads switched from sand track to soft sand to gravel and rock, and then we would veer off and sweep across the steppe, our progress marked by a series of dust plumes rising in the clear blue skies.

It was all very exhilarating and we had thrown caution to the winds as we crashed and bumped our way at speeds of up to 60 miles per hour across this magnificent landscape of mountain passes and valleys 50 miles wide. Herds of wild horses, black and white yaks, cattle and flocks of sheep and goats grazed the grasslands, watched over by horsemen dressed in traditional Mongolian felt coats and ornate hats, and sometimes in an anorak. Snow-white canvas gers, alone or in little groups, dotted the plains. I once spotted a pink one and, horrors, a plastic one. Great falcons and occasionally eagles would stand child-high by the roadside and at our approach would clamber into the air like heavy bombers, only to wheel and dive in pairs at play in the sky.

We were going too fast to take in this spectacular place. Almost in a trance, one would focus all one's attention on the road just 80 feet ahead, shoulders hunched and fingers gripping the wheel. One would be drawn, as though by a siren, towards a large rock lying in the track and, having hit it at speed, one would again loudly curse one's stupidity. To help matters along, Mongolian Buddhists would place one rock upon another, in a spiritually satisfactory manner, and sometimes these arrangements were to be found in the middle of the road. I apologise: they were sometimes hard to avoid.

I can't remember hitting the particular rock that finished off my beautiful 6 mm aluminium sump guard. I had been 'bottoming out' all day, wincing with every crash and thump to the undercarriage as we came down a switchback hill or swept into a well-cambered curve. I slewed to a halt and peered under Hortense. Sure enough, the beefy sump guard had sheared off at the back and was hanging down, held by just two bolts at the front. Dave attempted to jury-rig the thing, but we decided to remove it, leaving just the factory guard, a rather feeble tin affair, to protect the precious sump. I felt like a batsman sent out to face Fred Trueman but with no protective box. How could Hortense survive intact? Clearly it would not be possible. It was only a matter of time.

The rest of the day was spent racing down ridged and rutted roads, sometimes of the dreaded 'washboard' variety, the car-killer of Mongolia. The lead car, usually the Polo driven by a brace of testosterone-fuelled lads, set a mad pace and as the day drew to a close I knew that Hortense had sustained serious injuries. Dave was called to cast his eye over the damage to the suspension, the exhaust and fuel systems, and the beautifully crafted aluminium air intake and sand-trap contraption. Ever helpful, he murmured that it was not so bad, but I saw him rather as a priest administering the last rites.

As we neared Hovd, Dave and the boys decided to carry on in an attempt to make up time and camp later that night, while I said that I would book into a hotel and have a decent night's sleep and consider my options. With a sense of foreboding I said farewell to Dave, a kind and helpful man, and peeled off into Hovd. The probability that the next stage towards the city of Altai, 270 miles distant, without a town or village between, would be a solo effort filled me with apprehension. Little did I know.

I pulled into Hovd, and consulting my *Lonely Planet* guide, pulled up to the Buyant Hotel and checked in. There were no other Mongol Rally cars around, so my feeling of isolation increased. The next day I had to face the long trip to Altai alone, with no other settlements in between apart from the occasional roadside café and petrol stop.

I trudged into a local restaurant to find two carloads of Spanish Mongol Rally folk, and a group of four young English lads driving a large LT minibus, converted for the elderly with wheelchair ramps. I found this particularly comforting and it was agreed that I drive convoy to Altai in the morning with the bus. We dined on grey mutton and grey gravy and my spirits rose accordingly.

In the morning, we hit the Altai road, which from the outskirts of town became a frenzy of rock-hard lateral ridges, a corrugated road which set the teeth chattering and the steering wheel bucking, sending the four wheels into a manic, speed-shuddering dance. It was impossible to imagine that any car could survive this punishment and sadly, after three hours, Hortense let me know that the front offside shock absorber assembly had collapsed completely. It would have destroyed both me and what was left of the suspension to carry on and so, bidding farewell to the bus for the elderly, I limped back to Hovd. It took five miserable hours, and I checked back into the Buyant Hotel, feeling rather less than buoyant myself. This was a low time, for having seen what the Altai road had to offer, the thought of returning to it was draining.

I managed to track down a mechanic late the following morning and we assessed the damage. The offside shock absorber mountings had all sheared off and the shock absorber itself had bled fluid all over the assembly and the brake disc. A welder was summoned, all the shock absorber mountings were strengthened and a second-hand shock absorber fitted.

I must have been mad to think that a second-hand unit was any good, but was conned into it by a charade conducted by the mechanic and his pal the welder, who huffed and puffed as they pulled on the shock to demonstrate just how strong it was. By the time all this was completed, it was too late to start out again, and anyway I had decided to cheat and hire a truck to carry me overnight to Altai. I was just too damned tired.

My third night at the Buyant. The following morning, I went in search of the head cop in Hovd, armed with my magic letter from the Mongolian ambassador in London. He had kindly provided me with a sort of *laissez passer* introduction which said, I think, something along the lines of: 'Help the old chap out if you can, he's alright.'

Eventually I was passed up the line to the chief of police, Detective Doll, a tall, burly man of few words who studied the letter slowly, mouthing each word as his eyes passed over them. He barked an order and before I could gather my thoughts, I was shown into the back of his white Toyota, beside a crisply uniformed officer, while Doll squeezed into the front. His driver completed the quartet.

The rest of the morning I accompanied Doll on his business, interviewing snitches and grasses deep in the market, greeting friends, loading sacks of watermelons into the boot of his car, swapping cars and then changing back again; it was a blur of activity and the same people, snitches and all, kept reappearing in different cars doing different things. At one stage, his wife appeared and we loaded her luggage into a Jeep, from which more watermelons were unloaded and squeezed into the back of the police car, while we transferred into a battered Datsun with Doll at the wheel. The last appointment was an official one in which I stood stiffly to attention next to Doll as a plaque was unveiled and a politician droned on for half an hour, after which a Mongolian songstress twittered, accompanied by a string quartet all dressed in surprisingly garish outfits.

We were off again, this time to a compound into which Doll disappeared, indicating sternly that I should remain in the car. I could hear voices, the imperious tones of Doll and what sounded like pleading from the other party. It went on for quite a long time until eventually Doll reappeared, towing in his wake the pleading voice in the shape of Inky-yeah, clearly someone well known to the police of Hovd. Inky-yeah was to bear Hortense and me to Altai that very night on his lorry for $400. I was to meet them at 6:00 p.m. at the post office for the loading ceremony.

Quite a small lorry arrived and it appeared that it was already overladen. I followed Inky-yeah to a yard where a crane and Doll, now in plain clothes, were waiting for us. I spotted Inky-yeah attempting to fix the crane's hooks through the protruding safety belts of the car. Clearly, he was a fool and I ordered him to use my fifteen-foot tow rope. Detective Doll took charge and Hortense was hoisted clumsily aloft and eventually jammed onto the back of Inky-yeah's truck, her hind quarters protruding over the end of the tailboard. I was informed that the expedition would pull out of Hovd at midnight and that I would be the guest of honour for supper at the Doll family ger out in the Steppes, in which guise I was lifted onto the back of the mighty Doll as he waded across the Buyant river.

After a wonderful family supper, at which the children danced for me, it was time to set off. What followed was the stuff of nightmares. The washboard road continued for seventeen hours and at times I thought my internal organs were sure to be torn from their moorings. I shuddered to think about Hortense, now perched behind me, with Doll's watermelons bouncing all over her bonnet like cannon balls.

Finally, we pulled into Altai and drove around looking for a crane. We spotted an ancient Russian lorry with one on its back and, after a bad-tempered negotiation with the owner, Hortense was lifted out and dumped on the ground. I levelled a volley of abuse at Inky-yeah's head when it became clear the watermelons he had loaded on her bonnet by the sackful had produced huge, concave dents. I left him looking rather dejected but with $400 in his pocket, less Doll's commission.

I went in search of a hotel, planning a restful day and an early night before setting out early the next morning for Bayankhongor, about 250 miles to the east. The next day I set off in convoy with the Three Tall Americans (John, Sean and Eric) in their Nissan Micra in the lead, and we swept eastwards but almost immediately we took a wrong turn. By early afternoon we had plunged into and were lost in the northern Gobi, a stony and inhospitable landscape interlaced with sandy roads that tease you deeper into this dangerous place.

The Three Tall Americans consulted their compass, the sort often found in Christmas crackers, and we all agreed that we were probably somewhere near Bayan-Öndör, way off track, and would have to camp for the night and try again the following day. An enormous full moon illuminated the desert and after debating the probability of snakes and scorpions inhabiting the many holes in the desert floor, there was a determined and collective zipping shut of tent doors and we settled in for a cold and watchful night.

By 7:00 a.m. we were on our way, taking a north-east route and praying that we would hit the Bayankhongor road by midday. Speed became an increasingly central feature of the day as we rocketed across this bone-dry and rocky landscape, with no sign of habitation and only occasionally a sighting of wild camels turning their haughty gaze at us as we crashed and bumped our way past in a cloud of dust. As we pulled into Bayankhongor late that afternoon, weary and caked in dust, Hortense had lost about 30 per cent of her power. It was agreed that the others would carry on that night and I would hang back for essential repairs.

By nightfall I had beefy new Korean shock absorbers, and the exhaust system had been welded back into one piece and reinstalled; the front wheel arches were cut away to give greater clearance. A quick look at the map confirmed that with luck I was only two hard driving days away from Ulaanbaatar and suddenly a dash to the finishing line seemed possible. I spotted two Mongol Rally wrecks pulled into a roadside yard and, as I looked them over, a third limped in, driven by a couple of local Mongolians. They would be trucked to Ulaanbaatar, where they would be cleaned up and auctioned for charity.

I left town the following morning, joining up with a couple of County Clare men a few hours out of Bayankhongor. We drove in convoy for two days, entered Ulaanbaatar in the evening rush hour in a downpour and made our way to the finishing line.

Was it fun? I can't think of a better adventure for people younger than me, and I would urge those looking for some sport to enlist for the Mongol Rally. But for a sixty-four-year-old driving on his own it was a tall order. Up to the Mongolian border it was a fabulous trip, but it all got rather more serious as I started to get deeper into that magical and majestic country. But I ended with a tally of nearly £12,000 for the charity Hope and Homes for Children (*see* S: SIERRA LEONE), so that gave me a sense of satisfaction.

I dumped Hortense in the Mongol Rally compound with all the other cars and looked around. I spotted the Italian Renault 4L slumped in a corner, the bus for the elderly was there too, as was a London taxi I had met in Barnaul. It had been my intention to ship Hortense back to England but she was too far gone: her doors were ill-fitting now, probably the result of a twisted chassis; the hinge had severed on the hatch-back door, and the cut-away bodywork could never be repaired; her wishbone suspension was shot and the beefy Korean shocks, fitted only a couple of days previously, were leaking and no longer of any use. Mechanically, she had survived everything Mongolia had thrown at her, but structurally she was done for.

I unscrewed Hortense's steering wheel, the rather racy number originally from a Renault Gordini, and packed it in my luggage. It is now installed on Maude, Hortense's Renault 4L twin sister who resides in my barn in France. I hope that one day, when they are a little older, my grandchildren – Freddie, Theodore, Katie Grace, Raif and Clara – will be allowed to go through the creaking barn door and clamber into her, and Maude will somehow tell them of Hortense's adventures in Central Asia and excite them into exploring this wonderful world.

I left Ulaanbaatar and flew to Nice via Beijing and Paris. As guests of Sir Alan and Lady Sugar, Catherine and I were soon on board a 2,000-ton, 230-foot super-yacht cruising in the Med. Asked what I would like for dinner, as we lay just off Juan-les-Pins, I ordered grey mutton and a few potatoes. 'Not possible,' I was told by the steward. 'Would a lobster do?'

N

Nicotine

How cigarettes kept me dangling, literally

My doctor was quite explicit about the potential side-effects of Zyban. 'It's been having quite a lot of bad press,' he said. 'There have been reports that some people have had fits, but none of my patients has so far complained.' 'I'll have it,' I said. 'I'll take a chance, because for forty years I've been regretting this smoking lark and now it's sink or swim.' He handed over the prescription and off I went.

I don't know if Zyban is still available, but in my day, twenty years ago, you took a little Zyban tablet every day for ten days having made a mental note, but not a promise to yourself, that you'd be giving up somewhere in that period. So, there's nothing definite, you can carry on smoking. I took my first pill and on day two I didn't want to smoke anymore. I kept taking the tablets because that was the agreed regime, and at the end of ten days I stopped taking them and I've never smoked since. Thus came to an end four decades of misery that started with those Joysticks on the school train to Clongowes.

Looking back, I realise that my parents' friends, quite a few of whom were local doctors, had all died in their fifties clutching a lit Craven A, claimed at the time to be 'good for your throat'. At Clongowes, with your parents' permission, you could buy cigarettes in a pack of tens or twenties in the tuck shop and you could smoke in the library or the billiard room after supper. The popular brand was Sweet Afton, made in Dundalk, Ireland, but named after the eponymous poem by Robbie Burns – 'Flow gently, sweet Afton, among thy green braes. / Flow gently. I'll sing thee a song in thy praise' – which was written in flowery font on the front of the packet. Clutching your Aftons you would then retire to the old Higher Line library, which had a long central table and seats all around it, and in the far end by the fireplace, barely visible in the cigarette smog, was stationed the boy in charge of the radio. This he had permanently tuned to the subversive pirate station Radio Luxembourg, which would be immediately turned off if the face of authority ever appeared at the door. Bizarrely, smoking outside of the designated areas was a very serious offence and involved sliding into the hedges in the far fields and covering up the smell on your breath after-wards with strong peppermints.

When I first went to Clongowes, Joysticks – very, very long cigarettes – were a popular brand on the market, and to smoke those on the train on the way to school made one feel terribly cool and 'hard'. We also wanted to smoke exotic cigarettes like Passing Clouds, oval cigarettes in coloured paper with gold filter tips, and Sobranie, once the supplier to the Imperial Court of Russia. But our whole smoking experience was hugely enhanced by a boy in our year who came from Cobh, formerly

Queenstown, the harbour for Cork. Through some family connections, he was able to entice contraband cigarettes off the transatlantic liners that stopped at Cobh. These he would bring to Clongowes in huge suitcases and quietly sell them to the boys, which of course was denying the tuck shop of a useful revenue stream.

You can imagine the surprise of Father Spillane, who managed the tuck shop, to find discarded cartons of Pall Mall, a favourite of the boys because the advertising slogan was 'Wherever Particular People Congregate', as well as Camel, Lucky Strike, and all the American brands, with occasional surges of Gitanes, presumably taken from that graceful liner, *France*, whereas the tuck shop only had Senior Service and Afton. Our supplier, who it is rumoured later joined the American army and fought in Vietnam, was under constant surveillance, but was never trapped.

By the time I left Clongowes I was hooked, and so began quite an unhappiness because in fact I never really liked smoking and I knew it was a terrible addiction. When I started work I abused my body, in the sense that I never ate during the day, I simply smoked and drank coffee non-stop. It was a terrible burden, because when I was living in London, alone, particularly after my divorce, many was the morning I would lie in the bath with a migraine that would bring a house down, and it was to do with starvation and coffee (years later, Catherine said that she'd never known 'such a thin man', agreeing quickly that she had, of course, not known many men at all). By the 1990s, I determined to get a grip on this and took myself off with a great friend to an Allen Carr clinic somewhere out of London, where we smoked a thousand cigarettes while listening to a former boxer who couldn't breathe through his nose rolling out the reasons for giving up. We had already stocked up with honey herbal cigarettes which we began puffing as soon as we got back in the car and headed for London. It didn't last long for either of us. I was pretty much back to the real cigarettes within days.

It all came to mean something important when I was working late in the office one summer night and I'd run out of cigarettes, and at about ten o'clock I determined to go out and buy some. Leaving all the lights on, my jacket over the back of the chair, I let myself out of my third-floor office, down the stairs and through the front door into Garrick Street in Covent Garden, then on to the local pub to buy the fags. On my way back to the office, my stupidity became clear: I'd left my keys (including those to my flat) in my jacket pocket. What to do?

I roamed the outside of the building and let myself into the rear courtyard where my car was parked. I looked up and noticed that a sash window on the third floor was just a little bit open. I also noticed a painter's boat which had been hauled right up to the top of the building, but dangling down almost to the ground was the sturdy rope used to pull the boat up and down. I tugged at it tentatively. It was firm. As a young boy at school I was very adept at climbing ropes in the gym – all you had to do was wrap your legs around it and shimmy up – so I thought, Okay, although I'm fifty I can still do this thing, spurred on by the knowledge that I had to do something, otherwise I'd be sleeping in my car for the night.

I began to climb the rope. Slowly, I hauled myself up, and was level with the second floor when I heard the creak of the gate opening below. Somebody was coming into the courtyard. If they looked up, what they would see was a burglar suspended on a rope. The natural inclination for a right-minded citizen would be to grab the rope and shake the burglar free. I stayed completely motionless, frozen with fear, and watched as the figure below made his way into the rear entrance of the Garrick Club. I continued on up the rope to the third floor, but when I got level to the window sill of my office, I was disappointed to discover that I was about 2 feet away from the wall. This was complicated, because I had now to release one hand from the rope and adopt a swinging Tarzan-like motion to bring myself into the window sill, and out again, and in, and out, making a tentative attempt to grab the window sill and failing to stop the swing, the pendulum motion, and out again, maybe next time trying to get just my fingers over the sill and hold myself there against the natural force of gravity. Finally, I got a hold.

The next problem was to prize open the window. To release the left hand would mean that gravity would once again take over and I'd be swinging away from the building. So, gripping my legs around the rope and bringing it into my chest, thus freeing both hands, I was able to hold the lip and ease open the window with the other hand. This was a very dangerous manoeuvre. I grabbed the sill with both hands and flopped over it, absolutely exhausted, my shins grazed and bleeding from rope burn. The only lesson I can take from this mad escapade is that I tend to succeed when I'm determined. If I was asked to undertake the same journey up to the third floor in order to give someone CPR, I have to admit I would probably decline.

Unfortunately, I did exactly the same thing about three weeks later, leaving the office to get cigarettes and locking myself out. I don't know if the painter's boat had gone by then – I didn't even look. Instead, I stopped two policemen on the beat and asked them if they had any sort of skeleton key as I'd locked myself out of the office.

'What sort of lock is it, sir?' one of them asked.

'A Yale,' I replied.

'Don't worry, sir. We can pop that, we can pop that no problem at all. No damage, we'll just give it a bit of shoulder and it'll be fine.'

'Brilliant,' I said.

'Which way, sir? Up the stairs? That door? No problem. Stand back, sir. We'll just give it a nudge, stand back.'

And with that, they both launched themselves at the door and completely smashed it. The architrave was shattered, and on the other side several bricks had fallen out of the wall.

'There you go, sir.'

That's when I went to see my doctor to talk about Zyban. Two days, it worked for me. I've had twenty years without smoking and I feel a hundred, no, a thousand times better for it.

O

Old

Please, not the 'Idaho potato'

Now that I have passed three-score-and-ten, it has slowly dawned on me that a dreadful future may lie ahead. My great-grandmother, Elizabeth Tuckey Hewer, lived to be ninety-nine, and my father was ninety-six when he died. Two or more decades still to come for me seems like an improbably long time; the same span in reverse would bring me back to my early fifties, when, seized by the first intimations of mortality, I set out to find myself a burial plot. This mission remains unaccomplished, as I never heard back from the church warden at Sevenhampton (*see* H: HEWER) and I let the matter drop and got on with the business of living.

Now I wonder, what are the chances (or desirability?) of achieving the longevity of the Hewers? And how many times in a life does one's hand brush against death's doorknob before one finally crosses the threshold? My father had a near-miss in his late forties when he found himself on holiday with my mother in Arcachon, on the French Atlantic coast, with a burst appendix. It was only my youthful agility in getting down there with a wallet full of francs to pass to the outstretched hand of Dr Wolf at the Wolf Clinic – he wasn't going to operate until he had the cash – that saved him. Appendicitis has stalked all us Hewers: my uncle Tom (Dad's older brother) died of a burst appendix in Reading General Hospital, still in his twenties, on the very day he was due to marry. No doubt my father's fear and horror of death started when Tom lay for nearly a week in the August heat in the drawing room at The Grange because my grandmother couldn't bear to let the body go. I too had appendicitis at the age of twenty-one, but they got there before it burst. My sister Annabelle was less lucky: hers popped when she was a teenager (a very bad case of misdiagnosis) and she was perilously ill for some time.

My father survived a terrible riding accident when he was nineteen, in which he seriously damaged his back. Thereafter, for some time, he had to wear a leather and steel corset, which was a vision of horror to us children when we saw it hanging in his wardrobe, no longer required but kept, just in case. For no obvious reason, in my mid-twenties I suddenly noticed that the muscles on the right side of my lower back had begun to wither, causing painful and unexpected jolts to the spine. I went to St Thomas' Hospital in London to be seen by a very pompous surgeon with film star looks who swept in accompanied by a phalanx of nurses. Without bothering to look me in the eye, or indeed at his notes, he said, 'Now then, which leg seems to be giving you the problem?' I said, 'It's my back, actually.' He was unresponsive and I knew from that moment on that my relationship with St Thomas' would be brief.

I took myself instead to the Park Street Clinic in Mayfair

where Mr Tucker, an elderly orthopaedic specialist famous for strapping up jockeys' injuries before the next race meeting, held court. He spotted the problem within seconds. With framed photographs of various members of the royal family witnessing, and his red carnation crisp to the touch, he ordered me to stand still and then walk up and down his consulting room. 'As clear a case as you'll ever see,' he announced impressively to his assistant. Turning to me, he said, 'Young man, you will have your right heel built up by an eighth of an inch with an instep, and Nurse Nord will give you massage therapy over the coming months and this will put you right.'

Nurse Nord. The name conjured visions of a tall, Scandinavian nurse with beautiful, deep-set blue eyes. Perhaps this back problem was a blessing in disguise. Not so, for it turned out to be Nurse Gnawed, who pummelled and beat me into submission on a weekly basis. But true enough, Mr Tucker did the trick, discharging me with orders to wear an orthopaedic corset for a while. When I told my father about him, he said, 'Tucker? Is he still alive? He was the surgeon I saw after my hunting accident in 1937, and it was he who devised the corset I had to wear when I left the nursing home after a year, to strengthen my back.' So, there you have it: my father and I, who didn't have much else in common, both closet corset-wearers.

My head has always been a big problem medically. During the dark years following the end of my marriage, many a morning I would lie in a hot bath in a futile attempt to soothe away yet another migraine. Migraines for me were never more than ten minutes away, brought about, I later realised, by smoking too many cigarettes, drinking too many coffees and neglecting to eat properly. At one point, I decided to have a brain scan. I was slid into the CAT scanner at the Lister Hospital, even as a torpedo is slid into its close-fitting launch tube, to discover nothing. Panic over. There being no neurological cause for the migraines, it was clearly down to me. These days, this happier person has been headache-free for twenty years (*see* N: NICOTINE).

Although it's hard to believe anybody could possibly be interested in this, we can now add the Hospital of St John and St Elizabeth in St John's Wood to the history of my medical wanderings. This visit was occasioned by some tomfoolery in a lift. I can't remember the name of the woman, but I think she must've been quite a lot younger than me (I was in my mid-fifties), because I was attempting to draw a picture of the future should anything come of this relationship. The lift was heading down to the ground floor, and I was crouched down on all fours with my fingers spread on the floor by way of illustrating the view she would have of me as she pushed me in a wheelchair in old age. The lift reached the ground floor with a bump and the weight on my fingers bent one of them backwards at the middle knuckle, accompanied by a yelp of intense pain. A few days later, the rheumatologist at St John and St Elizabeth eyed my swollen knuckle and, to my mounting horror, produced a syringe with an extraordinarily sleek needle which he grated and ground into the joint. Before I had time to faint, he took some bloods and told me to come back for the results in a few days.

The bloods told an unusual tale. 'I'm sorry to have to tell you,' intoned the rheumatologist, 'but it very much looks like you're suffering from lupus, an autoimmune condition most commonly found in African-Caribbean women of child-bearing age.' 'Then why me?' I whimpered. 'Well, occasionally, lupus draws in an innocent bystander.'

It was at about this time that the City Slickers scandal was raging, in which two young journalists were accused of insider dealing or some such offence and I was due to testify for the prosecution in their trial at Southwark Crown Court (the *Daily Mirror*, for whom they worked, had tipped the shares of Alan Sugar's Viglen company, a client of mine). It was a cause célèbre, and one of the journalists entered a plea of guilty and then, I seem to recall, made a beeline for Dubai, while the other one found himself heading for a short spell in chokey. I had just sold my company and headed off to my house in France and was feeling out of sorts; retirement didn't suit me, a condition exacerbated by my recent diagnosis of lupus. The thought of returning to London and giving evidence was not attractive, but the Department of Trade and Industry, who had brought the prosecution, was offering to set up a video link from a French court. This seemed an extravagant waste of public money, and I committed myself to the journey back.

The day arrived and, waiting to be called in the lobby outside the courtroom, I sensed that all the court officials were being very solicitous. 'How are you feeling today, sir?' said one. 'Very good of you to turn up under the circumstances,' murmured a senior counsel as he swished by. 'I hope this will keep you going,' chirped a young female official from the clerk's office who appeared with a cup of tea and a biscuit. Obviously, the view was that I was seriously ill. I began to settle into the role. The cry went out, 'Mr Nicholas Hewer!' and I levered myself out of my chair and was escorted into the courtroom. Slowly, carefully, I paced the length of the court to the witness box, which was placed within arm's length of the judge. I stood there and took the oath and, turning his bewigged head to me, the judge said in a very low murmur, 'Very good of you to come under the circumstances. Now, if at any time you need to leave the court or you need to sit down you have merely to tell me.' Firmly gripping the edges of the witness box, I squeaked, 'Thank you, I'll do my best to remain standing.' The court case passed and, mysteriously, so did the lupus. A misdiagnosis, surely, else why did it disappear?

Next, to the Lister Hospital again, this time sporting large, uniform roundels of red weals on my upper body, and, discouragingly, on my face. A dear friend of mine having asked, 'Are you offering yourself for target practice?', I swiftly carried myself off to see the epidemiologist, who told me that I had a nasty case of 'hit and run rheumatism'. Seeing that I was processing this phrase rather slowly, he clarified: 'We call it palindromic rheumatism, which means, luckily for you, that it may reverse itself and leave just as quickly as it arrived.' I reported back to my dear friend later that day, and she said, in her rapid-fire fashion, 'God-Dog, that's awful. Poor you.'

As I write this I feel stronger than I did yesterday, and this is due to Nurse Elizabeth Sylvester at the Belgravia Medical Centre, my NHS GP surgery. Before I tell you why, we have to journey back a decade, to Rwanda, where I was filming for the charity Hope and Homes for Children (*see* S: SIERRA LEONE). I was in my hotel room in Kigale, squinting at my laptop screen, when I realised that something was seriously off. When I flew back from that trip, I had just one day before setting out again for Central Asia, which required a yellow fever jab. As my (private) GP in Northampton gave me the jab, I told him that my vision was a bit funny and I didn't feel great. He took my blood pressure, and when it returned 160 over 116, his eyes widened in alarm. 'How long has this been going on? We'll have to put you on hypertension pills immediately. And you should also get your eyes checked.' I took myself straight to Moorfields Eye Hospital in London, to discover that I was literally about an inch away from a stroke: instead of a blood vessel bursting in the brain, it had cleverly popped behind the retina of my right eye – a very near-miss indeed.

I've been taking the hypertension pills since then and, after an intense romance with my very own blood pressure monitor, I stopped thinking about it. But in recent months, a terrible weariness, like a lead cloak, has been weighing me down; my legs have gone, to such an extent that when exiting my low-slung car with my right foot, as I move to put weight on it, it judders and goes into spasm. It's only when I've got my other foot on the ground that I begin to feel safe, but it's at least six steps of walking like the wounded war hero and ace fighter pilot Douglas Bader before I synchronise. So yesterday, Nurse Sylvester suggested we check my blood pressure. It returned an 85 over 51. 'How long has this been going on?' she gasped. 'I've no idea,' I said, 'but I feel exhausted.' After a brief discussion about the dangers of being clinically dead, we decided to cut back on the hypertension medication and see how we got on. Today, for the first time in months, I bounced out of bed, my legs were those of a young racehorse, and I had the hips of Nureyev.

So far so good. With the help of the NHS and a healthy private insurance policy, I have managed to construct a stout defence against the grim reaper, forcing into retreat a series of potentially deadly onslaughts. This includes all manner of pre-emptive kicks against disease and faulty parts, which is why my visit to the London Clinic proved so satisfactory (see E: ENDOSCOPY). Sadly, both Marlon Brando and Maria Schneider have died, but nobody who saw *Last Tango in Paris* will ever forget Brando's admission to Ms Schneider that his prostate was as big as an 'Idaho potato'. One has to take care of one's Idaho potato, and no sensible man ignores the call of the donning of the latex glove.

As I enter my seventy-fifth year to heaven (*inshallah*), I need more than two hands to count my blessings. I have at last reached a state of contentment which kicks in at morning shower time – for between waking and bathing I, like many as they enter old age, suffer from what can be considered a dark cloud of depression and anxiety which can reach apocalyptic dimensions, though this is, I suspect, a kind of perverse indulgence given how speedily it's washed away by my hypoallergenic shower gel for very dry skin. I'm still here and, the blood pressure seesaw excepted, I believe I'm in pretty good shape. To see my grandchildren so delightfully nurtured has relieved me, to some extent, of the guilt that a divorced parent always feels. They are the next shift, and I'm sure they'll make a good job of it. And Catherine, the kindest person I know, a chum to the weak and the weakening, as Betjeman put it, will care for me when the time comes. She has said as much, and having seen the way in which she comforts the dying in her family and in our circle, I need have no fears that she'll shovel me into some care home, there to waste away on a blue plastic chair.

Inevitably, in old age one's mind turns to the manner of one's death. I've long thought that if I could find a way to turn impending death into an easy one by addressing it philosophically and not fearfully, then I would indeed be a fortunate man. My mother, sadly, died at a youthful eighty-two in November 1999, in spite of the fact I'd told her I had a large amount of money on at William Hill that she would see in the millennium.

When she was still in the hospital with heart problems, there was a priest cruising the wards but when asked if she wanted to speak to him she said, no, her family was her religion. She left the hospital thanking the heart surgeon by saying, 'You have done your best and I will now go home.' She died the next day with her family around her. A woman of great calm and good humour, she met her end gracefully. I think she'd reached a place where death held no terror because it was a time of expectation, and now that I'm in my mid-seventies I don't think I would feel cheated or conned.

My poor father, by contrast, was fearful of death, maybe occasioned by his brother Tom's tragic end, about which he never spoke. Aged ninety-six, but still well enough to live on his own at home, Dad fell one day and pressed the alarm system on his wrist. The ambulance arrived within ten minutes, and the next morning he called me cheerily from his bedside in the hospital in Swindon. He was fine, basically, just a bit shaken by the fall. But a week later, he was dead, for reasons none of us could fathom. I think he'd caught something on the ward. Poor man, he was on a morphine drip and hallucinated a great deal. He would wake and ask whether he was at the Pearly Gates yet, and when we said, 'Not yet, Dad', he would become quite distressed. It was deeply upsetting, as he didn't seem to have conditioned himself to meet his end.

As Groucho Marx famously quipped from his own deathbed, dying is no way to live. How wonderful it would be to have the presence of mind to check out of this life with a memorable last word. Oscar Wilde did not disappoint. Lying in a fleapit hotel on the Left Bank of the Seine, he rasped, 'My wallpaper and I are fighting a duel to the death. One or other of us has to go.' Then there's the story, possibly apocryphal, of the surgeon

Joseph Henry Green who was checking his own pulse as he lay dying. His last word? 'Stopped'. An old school pal of mine, who came from a big medical family, told me the story of his father's deathbed scene. His brothers and sisters, all doctors, were gathered around having a vigorous argument about whether or not they had just heard the death rattle, whereupon their father, also a doctor, opened his eyes and said that it most certainly was not a chain rattle. Needless to say, he did not recover.

P

Proof of Life

Health and safety with the SAS

I returned a call to BBC Bristol to find out more about *Around the World in Eighty Days*, a series planned in aid of Children in Need. The producer came to the point very quickly. 'Do you think you could get Sir Alan to accompany you on a road trip from Istanbul to Almaty in Kazakhstan?' I suspected I was being used as a lure to bring in a bigger fish, who would form part of a six-team adventure circumnavigating the globe in true Jules Verne style. I put in a call to Alan. He cut me short very quickly with the words, 'If you think I'm going to tramp across some barren desert in some rusty jalopy when I've got a perfectly good plane sitting at Stansted and a yacht at my disposal anywhere in the world, you must be crazy.'

I reported this disappointment back to the producer who said, 'Why not try Margaret?' Another disappointingly brief call. 'I think I'll let this one pass,' she said brusquely. My thoughts alighted on Saira Khan, runner-up in the first

Apprentice and generally known as a good sport. She jumped at it, and before you could say 'hot-air balloon', we found ourselves in a huge country mansion surrounded by parkland, locked into a six-day intensive training course, required by the BBC for those travelling to potentially hostile environments. Normally, these courses have as many as thirty participants, but because neither Saira nor I could devote six days solid but only three days followed by another three days a week apart, we found ourselves the only people on the course.

The course was run on behalf of TOR International by Karen P, a slight and athletic-looking ex-army major who had served with the SAS. Karen took us hour by hour, day by day, through a challenging programme, beginning with Risks and Threats, which was followed by Basic Life Support. I recall lying on the floor with Karen on top of me, ensuring that my airways were open and that I hadn't suffered a fractured skull. It's possible, I learned, to detect whether your subject has incurred a fractured skull by studying whether there are signs of panda bear eyes and bruising behind the ears. A trickle of blood from the ear is also helpful.

After lunch, we went on to Personal Conflict Management (long overdue in my case), Use of Body Language, Crowd Dynamics, Kit and Equipment. Then we shuffled outside to examine a vehicle containing a dummy body that had crashed into a tree. The engine was still running. What should we do? Would we remember what we'd been told before lunch? Drag the body out, turn the engine off, ensure the body is able to breathe. Yes, but in what order? One tipping point followed another, and so the course proceeded. Ballistics Awareness was a favourite of mine. Could I differentiate between outgoing and

incoming fire? Could I master non-lethal crowd control meas-
ures and trauma management? Most interesting.

Next, Personal Security/Robbery/Carjacking. 'We now move
into the woods,' said Karen. 'Be careful where you tread, as the
area has been mined.' We tiptoed forwards. 'Stop,' she said.
'Look, you're about to blunder through a tripwire.' Saira and I
froze. 'And now,' Karen said, handing us each a 10-inch length
of metal, 'this probe may well save your life.' We gently prodded
the soil at a shallow angle, trying to detect hidden landmines
without actually blowing ourselves up. We inched forward gingerly, at which point my mobile rang. I sprang upright. It was
Alan, ringing to tell me that he was seriously contemplating
pulling out of *The Apprentice* for various contractual reasons. I
paced to and fro on the minefield, trying to dissuade him from
such rash action and seeing my income plummet. Karen was
most unhappy, and as I resumed my position she shot me a
killer look (in real life, she could probably have killed me with
one disciplined finger to the carotid artery on my neck).

Back into the classroom for Trauma Management and Triage,
in which one decides whose injuries to treat first. One crisis
situation tumbled into another – Vehicle Checkpoints and Road
Blocks, Vehicle Security, Travel Health, Surviving in a Disaster
Zone – until, at the end of day five, our ring binders bulging,
we felt exhausted but really rather excited because we knew
that on the morrow all we had learned would be put to the test.

Rising early, we were told by Karen that our task for today
would be to make our way to a helicopter landing zone inside
a United Nations safe area where we would be airlifted out of
a very violent and dangerous area, a war zone in the country
'Hostaelia'. Maps in hand, we made our way out of the grand
house and on the gravel drive there was a Land Rover and a

I Catherine pictured in Jaipur. 'What have you done to her?'

J The Great Avenue at Clongowes, with the castle in the distance.

J With Gerry Wilkinson in the Serpentine Gallery at Clongowes, flanking the portrait of our classmate Archbishop Michael Courtney, assassinated by rebels in Burundi.

J The day an Australian rugby international came to the pitch. Author seated second from left, front row.

K A young Dylanesque Nick in a pensive mood.

L My beloved Willys Jeep in the barn at Lacroix.

M Deep in the Gobi Desert, with front suspension all but destroyed.

M Hovd police chief Doll bears me on his back across the Buyant River as we head to the family yurt.

O Michael Whitehall and I discuss the chances of passing our OAP driving test.

P Your Astrakhan hat is taller than mine. And you have gold teeth. You win.

P Tending to the wounded in Hostaelia, Surrey.

P Exiting the clapped-out Russian MIL8 helicopter somewhere in Kazakhstan with the Children in Need bag, en route to the Almaty handover.

Q Princess Diana visits Gulu, son Zoran and daughter Divia at their London home.

R Sheikha Bouchra and one of her paintings.

S James, his son Nicholas, his wife Abie and his daughter Hawa at his busy Jamenick timber business in Freetown, summer 2018.

▼ Catherine adopting a sexy pose in waders while cleaning out a pond at Rectory Farm.

▼ Catherine.

W I picked up a different hat in each country we passed through from Istanbul to Almaty. Here are a few on the heads of Ged Healey, me, Saira Khan, cameraman Johnny Martin and director Matt Brandon, in Baku on the shore of the Caspian Sea.

X The ever-young John Croft, code-breaker.

sullen Hostaelian driver ready to do our bidding. Our training kicked in. 'Saira,' I said, 'inspect the vehicle while I frisk the Hostaelian.' I patted him down and pulled from his waistband an automatic pistol. Saira reported, 'There are wheel nuts missing, and one of the tyres looks a bit flat.' How pleased we were. The tyre was pumped up, and after rootling about we found the missing wheel nuts (which had been removed on purpose to test our powers of observation) and with our recently acquired orienteering skills we sped off into the Surrey countryside.

After an hour and a half, we arrived at a pair of huge, solid-steel gates, besides which were draped two billowing UN flags, flanked by armed guards with machine guns across their chests, legs akimbo. We were approached and asked to give our names. The gates swung open and we reported to the guard-house where a detail of UN soldiers complete with blue berets was waiting to greet us. On the map table were spread huge charts indicating where the minefields lay and where disparate bands of robbers and rebel forces had last been reported. At the far end of this 5,000-acre British Army training camp sat the helicopter landing zone, our destination.

With a cheerily ironic 'Good luck' from the UN officer in charge, we clambered back into the Land Rover and our Hostaelian driver shot off. He insisted he knew the fastest way to the landing site and began to challenge our directions. Only our determination to follow our training saved us from driving straight into a minefield. Then we were flagged down by a lone UN soldier, but something in his uniform told Saira that he was fake. He insisted on searching the vehicle and to our horror discovered a bullet in an ashtray which we had failed to find during our initial vehicle check. As he shouted at us, we were suddenly surrounded by a ragtag bunch. I ordered the driver to move on and we left them in our wake.

Driving along a tree-lined road, we heard the sound of gunfire and saw, emerging from the nearby woods and streaming across the field towards the road, fifteen to twenty heavily armed soldiers, firing as they ran. Our driver, sensing imminent danger, jumped out of the vehicle and dragged us into the ditch with him. We cowered there and watched the Land Rover be driven away. Stunned, in the ensuing silence we stood in the middle of the road wondering what had just happened, when an army lorry rumbled towards us. It came to a halt, troops emerged and we were bundled roughly into the back. Our driver, meanwhile, had made good his escape.

We were taken to a clearing and thrust onto our knees in front of a rebel commander. Everybody appeared to be drunk and it was with difficulty that I persuaded three rough rebels from dragging Saira into the woods. It all felt very real at this point, and she was justifiably terrified. We were hooded, spun around and thrown into the back of a Jeep which drove for ten or fifteen minutes, whether it was in circles or not I have no idea, until we arrived at a building and were dragged up several stairs into a concrete-floored room. There, we were put into stress positions against a wall for what seemed like an age. Occasionally our hoods were lifted up just far enough so they could jab a bottle of water into our mouths.

Eventually, I was hauled to my feet and dragged outside. My hood was whipped off to reveal the rebel commander who barked that I should now make a plea for my life in return for a heavy ransom. He thrust a copy of that day's *The Sun* into my hands, while another rebel set up a video camera. For my captors, this is what is known in the hostage-taking business as their 'proof of life' to my negotiators that I was still alive on the date of the newspaper. Proof of life also refers to hostage negotiators asking captors to prove their captive is still alive by asking the hostage a question that no one else could answer or research.

When BBC journalist Alan Johnston was kidnapped in Gaza in 2007, his parents were asked by negotiators to supply a proof of life question to be put to him by his captors. 'Ask him what was the name of our cat when we lived in Africa,' they said. Being a good Scottish family they had called it Whisky. The unfortunate reality was that the question got lost in translation and Alan was asked, 'What is the national cat of Africa?' The way to avoid such potentially fatal confusion is to prepare three questions in advance, to be held secretly by a next of kin, if you're entering an area where there is a threat of kidnap.

I'd left poor Saira in terror, and to be frank, I too felt pretty shaken by now. However, pulling myself together and feeling awkward about having to plead publicly for my life, I devised a plan that would save me that humiliation. I said to my kidnappers, 'Actually, I've already said goodbye to my family because I'm in the grip of a dread disease and about to die anyway, so this is all rather academic.' The rebel commander frowned and, with a puzzled Glaswegian accent, turned to his second-in-command and said, 'What do we do now?' After a muffled confab, I was reunited with a brave but tear-stained Saira and our Hostaelian driver, who had miraculously reappeared. We were released and set out once more for the helicopter zone.

When we got there, we were dismayed to find on a flat piece of ground the upturned hull of a Puma helicopter which was in flames; scattered around it, moaning, were a dozen terribly wounded UN military personnel. The carnage was dreadful.

Many had lost their arms and some their legs. Time for triage. Saira and I scurried among them, our training surging to the fore: elevation at all costs. TOR International doesn't do anything by halves; lying on the ground were their trainers with false arms amputated at the elbow, but hidden under their real arms were pumps used to squirt alarmingly convincing fake blood. It was our job to apply the tourniquets, and so we silently administered to the injured, leaving the dying to their God.

It was the end of the war game. Saira will attest that we were both exhausted, slightly ragged, but hugely impressed by the depth of the training. To this day I think of DRAB – Danger, Response (always pinch the eyebrow of the patient, it's highly sensitive), Airways, Breathing.

We now felt equipped to take on any dangers that Central Asia could throw at us. As it happened, our trip from Istanbul to Almaty was dangerous only in as much as we could have died laughing.

There are those trips where the crew and the so-called 'talent' hit it off immediately. We were on the road for nineteen days and apart from me throwing a mardy, of which more later, we had a blast. Never more so than in Georgia, that beautiful, bountiful land of song, fresh food and lots of white wine. At least that's how I remember it. A village dinner was arranged, before which a famous and incredibly tall and thin Georgian musician would perform for us. He wore a very formal suit, a very tall astrakhan hat, which I envied quite a lot and made a mental note to acquire, and a full set of gold teeth – when they caught the light, they were really quite startling. He entertained us for quite a long time on his stringed instrument and with his oddly high-pitched voice.

Time for dinner. Men only. Saira retired to the kitchen, where she spent her time dancing with a teenage boy, swooping around the room to the singing and general encouragement of our hostesses. Meanwhile, I was ensconced at one head of the table while the village headman was at the other. Apparently, it is the custom in those parts for the headman to propose a toast, to which the guest responds. A translator stood by. Unfortunately, there were many courses, and as the toasts piled one upon the other, things got just a little out of hand. 'People of Romania,' I began at one stage, before the translator suggested that we were actually now in Georgia. 'People of Georgia,' I continued, 'we have much in common. Both our flags feature the cross of Saint George and we were both conquered by the Romans.' 'So was Romania,' the translator helpfully whispered, 'that's why it's called Romania.' Eventually we were helped into our bus and waved away. I'll never forget Georgia and its white wine.

The whole enterprise, however, was thrown into jeopardy when we sped into Baku, capital of Azerbaijan, lying on the banks of the Caspian Sea. There, we expected to see our ferry waiting to take us across the Caspian to Aktau, in Kazakhstan, but there was no sight of it and we were alarmed to learn that there would be no ferry for a while due to 'high winds' on the Caspian. We gazed at the limpid surface of this, the largest inland body of water in the world, and were surprised to spot, out at sea, the outline of what was clearly a ferry, *our* ferry. It appeared to be at anchor. Investigations were made and it became clear that a dispute was in full swing and the ferry was some sort of bargaining chip. The problem was that we were in a serious race – eighty days to cover the globe – and absolutely had to get to Almaty, the old capital of Kazakhstan, on a fast-looming date otherwise the whole schedule would fall over.

There was no other way to cross and nothing for it but to wait it out in Baku, sitting in our harbourside hotel, astonished at the casual way some of the ships disgorged bilge filth into the once crystal-clear waters of the Caspian. This used to be home to the mighty sturgeon, but apparently no longer; the oilmen, drilling across the Caspian, have put a stop to that.

Oil has brought great wealth to the region and to Baku in particular, which has made it the most expensive hole in the world where a pair of flip-flops will set you back £40. I make it a point when travelling in far-flung or interesting places to pick up a local hat and had already added to my collection in Georgia. These hats, now numbering more than twenty, hang in a neat row on a beam in the house in France, and are donned at riotous dinner parties, normally at the end of the main course, and certainly by the time dancing ensues. I discovered, as we lay over in Baku, that Azerbaijan is the home of the finest astrakhan hats, or that's what the shopkeeper told me. In halting English, he explained that these hats are made from the 'fur' of the Qaraqui sheep, and the finest are from the aborted lamb foetuses because, the hatter was keen to explain, the curls are tighter and therefore more desirable. Curbing any notions of decency, I snapped one up for £100 and subsequently presented it to Catherine. With barely a pause, she popped it onto her hat shelf at Rectory Farm, remarking that it would be useful for winter funerals, a number of which, she suggested, were in the offing.

We spent some three days in Baku and when we eventually boarded our ferry, the litigation now apparently settled, we were hopelessly behind schedule. By way of relieving the tension, we decided to celebrate our departure with some vodka with vodka chasers (Saira bravely stuck to apple juice). I suppose it was shortly after midnight that the ceremony to grant

British citizenship to Nick the Red, a fixer we had picked up in Georgia, was performed. It must have taken place in the galley of this barely seaworthy hulk as I found myself knighting him with an enormous soup ladle while intoning a solemn oath which he was required to repeat. Saira held a tea towel over his head while Johnny the cameraman and Ben the director held his shoulders.

We had taken with us Ged X, a former special forces medic (*see* S: SIERRA LEONE), but the only time his expertise was required was after this drunken crossing of the Caspian Sea when, the following morning, the cameraman felt disinclined to get out of his bunk on the grounds that he was still so drunk that he would be unable to lift the camera onto his shoulder. Ged rigged up an improvised intravenous drip, and within twenty minutes the cameraman was back in business. I made a mental note of this ingenious approach to curing hangovers.

The overnight sea crossing still left us at least two days behind schedule and I knew, from my Mongolian jaunt the previous year (*see* M: MONGOLIA), that we could never make it up no matter how hard we drove. One of the key rules of *Around the World in Eighty Days* was no flying, but what to do? We could stick to the rules and be late in Almaty, giving the next team of Julia Bradbury and Matt Baker no time to get to the Pacific coast where *BBC Breakfast* presenters Louise Minchin and Bill Turnbull would be waiting to board a tanker to get them to California. So, it was with gay abandon and in contravention to all the rules that we chartered an enormous converted Russian Mil 8, ex-Afghanistan war helicopter gunship, to fly us on a six-hour hop across the Kazak desert, interrupted by a fuel stop in that barren wasteland, signalled only by a petrol pump and a battered old caravan.

Because of the intense heat, this venerable old chopper, loaded to the gunwales with nearly a ton of equipment and seven of us plus three Russian crew, each inscrutable behind their mirror sunglasses, soared and plunged according to the terrain we were crossing. I don't know how many rivets that old helicopter boasted, but I do know that each and every one of them danced loosely all the way to Aral city, one of the most desolate and depressing ex-Soviet outposts. There we were to catch a train and managed to do so by the skin of our teeth. We learned that the train had originated somewhere in Russia and was snaking through Central Asia, heading for Uzbekistan, jam-packed with every nationality of the region, many defined by their clothes and hats and by the food that was cooking in the aisles of every carriage; a moving Tower of Babel, in truth, with women doing their washing, feeding their children, and old men asleep in their string vests.

I was pretending to negotiate the purchase of a string of dubious pearls from one of the many hawkers on board when the train security detail bustled up, demanding to see our filming permit. Basically translated, it was made clear that while the train was travelling through the Kazak desert, the train itself was Uzbek territory and therefore our permit was insufficient, and would we kindly hand over all our film, pronto. Sensing the problem, our cameraman Johnny, a world traveller indeed, palmed the memory card and handed over an empty one, sliding the precious version into his pocket. The foul-tempered Uzbeks hadn't finished with us yet, for when we reached our stop, they gave us three minutes to unload our near-ton of equipment. Camera cases were being thrown out of windows as the train accelerated out of the station and, had he bothered to look, the driver would have seen a sea of V-signs raised high in his honour.

Our researcher had organised a dinner in an outlying farm-house to show us Kazak hospitality. We sat for what seemed like hours waiting for the main dish to arrive. I sensed trouble, and trouble arrived on a big tin tray in the shape of a sheep's head. I knew I was the designated target for a bit of sending-up.

'It is our tradition to offer to our guest of honour one of the two eyes,' said the English-speaking headman as he gouged out an eyeball, complete with its long, trailing optic nerve.

'Stop right there, my friend,' I interrupted. 'Please forgive me when I say that, in my country, we would find it very difficult to eat a sheep's eye, as indeed you might find it very difficult to eat an oyster, a dish that we love. So please do not be offended if I ask to be excused from your delicacy.'

'But I love oysters!' he replied, to my astonishment.

Now what? I spotted the headman's four-year-old daughter eyeing the eyeball greedily, so I asked whether perhaps she could have it and I would make do with a little of the sheep's lip. He nodded, in a jaded sort of way, and taking a knife I sliced off a thin sliver of lip, placed it in my mouth and pretended to enjoy it. Inwardly, I was livid at being put upon by some clever dick researcher and, I'm ashamed to say, I sulked for a day or so.

By the time we reached Almaty to hand over to Julia Bradbury and Matt Baker, who were taking on the next leg to the Sea of Japan, we had had the most amazing trip due to the camaraderie of the crew, director Matt Brandon and camera-man Johnny, good old Ged, the sporty Katharine Arthy and Saira being the best fun. She has remained a great friend to this day. Proof of life indeed.

Q

Queen

On not meeting her

My first brush with royalty came in 1953. I had watched the coronation of Queen Elizabeth II in the house of friends of my parents because we didn't yet have our own television set. The owners had moved out and their house was completely devoid of any furniture apart from the television, so we camped in the sitting room and watched the ceremony, although I remember spending most of the time in the bathroom teasing and torturing a large spider. Shortly after that, Swindon's borough parks department descended on a small traffic island opposite our home and turned it into a floral tribute which said, 'Welcome to Swindon'. As a nine-year-old boy, I quite reasonably assumed this was a kindness to our family, and it was something of a disappointment to learn that it was, in fact, for the Queen and her husband, who would be passing our house in a motorcade. We stood dutifully in the gateway to The Grange to mark the occasion – the car flashed past and she was gone, but I like to think she gave us a warm wave and made eye contact with me.

My second and only very slightly longer encounter with a royal was at the Warneford Clinic, a psychiatric unit in Oxford. The occasion was a conference on alcoholism, which was being sponsored by Securicor, one of my clients at Michael Joyce Consultants. I found myself standing in a little receiving line to be introduced to Diana, Princess of Wales. She approached, I bowed, there was a handshake. I think it was all over in twenty seconds, enough time to be struck by Diana's remarkable eye contact. I suppose the royals are all trained in this, the idea being to leave the civilian with the clear impression that you'll be receiving a phone call within the next week with an invitation to go to the cinema, somewhere in Fulham perhaps. Diana was very beautiful, but it was the smile and the eyes that had it.

Next was a reception at St James's Palace, and the host this time was Prince Andrew. He was less impressive, bowling up to our little group, which had been formed by his lackeys. The scheme is as follows: lackey approaches to say that you will shortly be introduced to Prince Andrew and you should therefore form a small horseshoe of four people and look out for the discreet nod that indicates you are next in line. Thus, there are little horseshoes all over the room and Andrew makes his progress through them. We knew immediately that he was honing in on our horseshoe because we could hear him from 30 yards away – he has a sort of booming, unattractive manner about him. He huffed and puffed in the middle of our horseshoe, was obviously not the slightest bit interested in any of us, and before long he was gone, which was fine by us.

The lengthiest and most rewarding encounter came when Malcolm Miller, marketing director of Amstrad, another client, called me. 'The palace has been on the phone,' he said. 'They want to have a look at our new laptop computer. Here's the phone number, can you handle it pronto? And better take Cliff with you, as you know absolutely nothing about technology.' I rang the number and it was answered by the secretary to the Princess Royal. A date was arranged, and I was told to enter through the Privy Purse door, which lies to the right of the palace's facade. Come the day, Cliff the technical guru and I took a cab and, as instructed, entered at the Privy Purse door. There, in a terrible state of faux flustered nerves, was Princess Anne's secretary – or maybe it was her lady-in-waiting, given how posh she was – who apologised profusely and explained that because the Princess had been delayed at her last appointment she was going to be about twenty minutes late and was it *at all* possible that we could hold on; she knew how busy we must be and wasn't this just an *awful* situation, so regrettable but I'm afraid unavoidable, but if there's any possibility *at all* that you can wait, the Princess would be *most* appreciative. 'But of course,' I said.

We were ushered into a nearby lift, which was basically full of a sofa, so the three of us sat on the sofa and went up to the long first floor of Buckingham Palace, which stretches the entire length of the building's frontage. My memory tells me that every 15 feet there was a footman in full livery standing pressed against the wall, eyes cast downwards, and that each door had a small card slotted into a little brass sleeve, much as you would find on a filing cabinet. We arrived at a door which said, 'The Princess Royal', were shown into her private quarters and the secretary/lady-in-waiting, oozing apologies, disappeared. There we were, Cliff and me, looking around and not touching anything – the family photographs, the very beautiful furniture, not least a glorious oval table, made of a light golden wood, possibly maple, and possibly from the reign of George III. It was onto this table that Cliff suddenly unloaded a lot of spanners and screwdrivers from a briefcase, all of which skidded and bounced across the highly polished surface of this exquisite piece of Sheraton or whatever it was. 'Cliff! Cliff!' I whispered fiercely. 'What are you doing? This is hugely valuable, we mustn't scratch it.' Cliff scooped the tools up, while I searched for marks. Nothing obvious, crisis over.

We waited, gazing out of the window onto the Mall, and eventually a side door opened and in strode Princess Anne, hugging under her arm a very heavy piece of marble. 'We're on round plugs here and they all fall out of their sockets,' she explained, 'so we've all got a piece of stone to lean against the plugs.' She was exquisitely dressed in a beautiful green suit, and was the most charming, interested, amusing company. These were the very early days of mobile computing, when laptops were called luggables – they were portable but only just – and she wanted to study this Amstrad model because she was thinking of getting one for her father.

I realised the meeting was over when I sensed a change of mood – it was just a look, the royal look, the 'see you next Friday at the Apollo cinema' look. Cliff was oblivious, and to my horror I saw that he had taken a strange stance, leaning backwards against the wall, legs astride. Fishing in his breast pocket he produced a business card and said, as if he were in the staff canteen, 'Look, if you ever need to give me a call for a chat about the technical stuff, here's my card.' He still hadn't clocked that it was time to go. I turned to the Princess and said, 'Well, thank you so much', and with that I nudged Cliff to get him moving towards the door.

That was the first and last time I met the Princess Royal, but a story told to me by a great friend confirms my opinion of her as a good sport. The Princess was in a lift at the Granada TV studios with a producer who had just filmed a documentary about her. They were going to view the rough cut, and the two of them squeezed into a tiny, shabby lift with double doors. As they closed, two pieces of graffiti, written across the two doors, were brought together. To the producer's horror, inches away from his and the Princess's nose, the graffiti became legible: 'BEAM ME UP SCOTTY', read the first, and beneath it, 'WHO PUT THE CUNT INTO SCUNTHORPE?' The producer could hardly breathe. Princess Anne was silent. And then, very slowly and deliberately, she said, 'What does "Beam me up Scotty" mean?'

My next royal is Camilla, Duchess of Cornwall. As a supporter of the National Literacy Trust, a charity of which she was the patron, I attended an event at a school in London's East End. I was allocated a table of schoolchildren, as were a number of other ambassador types, and with a hesitant and rather shy progress she arrived at my table and sat down. She was the most charming person, very relaxed and approachable. 'You're not still doing that *Apprentice* thing, are you?' she asked with that dark, warm, tobacco voice of hers. I told her I was about to give it up, and I got the impression she approved of this decision. She was funny and engaging. Together we interrogated the children.

Prince Charles, on the other hand, whom I've met briefly a couple of times, is, in my opinion, very mannered. He has mastered an approach which I can only describe as the 'save your energy' technique. When he's in a large room being introduced to lots of people, he can't really be blamed for not being interested in and perhaps hopes never to meet again, he adopts a sliding motion with his feet, a kind of soft-shoe shuffle which spares him the bother of actually having to lift his feet off the ground.

I've studied his technique, both in person and from watching him on television. Here's how it goes: when he does the round of horseshoes, he speaks to the person on the far right (or left), and then he bypasses the one in the middle (on this occasion, me), and then talks to the person on the far left (or right). He makes as if to move off, takes two slides, then half-turns and, with a raised forefinger, a raised eyebrow and a smile, addresses the one he's missed in the middle. He asks one question, then says, 'I'm so grateful for all you're doing', and with that, he slides towards the next group. It's a very economical process and I wonder if it could possibly go back to the court of Queen Elizabeth I.

The youngest member of the family, Edward, is quite the opposite. He hops around a lot. He has taken over the Duke of Edinburgh's Award scheme and in that context I've met him a couple of times. He's taller than you think, partly because he bounces on the tip of his toes. He is generally a little bit overenthusiastic, a bit theatrical. I'm sure he means well. Interestingly, I met and admired his wife, Sophie, when her PR company, housed over the world's poshest crockery company, Thomas Goode in Mayfair, was hired to help launch a short-lived Amstrad venture into healthcare. It was a sort of muscle-toning roller skate event, which probably explains why I don't remember much about it.

Turning now to the eldest member of the family, in the summer of 2016 I was fortunate enough to be invited to Buckingham Palace to celebrate the sixtieth anniversary of the Duke of Edinburgh's Award, where a lot of celebrities, some

Z-list like myself, were each allocated a group of maybe fifty young DoE Award winners who were there to meet HM The Duke. My group was one of the last, which meant I had to do my best to deliver an inspirational run of chatter for an hour before the Duke reached us – all rather awkward because all anyone is doing is looking over your shoulders to see if he's approaching. Occasionally, a lackey would appear to update us on his progress. And then there he was, slightly taller than I'd imagined, ramrod straight, tanned, a hearing aid discreetly tucked behind his left ear. He walked into our little semi-circle, shook hands and chatted with the young award winners, and then he was steered over to Catherine and me.

'What are you doing here?' he asked me, accusingly.

'Well,' I answered, 'I've been told to talk to these young people.'

'And how did you get involved with this?'

'I was a supporter of Young Enterprise when Peter Westgarth ran it and then you hauled him in to run your award scheme so Peter brought me in as a supporter.'

He looked me straight in the eye and said, 'You should be much more careful about the friends you make.' And with that he disappeared off to the next group.

So, there you have a tale of my short brushes with the Windsors, to me both interesting and perhaps rather flattering, but my last anecdote is a great deal sadder.

I was lying in bed in my Dolphin Square flat early in the morning on the last day of August 1997, when the phone rang. It was Gulu Lalvani, the successful Sikh businessman and prominent member of the Asian business community with whom I'd done some work over the years. He said, in his unmistakable, deep voice, 'Nick, have you heard the news? We must issue a statement.' Shaking myself awake, I said, 'Gulu, what news?'

'Diana is dead.'

'Gulu, may I call you back while I check the news?' I turned the television on, and of course the whole world was in turmoil. I rang him back.

'What a terrible, terrible thing,' I said.

'We must issue a statement.'

'I think at this particular moment we'd best leave that to her family and the heads of nation states. And only then her close friends like you.'

'Do you think so?'

'Yes, I think it's for the best, Gulu.'

'We will go to Kensington Palace. I have ordered gardenias. Come to my house in Eaton Square at ten o'clock.'

I dressed and headed to Belgravia. I rang the bell, and Gulu came to the door. Throwing me the keys to his Bentley, and clutching a large bowl of gardenias, he said, 'We will go to Kensington Palace now.' Many people have driven Bentleys, but I at the time was not one of them. Not only was it very large, there didn't seem to be a gearstick. Gulu sat in the back seat immediately behind me, and I found the gearbox on the steering wheel, crunched the brute into gear and off we went. As we approached Kensington Palace, the crowds got thicker and thicker and we crept to a crawl. 'Keep going,' Gulu said.

'Gulu, we're not going to be able to park.'

'We're not going to park, keep going and turn left there,' he replied, pointing to the private entrance, a short side road called Palace Avenue. As I started the turn, I could see that the gates ahead were closed. 'Don't worry,' said Gulu. 'They will open.'

'By magic?' I asked, incredulous.

'No, they know my car.'

Sure enough, the gates opened and we drove up the avenue with the eyes of the world on this lone black Bentley, obviously containing some dignitary, maybe a member of the royal family, instead of Gulu holding his bowl of gardenias and me wondering what on earth we were going to do next. We got to the end, where a policeman emerged from a police box and tapped on the driver's window. I pointed my thumb at my passenger, and Gulu lowered his window and said, 'We have come to see Paul Burrell.'

'Mr Burrell has gone to Paris,' replied the cop.

'I've come with these gardenias to give to Mr Burrell.'

'Well, you'll give them to me, sir.'

The gardenias were passed through the window.

I now had to perform a three-point turn in this narrow road and I could see tens of thousands of people watching with their arms folded. By some miracle, I accomplished the turn and drove back down the avenue, then inched out onto Kensington High Street. The road was lined with outside broadcast vans festooned with rooftop aerials, and I asked Gulu if he wanted to talk to some of the correspondents. We stopped the car, and with difficulty Gulu got out and we proceeded on foot towards the vans. I introduced him to a few journalists as a close friend of the Princess of Wales, and for the next couple of hours he poured out his condolences and his memories of her. He had got to know her very well – he had supported one of her charities, and she would go to his house, where the framed photographs in his drawing room showed her bouncing his children on her knees. He was once photographed driving her to Annabel's nightclub, and, at the more unworldly end of things, they shared an interest in Eastern mysticism.

Gulu is an amazing man, very generous, very funny, a one-off who came to England from India to go to Leeds University, before starting a low-cost electronics brand called Binatone (named after his sister Bina). Passing that successful international business to his son, he took himself to Thailand and from an old mangrove swamp created the Royal Phuket Marina, an opulent hotel and luxury apartment development around a swish marina.

I can see why Princess Diana enjoyed his friendship. How sad she wasn't there to receive him with his bowl of gardenias.

R

Regrets

I've had a lot, culminating in a kidnapping

I was introduced to Her Highness Sheikha Bouchra bint Maktoum Al Rashid Al Maktoum by a close friend of Alan and Ann Sugar. The Sheikha was the Moroccan-born second wife of Sheikh Maktoum bin Rashid Al Maktoum, the ruler of Dubai. At twenty-seven years old, she was thirty-one years younger than her husband, had had three sons by him, and when I first met her in September 1999 she and the boys were ensconced in an enormous apartment in Lowndes Square, Knightsbridge, from where she could look out onto another apartment on the roof of the Carlton Tower Hotel (now the Jumeirah Towers Hotel), also owned by her husband. This rooftop apartment was for the sole use of her three tiny sons and their nannies and was decked out accordingly, turning it into an enormous playpen.

Maktoum was the oldest son of Sheikh Rashid who became Ruler of Dubai in 1958. When Rashid accepted an invitation from the Macmillan government to visit London in 1959,

Maktoum, then a teenager, was part of the royal entourage that stayed at the Dorchester Hotel and was shown the sights of London. For the first and probably last time in his life he saw the Underground. The royal party exchanged gifts with the war minister John Profumo. He was presented with a golden sword by the visitors and returned the compliment with an umbrella. That's British diplomatic hospitality for you.

Maktoum grew up to become a very shy and retiring man, more interested in horse racing than political grandstanding. His young wife was more ambitious. She believed that his younger brother, Sheikh Mohammed, the energetic one who was the real power (she referred to him as 'The Beard'), was overshadowing, even eclipsing her husband. She hoped that by raising her profile she might also enhance her husband's reputation and re-establish his public authority as head of the family. To this end, she wanted to mount a big art show in London, to which the whole diplomatic corps and London society would be invited. The artist was none other than Sheikha Bouchra herself.

And so I found myself in a lift that opened straight into the Sheikha's Lowndes Square apartment, which was staffed by barefooted young Arab maids wearing white headscarves tied in a knot at the back. One of them greeted me with a demure bow of the head, and took me silently down a long, thickly carpeted corridor into what appeared to be the principal reception room, dotted with small round tables and chairs, Arab style. The maid padded off silently and about ten minutes later the Sheikha made her appearance. She was very tall, demure, elegant rather than beautiful, her face made up to make her complexion paler. As mint tea in small gold-rimmed glasses was served by one of the maids, she spoke softly, in highly accented English, about how she was an artist and wanted to mount an exhibition whose centrepiece would be a *very, very* special painting, *very valuable*, and this would be auctioned for charity. The beneficiary would be 'the good doctors'. Gentle probing narrowed this down to the emergency medical charity, Médecins Sans Frontières. Was this something I could organise for her?

I said I thought I could do this but that my family was heavily engaged in looking after my mother who was, sadly, nearing the end of her days. Could the Sheikha hold off the actual event for a month or so? 'Of course,' she murmured. 'And I will pray for her.' I was very touched at this. My mother died not long afterwards.

I agreed to start the preparatory work and asked her if she had any ideas as to a venue for this event. She had no preferences but insisted it must not be in a public place (which knocked out my first suggestion, the Islamic wing of the British Museum). 'Perhaps you could show me some of your work?' I ventured. She rose and led me far into the depths of the apartment, until we reached her studio where freshly stretched canvases, as yet untouched, were neatly stacked against the wall. An easel took centre stage. Her celebrated method of painting was to squeeze a whole tube onto a palette, chuck the tube away, and then dip her brush in and smear it across the canvas, thus bypassing the irksome tradition of mixing the different paint colours on the palette before applying it. I began to feel nervous, but she was obviously very proud of her work. I admitted a lack of knowledge of this particular school which rather let me off the hook. Moreover, she was convinced that her Arab acquaintances would come thundering in on their 747s and buy it all up because owning her work would provide them with a direct link to the royal family.

On my way back to the office in Covent Garden, I passed the Hard Rock Café on Piccadilly, and immediately knew that I had, hopefully, solved the location. Alan Sugar had bought the whole building, Gloucester House, and above the Hard Rock lay six floors with an enormous lateral apartment on each, all of them unoccupied and unfurnished but beautifully finished pending sale. I rang him immediately to ask if we might carpet one of the apartments and, on the promise not to make a mess, could we hold the exhibition there? He very generously agreed. I brought in a team to carpet and dress the apartment: all the chandeliers were wrapped in white linen and free-standing lights were placed beside twenty or so easels running around the glistening white walls. I hired a catering team from some smart outfit in Mayfair who would dress in eighteenth-century costumes, with the boys sporting beauty spots on their cheeks. The grand ballroom of the apartment would be deluged in flowers, and the best canapés in town would be served. I got hold of a copy of the diplomatic mailing list to invite all the ambassadors accredited to the Court of St James.

When I went back to Lowndes Square a few days later to brief the Sheikha, she was delighted. She said she had started work on the *very, very special* painting; it would be called *La Nature*, a landscape with a mountain stream that would be studded with precious stones including aquamarine, topaz and green garnets, and above it a night sky full of diamonds for stars. I gulped, sensing a bear trap. Who would bid for such a valuable painting? If the Dubai set didn't turn up, this had the potential to become a huge embarrassment. Always go with your gut instinct. On this occasion, I didn't, much to my later regret. I believed in her confidence that her friends would all be jetting in with their credit cards (cash, more likely) at the ready.

The reception was held at Gloucester House on 16 March 2000. We had red velvet ropes outside, and a battalion of paparazzi. We had encountered some problems with the lift during the day and the thought of the great and good huffing and puffing their way up the rather grand staircase to the third floor gave me palpitations, so I hired a lift engineer to act as the lift operator, his tool bag discreetly stowed under a stool.

Upstairs in the apartment, the Sheikha, dressed in a long flowing gown, received her guests, announced by a splendid toastmaster in full regalia. In they poured, the diplomats and the mighty. I noticed the tall and elegant Jacob, Lord Rothschild, with his wife Serena, studying with interest the signing-in book, with a nod one moment and a raised eyebrow the next. Noticeable for their absence were the United Arab Emirates diplomatic brigade. None of them turned up. This was a warning sign, I now realise: they weren't there because the Sheikha's initiative hadn't been approved back in Dubai. Bouchra hid her disappointment well.

The crowd hushed as the toastmaster called the room to attention. Bouchra approached the lectern. She gave a little cry. I was standing next to Alan, who nudged me and said, 'You'd better get over there fast.' I shot across the room to discover that the speech I had so lovingly crafted was no longer sitting on the lectern. Someone had taken it. I didn't carry a copy and poor Bouchra was not one to make an impromptu speech. The toastmaster, a true professional, issued a low murmur, dived into his breast pocket and handed me his copy, which I smoothed out and popped onto the lectern. Order was restored. She gave her speech praising 'the good doctors' and conveying her husband's best wishes and regrets he couldn't attend because he was detained by duties of state. Although she spoke with conviction, a worm of doubt stirred deep in my colon.

The auctioneer from Phillips then got up and opened the bidding for *La Nature*, which had been featured on the court page of *The Times* that morning and was now proudly displayed in the centre of the room. It was expected to fetch around £100,000. It got off to a furious start: £1,000, £2,000, £3,000, £4,000, £5,000, £6,000, £7,000, £8,000, £9,000. Pause. 'Ten thousand pounds, anybody? Do I see ten thousand?' Silence. It came to an absolute full stop. Everybody was now looking at the floor.

Sold, then, for £9,000, to a smart young chap who turned out to be the boyfriend of the Sheikha's hairdresser and who, I later discovered, had been bidding on the Sheikha's behalf – it was her money. Meanwhile, I had the director of Médecins Sans Frontières there, who was expecting a big payday, and it was so awkward because nobody was buying any of the other squashed-tube paintings displayed on the easels all around the walls. I thought, Oh God, I have to do the decent thing here, so I bought one for £1,000 and Alan, God bless him, put his hands in his pocket and paid £1,000 for another one.

That was the end of it, and we all eased into the night. But we got a lot of press, including an arch little diary piece in the *Daily Mail* which, from memory, congratulated Alan Sugar, a well-known Jewish businessman, for providing the venue to a Middle Eastern royal family, this hopefully marking a thawing of relations etc, etc. When I showed it to Bouchra, she read it in silence then gave out a little shriek and put the paper down on the couch. She looked startled and I suddenly felt uneasy – how would her husband respond to the fleeting Jewish–Arab entente cordiale that had unfolded in Gloucester House?

Hello! magazine devoted an extravagant seven-page spread

to Bouchra. When my old school friend Gerry Wilkinson, close advisor to HH The Aga Khan (*see* K: AGA KHAN), saw it, he said, 'Nick, for God's sake, you can't show her dressed like that, in tight white jeans, lying provocatively on a divan!'

'She must know what she's doing,' I replied defensively. 'I don't know whether it's appropriate down in Dubai, which apparently is a land full of Russian girls with no visible means of support and young Dubai nationals getting busy on brandy and smoking and snorting things. I don't know what goes on down there, that's up to her.'

'Well, I've got to tell you, I've think you've got it terribly wrong.'

Gerry knew his stuff. The Sheikha, it turns out, did not. Nor did I.

As part of the PR campaign to raise her profile, I had organised for Bouchra to be photographed by society photographer Patrick, Lord Lichfield, who had his studio somewhere near Ladbroke Grove. He was ferociously expensive, about £10,000 a day, I think. At the end of the shoot, the Sheikha said, 'Nick, I have something for Patrick's assistants,' and handed me two great wads of fifty-pound notes. I took Patrick aside and said, 'The Sheikha has given me this for your assistants.' 'Don't be bloody ridiculous,' he answered, stuffing it in his pockets. On the way out, Bouchra handed me a roll of fifties. 'Nick, this is for you.' 'No, no, I don't need a tip; you pay me a fee.' 'No, no,' she insisted. I reluctantly and quite rightly caved in and discreetly trousered my little present.

She loved the portraits, and then *Vogue* rang up to say they were setting up for the summer season, and did I have anything to offer them on the Sheikha? Her husband, Sheikh Maktoum, reportedly worth over £10 billion, had just bought her a yearling, Royal Racer, so I thought we should do something around that. The horse was being trained by the legendary Criquette Head at her stables in Chantilly, near Paris. When I suggested it to Bouchra, she said, 'Let's go, and we'll take Patrick.' I rang Patrick, who agreed to come with his partner, Lady Asquith. Together with Terry Kelleher, a television journalist friend who'd made a short film of the 'art' auction, off we went to Paris, where we checked into the Bristol Hotel, while Bouchra checked into the family house on the Avenue Foch.

We got to Chantilly the following morning ahead of Bouchra, to meet Criquette and the glossy yearling and set up the shoot. It took the Sheikha forever to get there, we were losing the light and Patrick was getting irritable, and then she rocked up in a skin-tight, floor-length sort of ballgown, tottering about on the grass in impossibly high heels – to go to the stables and hold a horse's head. We were all stunned.

After the shoot, the others returned to London but I stayed on as Bouchra had asked me to go back with her the following evening. 'Tonight, we will go out,' she said. 'I will send a car for you.' The car was a very black and very stretched Mercedes and I was driven to the Maktoum home on the prestigious Avenue Foch. When the steel doors slid open into the courtyard, I was surprised to spy a line of black Mercedes limousines and 4×4s, all with diplomatic number plates. The whole place was crawling with security people in black leather jackets with strange bulges. I was taken into the house and shown into the drawing room, and there was Sheikh Maktoum's chair, next to which was a table in front of the TV on which all his spectacles had been arranged in a neat line. At first, I thought this meant he was at home, but when it became clear that he wasn't, I assumed that this little scene was repeated in each of his many residences, and that he therefore had hundreds of pairs of glasses. Finally, Bouchra appeared, wearing metallic silver dungarees. Next came her brother and a couple of cousins from Morocco, who were all obviously having a wonderful time just being 'on board'.

We each got into our own Mercedes, with a chase car in front of and behind each car. It was an unbelievable cavalcade. The way it works is, you drive along and when you get to a round-about, the chase car blocks the oncoming traffic, so you never stop. It's like a minuet. The cavalcade pulled up outside a nightclub on the Champs-Élysées called the Lido, famous for its risqué cabaret, although Bouchra had brought her three sons, all of them under ten. We were late and the show had been held up. We sat down and food arrived (by this time I was ravenous), but as soon as the plates hit the table the lights went down, so we couldn't see what we were eating. When we looked up from our plates there were girls with twizzles on their nipples and blokes with jewel-encrusted posing pouches thrusting their crotches at us. *In front of the kids.* Our bearded security detail, clearly UAE military personnel, didn't know which way to look. And then the lights went up and just when we were focusing on the food, the plates were whisked away and the lights went down and there was another act.

I returned to London the next day with Bouchra. She sent a Mercedes to collect me from the hotel, and I was driven straight up to the steps of her personal 737 – no security, no customs, no passports – at Le Bourget airport. The first thing I saw on the plane was a bedroom and then there was a lounge area with a thick white carpet, white sofas with gold seat buckles, and a table in the middle on which there were vases of roses and bowls of lobster tails for snacking on. There was another cabin beyond this for the security people, cabin stewards, chefs, nannies, maids and so on. We got to London, landing at Heathrow, and were poured straight into another cavalcade of cars.

With some relief, I got back to normal life, and then returned to France to be in Lacroix, my house near Agen (*see* L: LACROIX). A few days into my holiday, Bouchra telephoned. 'Nick, will you be at Longchamp tomorrow?' Every year, she would appear with her husband for the summer racing season at Ascot, Newmarket and Goodwood. They would then go to Deauville and Longchamp. Like clockwork.

'No,' I answered. 'Why do you ask?'

'Well, you see, my husband is flying into London tomorrow and he's expressed a wish to have a photograph taken with me and the children, and then we're going to Longchamp for the racing.'

'I'll try to contact Patrick and see if he's available. I'll ring you tomorrow.'

I rang back the following morning to report what progress I'd made with Patrick, but there was no reply on her mobile. Soon after, I received a frantic call from her brother, Atif, saying that the Sheikha had been kidnapped: 'You must get a lawyer, we must save her! I am at her apartment.' He was in a total state, and I could hear all sorts of shouting in the background. He told me that the Sheikha was meant to be going to Paris with her husband and the children but they hadn't arrived there. They'd taken off from Farnborough Airport in Hampshire, and he'd managed to speak to her briefly on the plane and she had whispered that she was being taken straight back to Dubai.

It was all very carefully orchestrated. The three boys were meant to be going to the circus that day, but one of them had the flu so he was kept at home in Lowndes Square with a nanny. The two other children never made it to the circus, but they'd been taken 'by four powerfully built men', according to a later press report, and driven directly to Farnborough, where the Sheikh's jet was waiting, engines running. On board were Maktoum and Bouchra, who was expecting a day out at Longchamp. When her children were bundled onto the plane by Maktoum's burly security detail, she realised they were all heading straight for Dubai. But now there was a child missing and Maktoum wanted that child. Back in Lowndes Square, Atif and his crowd wouldn't let the sick boy be taken and they had called the police. So, as I understood it, the noise in the background when I spoke to Atif was a huge argument between officers from the British Diplomatic Protection Squad and the Ruler of Dubai's diplomatic security chaps.

I managed to speak to one of the British officers. 'What on earth is going on?' I asked. 'Well, there seems to be a bit of a problem here,' came the answer. 'But I should keep out of it if I were you, sir. We've got it all in hand – we've got a gentleman here from the Moroccan Embassy, we've got a gentleman from the United Arab Emirates, and I think we'll be able to sort this out. Thank you very much, I appreciate your concern.' End of conversation.

By this point, following Atif's claim that the children had been kidnapped (as indeed they had been, although by their own father), a full-scale Scotland Yard operation had swung into action to rescue them. Officers from the Diplomatic Protection Squad had set off in hot pursuit of the 'kidnapper's' car and caught up with it near Farnborough and was tailing it. Local police were called in for backup. The children were seen being put on the plane, and a squad car raced onto the runway to prevent the jet from taking off, only to find that it contained the Ruler of Dubai and his family purportedly on their way to Longchamp for a day's racing.

At this point, trained negotiators from the Foreign Office were brought in along with a squad of marksmen armed with high-powered rifles. After a tense stand-off lasting several hours, in which time the third child was delivered to the scene, the police were finally satisfied that the whole episode was a misunderstanding arising from what a spokesman from Scotland Yard later described as simply 'a rather big domestic'. The red-faced Brits backed off, and the Sheikh's jet rolled down the runway, gathered speed and headed east.

I continued to call Bouchra's mobile for days and weeks after, but it had been disconnected. The debacle happened at the end of April 2000. In August, a diary piece in the *Mail on Sunday* reported that Sheikh Maktoum had attended Goodwood race meeting, where his yearling, No Excuse Needed (indeed), won him £30,000 in prize money. There was, the diarist added, less happy news of his wife, Sheikha Bouchra: she had been discarded in favour of a very young girl who was pregnant by the fifty-seven-year-old Ruler. Only then did it dawn on me: the Sheikha wasn't trying to raise her profile in order to promote her husband; her real concern was that she was going to be displaced by his new mistress. He wanted her out of the limelight, and out of London, and had duped her into boarding his jet in the belief they would be going for a day trip to Longchamp.

I never heard from her again. The security company who looked after the Lowndes Square apartment changed all the locks on the doors the next day and it was closed down. All the staff were paid off, and that was that. I had no point of contact so there was nothing I could do.

We don't know what happened to her. Maktoum died of a

heart attack in Australia in 2006. His obituary in the *Telegraph* reported that he was survived by his widow, Sheikha Bouchra. A few years later, someone told me they'd read somewhere that Bouchra had 'died in her sleep'. Who knows?

What happened to the *very, very valuable* painting, *La Nature*? Bouchra had given it to Alan to thank him for providing the venue for her first (and last) London exhibition. Alan stuck it in the garage, presumably, and then in June 2001 he held a big party at Searcys in Knightsbridge after being knighted, and he made a little speech in which he very graciously thanked me. 'Nick has been doggedly supportive of me,' he said. 'So, I've got a little present for him.' With that, he gave me a big parcel wrapped in brown paper: *La Nature*. I took it home, and Catherine and I hung it on the wall. One day, I took it down and drove to Hatton Garden in London to have someone assess it. Some of the gemstones were real – topaz, aquamarine – but of very poor quality. All the diamonds were fake – zircon, the expert told me. The £100,000 painting was worth £300 at the most.

I'm sure the Sheikha didn't know the stones were duds. Had she been done over by some opportunistic middleman who knew an innocent Moroccan girl when he saw one? I think she was probably taken for a ride by other sharpsters. And then she was taken on a final ride – back to Dubai – by her own husband, who no doubt shoved her into some obscure wing of one of his palaces and locked the doors.

I put the painting back on the wall at home to remind myself of the price of naivety. Not just hers, but mine. Big regret.

S

Sierra Leone

An adventurous start-up

Long-distance road trips have always been special for me, but this one was bristling with potential disasters. Robbery and kidnapping topped the list, along with the logistical nightmare of dragging a heavy trailer of valuable woodworking equipment along potholed dirt tracks through baking desert and steaming jungle.

The plan was to drag the unwieldy rig all the way from England through France, Spain and Morocco, then down the west coast of Africa through Senegal and Guinea to Freetown, the chaotic capital of Sierra Leone, which stubbornly remains one of the world's poorest countries. The reality was a series of crises in which the air turned a very dark blue. We ran into mechanical breakdowns, vandalism, tummy trouble, barefaced rip-offs and a shambolic lorry without brakes that drove straight into us. Despite all that, there was too much at stake to fail. I was determined that this project would not end with my ears ringing to those immortal words from *The Apprentice*, 'You're fired!'

The idea for the adventure came to me in 2011, shortly after I returned from a filming trip to Sierra Leone for the British charity Hope and Homes for Children. I had met the charity's founders, Mark and Caroline Cook, a couple of years earlier as I prepared to set out on my Mongolia odyssey (*see* M: MONGOLIA), and I was so impressed by their work that I adopted HHC as my charity for the trip. Taking a rather roundabout route to Mongolia, I stopped off in Romania to meet Stefan Darabus, the HHC director in that country, at his headquarters in Baia Mare in Maramures. From there he took me on a tour of orphanages he was closing – the objective of HHC being to remove children from orphanages into permanent family homes – including a truly dreadful place housing school-age children. One look at the manager, standing in the kitchen stirring an enormous pot of God knows what, was enough to tell me that this was an extremely unhealthy place for teenage girls and boys. Stefan told me he had reached an agreement with the Romanian government to close this miserable institution down over the next twelve months. Not a moment too soon, in my opinion. Two cars could be seen parked nearby, their occupants sitting there hour after hour, waiting perhaps for a stray teenage girl to slip out for a cigarette. Those traffickers would have had her in a Berlin brothel, or maybe one in Cardiff or Huddersfield, by the end of the week.

We then went to a small house occupied by a dozen children whose mental state or physical condition demanded that they be cared for by a couple of surrogate mothers. The children had been terribly damaged by their childhood in a local orphanage. As babies, they had learned not to cry because they realised no one would comfort them. Imprisoned in cots all day, with nothing but slops to eat, their only stimulation came from rocking incessantly. Never picked up, they had internalised their pain, causing lifelong mental and physical damage. When I met them, HHC had helped them escape the nightmare of the orphanage. They were being lovingly cared for but, now aged just nine or ten, the damage had been done. Some were unable to walk without the use of a cut-down Zimmer frame; others sported saliva sores around their mouths from chewing their tongues; others were unable to speak or, indeed, make a sound.

Mark Cook had been with the British contingent for the UN during the Balkan war in the 1990s and had been horrified at the conditions in orphanages in Eastern Europe. He was determined to make it his business to shut down these 'child warehouses', reuniting the children with their families where possible (the vast majority were not orphans at all: an estimated 80 per cent of the eight million children living in orphanages worldwide today have families, but have been abandoned because of poverty, war, disability or discrimination). Where reunion with the birth families wasn't possible, HHC would find suitable foster families. Today, the charity is at the forefront of a global movement to eradicate orphanages by transitioning children into loving homes – working directly in eight countries and supporting like-minded partners in another twenty.

During my filming project in Freetown I had spent a few minutes with James, a poor street boy who had been taught carpentry by HHC, of which, by this time, I had become a patron. James had been orphaned when he was eight during the brutal civil war that had engulfed Sierra Leone for eleven years, starting in early 1991. He had walked all the way from Bo, in the southeast, to Freetown, where he had attached himself to a family.

Now, aged twenty-three, he was working in a lean-to shed producing bedheads in a slum lane on a Freetown hillside. Quiet, polite and dignified, he struck me as an enterprising young man who wanted to succeed. As he proudly led me to his own tiny workshop and explained that he wanted to start his own business, it became painfully clear that he lacked the necessary equipment. I could see that he would become yet another victim of the continuing spiral of poverty in the former British colony.

Here, I sensed, were two opportunities. Firstly, I would have a real reason to undertake another rather adventurous road trip, but this one would have a purpose, an endgame. Secondly, I realised that if I could give this young man a dose of business advice and all the essential tools to launch his own carpentry workshop, then maybe he could make a go of it and build a little business. Initially, my plan was a one-man operation: I would beg, steal or borrow the necessary items from contacts and friends, top of the list being a 4×4 vehicle plus trailer onto which I would load an industrial saw and a massive diesel generator, and drive to Sierra Leone, where the vehicle would be donated to Hope and Homes for Children.

I couldn't believe how generous people were. First came the vehicle, following a meeting I had with Graeme Hossie, co-founder and chief executive of London Mining, which had iron-ore mining concessions in Sierra Leone. He generously handed over a brand-new, £60,000 Toyota Land Cruiser with a powerful 4.5-litre V8 engine, the necessary monster for an intercontinental towing journey. Next came the electrically operated saw, a Dalton 20-inch table saw which could slice through any African hard- or softwoods, donated by Tony Hoyle, boss of the Lancashire-based company Calderbrook Woodworking Machinery. To operate the saw in Sierra Leone, a city subjected to regular power cuts, James would need a diesel-fuelled generator. My cousin, Charles Hewer, who made a career in importing hardwood from Africa and elsewhere, sourced one for £4,500 and I bought it, along with a fifteen-foot, heavy-duty twin-axle trailer that could carry the one-and-a-half-ton load.

As I planned every tiny detail of the journey and gathered advice – most of it contradictory – James, the young carpenter, remained oblivious. I had asked the HHC staff in Freetown not to tell him anything in advance in case I didn't make it to Sierra Leone. It had been two years since we met, and I didn't even know if I'd find him when I got there. In fact, it later emerged that he was becoming pretty desperate, trudging around, knocking on doors, seeking work with his hand tools carried in a bundle on top of his head. Out of nowhere, I was going to tap him on the shoulder and say, 'Is this stuff of any use to you?' Would he just run away in terror?

Three weeks before I was due to leave Rectory Farm, everything was in place, even down to having a driver standing by in Tangier to take me through the most dangerous sector of the journey, the Western Sahara and lawless Mauritania, subject to marauding parties surging out of Mali in search of booty or hostages. And then everything changed. A Belfast TV production company with which I had worked in Northern Ireland expressed interest in my trip and asked if they could send a camera crew out with me if they could get a commission. I suggested that an approach to Jay Hunt, then the creative supremo at Channel 4, was worth a shot and we arranged to meet with her. The wonderful thing about Jay is that she takes decisions fast and there's none of the usual TV luvvie hugging and bullshit which invariably comes to nothing. Within minutes we had a green light.

I jumped at the opportunity to have the whole adventure filmed, believing that it would be a good way to get profile for Hope and Homes for Children and to show viewers the urgent need that the people of Sierra Leone were in. Additionally, I would be paid a fee which would more or less cover the money I had laid out on equipment, ferries, insurance, the horrifying fuel bills en route and so forth. My solo adventure, with all its likely pitfalls, had suddenly become a team event. This was going to be fun, no? Unfortunately, I failed to calculate the loss of control over my chosen route and much else besides, including how the eventual film would be edited, all of which would make this one of the most trying journeys I have ever undertaken.

I set off from Rectory Farm in my pristine Land Cruiser with its heavily laden trailer in early May 2012, Catherine's entreaties to be careful following me down the drive, and headed for our house in south-west France (*see* L: LACROIX), where I made final checks on my inventory of equipment. A few days later, I welcomed Nick Read, the director/cameraman who was an experienced Africa hand, and Tamara, the sound recordist. As we set out from Lacroix, my cousin Stephen, a near neighbour, waved me off with some bloodcurdling cautions. I admonished him, saying that, generally speaking, people are kind the world over. 'Yes, and then they cut your tongue out,' he added coldly.

The first stretch was uneventful, through south-west France to the Pyrenees, on to Barcelona, down to Algeciras and then onto the ferry to Tangier. From there, I had hoped that we would be traversing the Western Sahara and Mauritania, which held high risks, particularly for a sixty-nine-year-old in a brand-new Land Cruiser towing what could be rich pickings for any of the region's jihadist gangs. However, arriving in Fez after motoring down from Tangier, I was warned by a British security advisor (recruited by the TV producer for the role of Ancient Mariner) of the deathly hazards of entering the 'kidnap corridor'. To my dismay, Channel 4 denied clearance for us to travel into the desert, principally because the Moroccan authorities had refused a filming permit for that leg of the journey.

My plan was now being dramatically scaled back, and I was bitterly disappointed to learn that we were now to store the vehicle and its precious cargo in Morocco, in the care of a young Brit, a sort of fixer marooned in Morocco, living there with his mother who, joyfully, was once a body double for Goldie Hawn. Even better, his father, I recall, doubled for Roger Moore. Sadly, the son bore the physical similarities of neither. Leaving him with instructions to get rid of the wooden pallets on which the saw and generator were riding and bolt them to the steel bed of the truck, we flew back to London via Agadir. The Toyota and all the equipment were to be shipped to Dakar, the capital of Senegal, once all the arrangements had been made.

Back at Rectory Farm, I could do nothing but await news of the shipment. Eventually, I received an email with pictures of the Land Cruiser, now with our handlers in Dakar, showing the rear window smashed, the bonnet raised, and the floor festooned with what looked like ignition cables. I rang the handlers in a state of high irritation, demanding to know whether there would be anything left of the vehicle or my carefully assembled cargo by the time I made it to Dakar.

As it turned out, when I arrived in Dakar a few days later, all the gear was still intact and the only problem with the Land Cruiser was the damaged window. Young Mr Hawn/Moore had taken the money but had not properly secured the load, which caused us many problems, of which more later. A local fixer, Mohamed, joined us and, on meeting him, I liked him as he was an optimist and I always like optimists, as long as they're not bullshitters. It quickly became clear that he was going to be a hopeless chancer, but sadly his scams cannot be recounted here for fear of shocking the faint-hearted. The director, Nick, whom I liked and respected a lot, had disappeared and was replaced by Luke Campbell, whose claim to fame was that he had once directed an episode of *An Idiot Abroad*. Hmm. The team was strengthened by my old pal Ged X (*see* P: PROOF OF LIFE) and his colleague Tommy X, both special forces veterans who had operated in many war zones, including in Sierra Leone during the civil war.

Ged, a Geordie, amusing and stocky – that is to say, short but very broad – runs a remote areas medical support and training company. A very entrepreneurial guy in his forties, he and I travelled to Libya together not long before the overthrow of Gaddafi in a bid for his company to merge with a local clinic there which serviced the personnel of the desert oil drilling rigs. Tripoli was a strange place in those days and, fortunately for Ged, nothing came of this merger. However, the two of us spent an unforgettable day completely alone at Leptis Magna, one of the great wonders of the world, which in its day rivalled Rome in size and influence under the Emperor Septimus Severus.

If Ged was stocky, then Tommy was massive and clearly able to look after himself, and me too, I hoped. I was delighted to see them, and to have Wayne Cornish along for the trip. Wayne, the press officer for Hope and Homes for Children, was a real trouper and had fixed the initial shipping of the Land Cruiser from Japan to Gibraltar and unravelled the insurance problems and much else besides.

Soon, we were heading south through Senegal, towards the border with Guinea. As we got close, the tracks became sand roads, rutted and sometimes treacherous as they occasionally skirted the River Gambia which, Mohamed assured, was absolutely not infested with crocodiles. Progress slowed to a crawl as we lurched in and out of great depressions, pulling over to let the overladen and distinctly ropey local trucks smoke past us. Then came a sickening crunch on a remote track. The trailer had been grounding in the ruts and a bolt had sheared off. Local mechanics appeared from nowhere and fixed the problem by raising the trailer slightly. We were off again, albeit at a painfully slow 15 miles per hour.

Next came a bent axle, which heated up and then completely shredded a tyre. The spare was fitted but only lasted a couple of hours until it too started to smoke, burn and shred. The load was too heavy to carry on for long with just one wheel on one side of the trailer but we nursed it along until we spotted a roadside tyre sale and repair outfit, run by a couple of enterprising and deft young guys. Surveying their high, wobbly towers of worn-out tyres (there was no chance of buying anything with a decent tread), the correct tyre size was selected. They fitted one and threw two others in the back to use when the time, inevitably, would come.

Indeed, by dusk, we were two tyres down with one remaining spare. We stopped in a village to reassess the damage. Instantly, a crowd formed and a noisy debate ensued as to the best way forward. The night air was thick with mosquitos, to such an extent that I felt it wise not to open my mouth to speak. Suddenly men appeared with hammers and crowbars and much noise was made, but the problem, though eased, remained. Thanking them, we invited them to drain some of the diesel from the generator in payment. It was emptied in seconds.

Our first night in Guinea was spent in a breathtakingly dirty hotel. Ged produced some dry rations, which he cooked up on an open fire in the dirt yard and we squatted round the fire, dreading the moment when we would have to turn in. My room featured nothing but a bed and a shredded mosquito net. I was never a Boy Scout, but you can bet your boots I never travel without one of those silk sleeping bag liners and a very secure mosquito net. It was, nevertheless, a sleepless night.

Crossing the border into Sierra Leone was a lesson in patience, negotiation, self-control and gratitude that Sierra Leone's style of bureaucracy has not reached our shores. I can't remember exactly how many controls we had to pass through, but I think it was about eight, each one a couple of hundred yards apart, with wire stretched across the road. There was one for visas, one for customs, another for driving permits, another for an arms and drugs search, and so forth. Driving towards the capital, we were surprised to come across another control, wire stretched across the road, but this time there were no uniforms in sight. Instead, a small knot of young men surged towards the cab of the Land Cruiser, demanding money. I'll never forget Tommy's calm instruction: 'Put your foot down quite hard.' He then reared up in his seat and, with his window wound down, he let out a mighty jungle roar. Although a big burly fellow, he seemed to double in size and the would-be highwaymen fled into the bush.

When we finally reached Freetown, we found the teeming city in almost complete darkness. There were no road signs, so it was by some miracle that I found the headquarters of ARC, Action for the Rights of Children (a partner charity of

Hope and Homes for Children), where I parked the trailer safely before heading for the Hotel Barmoi and a much-needed shower and meal.

I had just five days to get the saw installed and working in the ARC compound before surprising James and ensuring he was trained up and ready to begin the long road out of poverty as a fledgling entrepreneur. But the following morning, I found myself stuck in the city's chaotic traffic jams for two hours, fuming and with an upset tummy. Perfect conditions for a classic local scam.

A British engineer, Steve Balchin, who had flown out to get the ripping saw commissioned and the generator working, had discovered that somebody had removed the transformer, which was vital to create the power. What chances were there that a transformer compatible with my generator would be found in Freetown? Well, not so unlikely if you happen to be approached by the person or people who stole it in the first place. Long story short, we were offered a 'new' transformer for $500, a huge sum, more than the annual salary of a middle-ranking civil servant in Freetown. It wasn't new; it had simply been re-sprayed in black to make it appear new. I was now seriously overheating and running to and from the lavatory, but I eventually conceded that you can't expect to travel in places of extreme poverty without encountering this kind of con. The rule of thumb is that everybody needs to earn what is referred to as the 'daily survivor', which is 80p in our money. We spend more on coffees in one week than most people in Freetown earn in a month.

Finally, we tracked James down and asked him to hop into the Land Cruiser and come with us to ARC's base as we had something to show him. On the way, hemmed in by the solid and stationary Freetown traffic, the Land Cruiser was blocking the road as I tried to creep into the oncoming line of vehicles. I was horrified to see, bearing down on us at speed, a big, heavily laden and ageing blue truck. It came barrelling down the road and we all saw, at the same time, that it was not slowing down. The driver was gesticulating madly for us to move, but there was nowhere to move to, for the traffic in front and behind was locked. Horrified, we braced ourselves as the truck slammed into the rear nearside quarter of our brand spanking new Land Cruiser.

I was now well and truly overheating. Furious, I leapt out and with the magnificently broad-shouldered Kelfa, the HHC director, at my side, I confronted the driver, accusing him of driving a wildly unsafe vehicle. 'You have no brakes!' I bellowed. The driver lowered himself from his cab and came nose to nose with me, full of fight. Within seconds, we were surrounded by a huge crowd and it was by no means friendly. Everybody had an opinion and I was becoming slightly wary that things might not go our way. In pidgin, the lorry driver, bolstered by his supporters in the crowd, blamed me for blocking the road. I countered that if he had not ploughed into me, he would have smashed into the next car, given that nobody was moving or had any chance of getting out of the way.

At this point, I was relieved to see a policeman shouldering his way through the crowd towards us. He produced a notebook and a stubby pencil from his top pocket and with a sinking feeling I realised that we were heading for a protracted, West African bureaucratic process that we did not have time for. I explained the situation and, grabbing the initiative, proclaimed that I would take care of the damage to my vehicle if he, the policeman, would ensure that 'this crazy driver and his dangerous lorry' were taken off the road before someone got killed. 'He has no brakes!' I kept saying.

At this, the lorry driver fell to his knees in gratitude and I suddenly realised that he had been terrified at the thought of having to pay for the damage. The policeman was thrilled at having resolved everything, and I was happy that we could get on with the day, though less thrilled with the big dent in the car. Fortunately, the damage was not serious and could be repaired.

James, by this time, was feeling rather undone, but when we finally reached the ARC base and presented him with the machinery, his face lit up. 'Is this for me?' he said simply. 'I am most grateful. May God bless you.' No cartwheels, no breaking down in tears, that's not in James's nature. I'm glad he didn't feel any need to perform for the camera. Over the next few days our engineer showed James how to use and maintain the machines. I checked out the opposition at the local joinery workshops, one of which was using the unpredictable national power supply – James, with his 24/7 generator, already had a competitive edge.

The table saw worked fine, but what I had failed to consider was that, after sawing, the wood needs to be planed into a smooth finish – without this, time and profit are lost. Sawing wood makes around 1,000 leones, or 15p, a go, while planing makes 6,000 leones. So, a planer was a vital requirement of James's business and something I would have to resolve back home in the UK. Meanwhile, I was keen to get James up and running, so off we went to buy his first load of planks: fifty softwood, fifty hardwood. At a local yard, I was impressed that James was able to drive the price down from 100,000 leones to 80,000 per plank. The total came to £1,500. Concerned that all the boards arrive back at the ARC base, I offered the sellers £1,000 up front and the following £500 on delivery. A noisy debate ensued and the police were called to mediate. James explained that I did not understand the system in Sierra Leone, but I was pleased to demonstrate to him that he should not pay in full until he was satisfied with the service.

ARC agreed to loan a space for James's workshop, and up went his business sign – JAMENICK Timber Merchants – and almost immediately a customer arrived, who asked for a discount. James negotiated and made a small profit, around 75p, which told me that he could hold his own.

The next task was to help James to open a bank account, into which I put a few pounds each month for six months, after which he would be on his own and, hopefully, able to grow his business. When asked by the bank manager to supply his mother's maiden name, James, who had earlier told me that not a day passed without thinking about her, faltered. Like so many orphans, he didn't know the answer.

Back home, a month later, I purchased a reconditioned industrial planer which was shipped to James free of charge, courtesy of Roy Duffy, a manager with the Welsh construction company Dawnus, whom I had met by chance in Freetown. It was the final piece in the jigsaw, so to speak. The rest, since then, has been up to James. From the beginning, I saw in him this entrepreneurial spirit and believed he'd be able to take it on and run with it.

I've stayed in touch with James over these past six years, and while times were hard, very hard, during the Ebola epidemic, he mothballed the equipment and was ready to go again when the emergency subsided. I have been gratified that over the years he has never asked for any financial help, but he calls me up to give me an update on his progress. He employs a number of apprentices and has what he calls his 'senior man', and has recently bought an old Land Rover for delivering the panel doors, which seem to be the mainstay of his business. In fact, I spoke to him just a few weeks ago when he told me that he has money in the bank and has found some land to buy, giving him a permanent base. He recently sent me some pictures of his house and his two children, the eldest of whom he has named Nick.

So, was the venture a success? Certainly, providing the young James Conteh, a bright but perhaps unexceptional street kid, with the right start-up kit to make a go of it, has been a resounding success. Perhaps it helps reinforce the argument that cash is fine, but tools to make cash is the better route to sustained prosperity.

Did the television film, *Countdown to Freetown*, cover all the points I had hoped for? I must admit that I think it was a failure, in as much as it did nothing to raise the profile of Hope and Homes for Children, one of my principal objectives in getting involved. There was one glancing reference, little more than a name-check, and there was absolutely no mention of all those people who had so generously made the trip possible, other than a few whose names might just be spotted as the credits at the end of the show flashed by.

It wasn't a bad film, indeed it was 'Pick of the Day' in many of the papers, and all I can hope is that it raised awareness of the plight of so many young kids orphaned by a brutal war. Just before going to press I flew to Freetown to help promote Street Child, which took over from Hope and Homes for Children when the latter withdrew from Sierra Leone to concentrate on orphanage closures in Rwanda and South Africa.

Whilst there I visited James and his family. He told me he has money in the bank, and has bought some land to give him a permanent base. His youngest child is called Nicholas.

T

Tottenham

The battle for the terraces

FIRST HALF

After a quarter of a decade, the memory of that titanic battle for Tottenham Hotspur will have dimmed for many, but for those who were intimately involved, the scars, I'm sure, remain. It was a complex affair, and if you really want to relive it moment by moment, then reach for Mihir Bose's *False Messiah: The Life and Times of Terry Venables*. I remember it as a story of the tortoise and the hare.

By the spring of 1991, there had been for several months a slow drizzle of press reports outlining the financial problems surrounding Tottenham Hotspur. There was talk of this famous club submerging under a mountain of debt. It wasn't a story that gripped me, as one of those rare people who did not follow the beautiful game. However, Alan Sugar did follow the game and particularly the fortunes of Spurs, as his family had done for generations.

In his autobiography, *What You See Is What You Get*, Alan recalls watching the FA Cup final on 18 May 1991, in which the managers Terry Venables and Brian Clough, both interesting characters, lead their teams – Tottenham and Nottingham Forest – out of the tunnel and onto the Wembley turf. Terry, with a big smile, had much to be happy about, as a deal had been struck to sell Paul Gascoigne, a key player, to Lazio of Rome. Just a few days from the end of the season, £5.5 million would be arriving in the club's seriously overdrawn bank account. But by the time the final whistle blew (Spurs 2, Nottingham Forest 1), the threat of overwhelming debt was back as Gascoigne, the club's saviour, had suffered a grievous knee injury. The Lazio deal was off.

With the press full of rumours as to the fate of Spurs, a line was coming through that Terry, with three seasons as coach behind him, was trying to put together a consortium to buy out the club's key shareholders, Irving Scholar and Paul Bobroff. When Alan got a whiff of this, he arranged to meet Terry and his financial advisor Eddie Ashby for a discreet chat. Naively, rather than huddling in a quiet, private corner somewhere, they chose the lobby at the Hilton Hotel on London's Park Lane on the eve of a major industry dinner that Alan was due to attend. Alan wondered why so many people were hovering around the lobby that evening, but it soon became clear that tongues were wagging and it wasn't long before a *Sunday Times* journalist tracked Alan down with the question, 'Do I hear that you're buying Spurs?' Alan demurred, but the following day the *Sunday Times* splashed with: 'Sugar to take over Tottenham', and all hell broke loose.

I was driving past the ponds in Hampstead one evening shortly after this brouhaha had started when my mobile phone rang. It was Alan. 'The deal to buy Tottenham happens tomorrow, so you'd better get up to Ansbacher in the afternoon.' I was stunned; I'd had no inkling that this little adventure was truly in the offing. 'Good Lord, have you told the family?' I stuttered. Why did I ask such a question? Because Alan is the master of compartmentalising his life. Frankly, he's got so many compartments going on, even today, that it makes my head spin. To which he replied, 'Don't worry, leave that to me.'

The following afternoon, 21 June 1991, I arrived at Mitre Square, deep in the City, to the offices of Henry Ansbacher & Co., a small but perfectly formed merchant bank that was handling the purchase by Alan and Terry of the majority shares of the club. Over the next few hours, I witnessed an extraordinary comedy of errors.

All the key characters were there except for the two lead actors, Alan and Terry. Almost everything was in place, as Paul Bobroff had agreed to sell his shares. Irving Scholar had disappeared to his Monaco home after instructing his lawyers to attend the deal meeting in his place. Tellingly, Scholar had not yet signed his shares over. At about 4:00 p.m., the preposterous Robert Maxwell entered the frame like a huge dark shadow. Maxwell claimed, in a call to Ansbacher, that he had 'turned' Scholar, who was now willing to sell his shares to him, Maxwell. The alarm bells rang, and Alan was urged to hurry to Mitre Square. As he drove to the City, tangible evidence of Maxwell's intervention became clear. A squad of bankers from Hill Samuel, Maxwell's merchant bank, had shimmied past the Ansbacher security and were making their way up to the floor where the deal was underway.

Maxwell called again, demanding that his representatives be let into the meeting. Bernard Jolles, the Ansbacher director handling the purchase, refused to yield, and one of his lieutenants, a young New Zealander called David Glenn, was sent to intercept the Maxwell deputation. He greeted them in the most courteous way, ushered them into an office, and promptly locked the door. No sooner had the first cries of protest been heard from those inside, a black Ford Scorpio car swept up, disgorging a squad of Maxwell's lawyers from the deliciously named firm of Titmuss Sainer. Down in reception, the security people, by now back from their tea break, were on their toes and, ignoring the lawyers' sophisticated legal entreaties, they barred them from the building.

Next, the squeal of tyres was heard on the forecourt, followed by the soft thud of the door of a Rolls-Royce closing. Sinews stiffened in the boardroom reserved for the Sugar delegation, for they well knew how irritable and vocal Alan could be once his dander was up. Word of his arrival quickly spread to the other rooms, one of which contained the Midland Bank party who were there to recover the £11 million they were owed by the club. The Spurs board had convened in another room, and Terry's advisors were cloistered in yet another.

I was in the room reserved for Alan's party when he arrived. The phone rang, and Jolles picked it up. It was Maxwell. 'Mr Sugar has just arrived,' Jolles said. 'Perhaps you should speak directly to him.' Alan took the receiver, held it to his ear, listened carefully for several minutes, and then put the phone down. 'The rudeness of that man!' he exclaimed. 'Do you know what Maxwell's just done? He's put the phone down on me, just like that.'

No sooner had he spoken these words, the phone rang again. It was Maxwell. 'Sorry old chap, had some people with me, wanted to clear the room so we could have a private chat, just you and me. I think you and I can do a deal on this. I'm buying Scholar's shares, and then Tottenham will have two sugar daddies, you and me.'

'This is my deal,' Alan snapped. 'If you want to invest in Spurs shares, buy them on the open market, and leave my deal alone.' And with that he replaced the receiver.

While Scholar was sensibly holed up in Monte Carlo, Bobroff, the other major shareholder, was in the Ansbacher building, and when it emerged that he too was going wobbly and was likely to follow Scholar in selling to Maxwell, he caught the brunt of Alan's famously direct vernacular.

I remember Bobroff appearing. He was a small, roly-poly man in a dark suit with black-framed glasses, sweating openly, standing in the door to the Sugar conference room looking absolutely terrified. He didn't have a friend in the place, and as all eyes swivelled on him he reacted by swaying awkwardly from one foot to the other. 'Well, I've always stuck with Scholar, and I don't want to act without him,' he stuttered. It was a bit like a kid at school caught off guard in the playground with a rival gang and without his bigger, stronger protector.

Bobroff was ushered into another room so that he could contact Scholar, and, at some point, he left the building to use his car phone. Suddenly, Scholar's lawyers arrived. I recall them as being a pretty slick, Armani-style crew. Alan called Scholar in his car, and in his inimitable fashion explained that all these antics were unacceptable. Before long, Scholar called back to agree the deal.

Next to arrive onstage in this overheated drama was Terry, accompanied by his legal wingman Jonathan Crystal, a journeyman barrister with a cigarette cupped in the palm of his hand and looking every bit like the actor Sam Kydd having a crafty smoke in a war film. Terry, not surprisingly, was confused as to what was going on and who was doing what to whom.

Tottenham was quoted on the London Stock Exchange, and Ansbacher's Bernard Jolles played strictly by the book and the City code, insisting that no announcement be made that could in any way break the rules. Bernard eyed me suspiciously, seeking a commitment that I would never leak what was going on, and I was sent to the room containing the Tottenham board to seek their assurance and that of their PR company that they too were watertight.

Having seen off the interloper Maxwell, Alan and Terry were now masters of Tottenham. Amazingly, Maxwell called to concede defeat and congratulate Alan. As all the phones in Alan's conference room were occupied, he had to take the call in the kitchen, knee-deep in McDonald's burger wrappers.

With the shares signed over, Alan produced the necessary banker's draft but when it came to Terry's turn, there was no response. If Crystal was Terry's legal enforcer, then Eddie Ashby was his money fixer. Ashby sidled up to Alan and, as Alan reports in his autobiography, said, 'Oh, by the way, Alan, there's a bit of a delay with Terry's three million.' 'A delay, what do you mean by delay? You sat there watching me beat up Bobroff, negotiate with Scholar and fight off Maxwell – you saw it all – and now you tell me your money's not here?!'

In the face of this onslaught, Ashby could barely stumble through a series of apologies-cum-excuses. All the while, standing nearby was Crystal, surveying the scene. He slid into the conversation, saying, 'I can vouch that Terry's money will be coming through next week. You can take my word for it as a barrister.' This was not an auspicious start to the partnership that had now been formed to run one of Britain's most famous football clubs. With a sense of surprise and perhaps some alarm, Alan wrote out another banker's draft for Terry's shares.

A press conference was called at White Hart Lane and I was able, gently I hope, to tell the PR firm retained by the Tottenham board, that I would now be taking over and to thank them for their time and trouble. Little did I know.

Alan and Terry were paraded for the football and financial press, with Alan announcing that he would look after the eleven in the bank (referring to the £11 million overdraft) and Terry would look after the eleven on the field. The Dream Team.

SECOND HALF

Between 21 June 1991 and 14 May 1993, the partnership between Alan and Terry descended into acrimony and distrust. And so it was that I found myself at the White Hart Lane ground on that May day to be on hand following a board meeting at which Terry would be fired as chief executive of Tottenham Hotspur plc.

The first shots of the PR battle had been fired by Terry the night before, while attending the Football Writers' annual dinner at the Lancaster House Hotel in London. Terry, at the instigation of his PR advisors, whom he had hired just the day before, had leaked the fact that there would be a board meeting on the following day when his future at the club would be discussed. With a wink and a nod, Terry made it clear that he, an acclaimed hero of English football, was to be dismissed by Alan Sugar, a multimillionaire computer tycoon who had never kicked a ball. The following day, ITN carried the story and storm clouds gathered over White Hart Lane.

Terry had put in the pre-emptive kick and stolen a lead in what was to become a ferocious press war. Alan is a man who likes to play by the rules, particularly City rules, and though I was beginning to take press calls he was adamant I should make no comment and that we observe the code. So, we were rather flat-footed. When I arrived for the board meeting, I had to elbow my way through a crowd of Tottenham fans, many of whom were carrying placards of a quality and consistency that quite clearly indicated they were mass-produced. Terry's PR operation had obviously geared up into an offensive play.

As soon as the dramatic board meeting was over, I issued a statement to the London Stock Exchange announcing the outcome, and the Sugar and Tottenham boards went into a huddle, while Terry and Crystal formed their own huddle elsewhere. John Fennelly, the press man on football matters at the club, told me with some pleasure that the massed ranks of reporters outside wanted to know what was going on and that that was now my job. Although unable to make any detailed statement, I found myself surrounded by quite a hostile crowd demanding to know why Terry had been fired. I explained patiently that given the legal complexities, I was unable to give them any detail behind the termination of Terry's contract, but that I would be able to do so as soon as certain legal issues had been clarified. Withdrawing myself speedily from this interrogation, I went back inside the club.

Surveying the scene outside from an upstairs window, I saw a young woman reading a statement to the demonstrating fans gathered on the other side of the closed gates, and I sensed that this was the hand of the PR company. Shortly after, I also saw various members of the board leaving the car park and was disturbed to witness the cars of at least two directors being kicked as they inched out. It became clear to me that should Alan decide to leave by the same gate, his Rolls would sustain some severe damage so, after a hurried discussion, it was agreed that I would take my BMW 7 Series, of which I was really quite protective, out through the crowd because I was not a particularly recognisable face in this drama. I would then drive around the stadium and wait for Alan to walk across the pitch and exit by a door on the far side.

I got Alan home safely, but before you could blink, Terry's lawyers had concocted the basis for an injunction to set aside the sacking. To everybody's amazement, the injunction was granted and both sides went into overdrive, determined that the next legal campaign, that of setting aside the injunction, would be hard-fought.

As the battle for the hearts and minds of the fans and the football and business media started in earnest, the Sugar camp was lagging far behind. The press onslaught was horrific, not just the venom, but the volume too. I recall with horror sitting in my Dolphin Square flat at six in the morning when the fax machine would start to whirr as the press coverage came pouring in and how the phones would ring late into the night with wrap-up calls. It reached such a fever pitch that the management of the building called me to ask if I was running a business there in contravention of the lease.

It was ugly, particularly with the footballing press. I was shocked when a well-known tabloid journalist, now writing for a national broadsheet, replied to my question, 'Why can't you take a balanced view?' with, 'Well, you've got to look after your friends.' Looking back, I guess the reason for this is not difficult to determine. Terry Venables, chirpy chappie that he is, was a master at manipulating the back pages of the tabloids and, in fairness, the press in general. He was a man's man, an arm around the shoulder, hugging sort of fellow with a ready wit and a quotable quote always on his lips. He had played at every level of the game, had achieved more as a manager than most and, by contrast to Alan, he was accessible.

The press went potty, and it looked as though Terry – former England player, Renaissance man of English football – had attracted pretty much all the support. But a lone figure, Harry Harris of the *Daily Mirror*, was trying to make friendly overtures to the Sugar camp. I urged Alan to engage, knowing that we desperately needed to get a red-top onside, and although *The Sun* had the greater readership, the *Mirror* was a powerful player.

Rereading Mihir Bose's book, I recall warning Alan that he could never win on the back pages. 'Remember,' I am quoted as saying, 'Terry has been living and drinking and travelling with these journalists for the last twenty-five years. He's probably godfather to half of their children.' My belief was that we could never win the Mr Football v. Mr Tycoon battle; as an icon of the beautiful game, Terry was untouchable. But if we could pitch it as a contest between Mr Tycoon and Mr Ambitious Businessman (Terry was, after all, the chief executive officer of Tottenham), then perhaps we could sway the odds in our favour.

Terry's Achilles heel was his team off the field. It dawned on me that his 'shadow', the barrister Jonathan Crystal, and his money man, Eddie Ashby, were not bulletproof. Sometime previously, when worries began to surface about him, a dossier had been prepared on Ashby, who had been declared bankrupt a while before his entry onto the Tottenham stage. This weighty and comprehensive dossier, only recently declared to Alan, detailed the short and unhappy lives of some thirty companies over which Mr Ashby had control. I knew that if such a document were to find its way into the hands of the press and be published, it would be a severe embarrassment not only to Ashby, but also to his boss, Terry Venables. It was early in the morning of Sunday 19 May, some two weeks after the fatal board meeting that fired Terry, that I waited impatiently for the first editions of the *Sunday Times* to come off the press to read a major article by Mihir Bose on Mr Ashby's unfortunate business career to date. A slow-burning fuse to a very large bomb had now been lit.

Terry was not giving up easily, and the hearing for the lifting of the injunction was scheduled for late May. It became the cause célèbre of its time. Terry's army pitched up in strength outside the High Court in Fleet Street, complete with banners and effigies of Alan to burn. A place on the public benches inside the court was at a premium, and of course the press pack was there in force. It reminded me of those great cases in the nineteenth century, like the trial of Oscar Wilde, when the whole of society would turn out.

The High Court had set aside just a single day for the hearing, but it was soon clear, not just by the number of barristers present but also by the high bundles of documents being wheeled into court on sack trolleys, that one day would simply not be enough, so the hearing was adjourned for a couple of weeks. When it resumed in mid-June, it ran on for three days. We were concerned at the potential for violence among a seething crowd hyped up by the press – we all know how mobs can behave in front of the camera – so I hired our own television crew to immerse itself in the crowd in order to give us a feel for those most actively involved in provocative acts, the plan being to pass the footage to the Metropolitan Police. And I'm glad that I did because it turned out that a number of those at the forefront of demonstrations against Alan were from some very dubious pressure groups, and were not Tottenham fans or Venables supporters. It suddenly clicked with me when I stood behind Alan as we entered a lift in the High Court, and a man surged forward and hissed 'Judas' in Alan's ear, that perhaps we were dealing with some Far Right racist or anti-Semitic elements, attracted by the opportunities for trouble-making. The police were very interested in our footage, and familiar with some of the faces shown in it.

Descending in the lift to the judges' car park at the end of that first day's hearing, three or four of us, intent on heading back to Alan's solicitors' offices, suddenly saw his car through the far railings as it approached the car park gates. If we got into his Rolls and then emerged into Fleet Street, we would find ourselves in the maw of a dangerously angry crowd. I immediately put into action the escape plan we had used for Alan after the board meeting at Tottenham, waving away his car and instead hailing a cab in the shadows of the judges' car park. I put Alan in the middle of the back seat, flanked by two lawyers and with me on a jump seat. I asked him to pretend to read a big folder close up, and we nudged our way out and through the crowd without being noticed. Terry, meanwhile, exited the court by the front, hand raised to an adoring crowd. But he had little to celebrate. On Monday, 14 June 1993, he lost his campaign to remain as chief executive of the club and was ordered to pay costs estimated at £100,000. Finally, Terry had been fired.

Sometime before the court case, Alan's main company, Amstrad, had been involved in a corporate manoeuvre and I found myself, as an observer, following some related legal application in the High Court. As the judge entered the courtroom, the barristers for both sides rose, and I was surprised to see Jonathan Crystal pop up among them. Surely Alan wasn't using *him* to represent Amstrad? But no, Crystal was there to excuse himself from a later, unrelated hearing in the same court. He told the judge that he could not attend this hearing as he had to appear elsewhere on a disciplinary hearing, but that he would be able to come back the following day. He apologised for the inconvenience and, after much grumbling, the judge agreed. Crystal left the courtroom, and the Amstrad matter in hand was taken up. Shortly after, it transpired that Crystal had in fact attended a Tottenham Hotspur board meeting that afternoon, and when this 'oversight' was referred to the Bar Council, it saw Crystal handed an embarrassing month-long suspension from the English Bar.

Things were beginning to unravel for Team Terry. The fuse on the *Sunday Times* article was burning fast and the investigative journalists began to take more interest in this hullabaloo than the football journalists. In September, four months after the sacking, the first of two *Panorama* programmes on Terry's business dealings was aired. Three days later, in a double whammy, Channel 4 screened its *Dispatches* programme, also concentrating on the Venables–Ashby business relationship.

Things were definitely going in the wrong direction for Terry's camp. After the *Panorama* broadcast, John Sadler, the *Sun* columnist, wrote: 'Football fans throughout the country feel cheated this morning. Disillusioned, dismayed, led up the garden path and seriously let down. And all by one man, Terry Venables, whom they'd come to respect, admire, worship as a hero. Not only the supporters of Tottenham Hotspur feel misled and duped by the disturbing allegations that now surround Venables' dismissal by Alan Sugar … Whether or not Venables ever acted illegally as Spurs manager or chief executive is a matter for examination elsewhere. What has hurt football is the feeling that Venables, with cheering hordes following in his footsteps, was not exactly straight with his disciples. The feeling is that the Pied Piper continued to play a happy tune, knowing all along that somebody was going to blow the whistle.'

The New Year looked brighter for Terry when the FA invited him in for a chat. On 28 January 1994, he was confirmed as England coach, and by March he was in action with a 1-0 victory over Denmark at Wembley Stadium. A series of other games followed, including a decisive 5-0 win in a friendly against Greece, also at Wembley. But, never one to keep his head down, by September Terry's autobiography was launched containing some defamatory comments (though all unsold copies were ordered to be pulped – Terry, always renowned as a stickler for the truth, reported that only six copies remained unsold – close shave for the publishers then), just a few weeks before the second *Panorama* programme dealt him another hammer blow. In November, the Department of Trade and Industry started investigations into some of Terry's many companies. Just as his star had begun to ascend again, he was summoned to face the DTI inspectors.

The DTI grinds exceedingly slowly and only in November 1995 did it decide to start a civil action against Terry. The first hearing took place in February the following year, but it wasn't until January 1998 that Terry, after four years of strenuously denying any improper business conduct, was banned from being a company director for seven years. There were nineteen allegations set out in an agreed statement of facts, and the DTI's counsel, Elizabeth Gloster QC, told the judge that Terry's conduct in relation to four companies 'has been such as to make him unfit to be concerned in any way with the management of any company'.

As part of this disappointment, Terry withdrew from applying for an extension to his England coach contract.

MATCH ANALYSIS

It had been a long and bitter haul, but the triumvirate of Venables–Crystal–Ashby had been dissolved, with Crystal temporarily suspended from the Bar, Terry disqualified as a company director, and Ashby jailed for financial fraud.

Score: Sugar 3, Venables 0. It was a hugely satisfying victory for me and the other members of a small, closely knit team, which included Lord David Gold, Alan Watts and the great Margaret Mountford, all of Herbert Smith, a City law firm which justified its reputation as one of the best in the country. There was also John Ireland, the in-house lawyer at Spurs, and the gutsy Colin Sandy, one of Alan's long-term in-house advisors.

For Alan, who had faced up to every disgruntled football fan in the country without once being rattled or intimidated, and who had countered every dodgy manoeuvre, every sly attack with dignity and courage because he was determined to do the right thing by the club, it was a great but exhausting success.

U

Underwear

When I discovered a dislike for frilly knickers

When I was about nine years old, I went to a little prep school called Bentham House, in the countryside north of Swindon (*see* B: BOYHOOD). One of the boys there was the son of a very rich local businessman, a large and boring man, Mr D, who was, essentially, one of the town's 'gombeens', an Irish expression to describe an entrepreneur with a finger in every pie. The family lived in a large secluded house in Westlecot Road, Swindon's answer to the Avenue Foch, and sometimes Mr D would arrive at the school in a big silver Bentley to collect his son and, on the odd occasion, me. 'Don't touch the paintwork!' he would roar as we clambered in.

I suppose the idea was that I would play with my school-mate and stay for tea, but I have no memories of this. What I do remember very clearly indeed is that my friend would trot off to feed his rabbit and that Mrs D, a vague, subdued and pretty woman in her thirties, would invite me up to the marital bedroom where we would sit down on the floor next to a large chest of drawers. She would then open a drawer and take out all her fine lace underwear, as it was worn in the 1950s, and lay it out on the carpet. I think some of them are known as French knickers, and there were camisoles and strange négligées and garments that one is unlikely to encounter these days, but the emphasis was on the exquisite quality of it all. Stockings were draped dreamily over her arm to show off the silky sheerness. I never understood why she thought I would be interested in this, but I was far too polite ever to say anything, other than to admire her collection. Then she would put it all back and close the drawer and I would walk back home, puzzled as to why I had been alerted to this cache of frilly knickers.

I've never worn any women's underwear, but I suppose that would've been the time that I acquired the habit if I had been so inclined.

Some sixty years later I was presented with a parcel which had been posted to me, care of *Countdown*, and I opened it in the general office at the studio in Manchester's Media City. Out fell a pair of red net knickers of appalling vulgarity and crotchlessness. Although the parcel was postmarked Swindon, I refuse to believe that Mrs D, now in her late nineties if she's still alive, would ever have countenanced a garment so vile. I hurriedly passed them to the production secretary for disposal and the matter was never discussed again.

V

Veuve-Verve

Dear Catherine ...

I think one should never rush into making an assessment of another. Always give it time. And so it is that, after twenty years, I feel ready to drop you a little note giving you my appraisal to date.

I well remember when we first met. You were a student living in South Kensington and I was a young chap, nothing to write home about, living in York Buildings, a quiet little street just off the Strand with my great childhood pals Robert Humphreys and Mike Roworth. Robert and Mike were both assiduous in their pursuit of a pair of student speech therapists who were at college with you. These were the days of hot pants, and you were very attractive in this Biba look, and I had sort of an inkling that I might just get a date.

I wasn't besotted with you, perhaps because I quickly understood that you were not besotted with me, for you had your eye firmly set on Paul, a medical student at Bristol University who, interestingly, was being tutored by my father's cousin, Professor Tom Hewer, a pathologist and at the time vice-chancellor. I subsequently discovered that your boyfriend was probably one of the medical students who had to do Professor Hewer's gardening every Sunday if they ever wanted to make a good impression.

You wed your young doctor, and I got married too, and we went our separate ways. I occasionally heard news of you – Paul was a partner in a general practice in the then new town of Milton Keynes, and you had set up a publishing company producing resources for speech therapists to help stroke patients and had turned it into a success. You gave up your speech therapy practice, although you were drawn occasionally, as you've subsequently told me, to lucrative private practices as far away as Switzerland. You had two children, Sarah and Ben. Robert, by now married to his speech therapist (also called Catherine), kept me in touch with your progress and I learned with sadness, some twenty-three years ago, that you had been widowed.

I think it was about two years later that Robert and I had a conversation, propped up at the saloon bar in the Reform Club. 'You know, you really ought to meet Catherine again. She lives in Buckinghamshire now and I think you might get on well together.' With that, he began to pour me a glass of champagne – Veuve Clicquot, no less, named after the widow who became the first woman to take over a Champagne house. '*Veuve*,' I whispered to myself. 'Let's hope she's still got that verve I remember.'

Robert arranged for us all to meet at the Reform, and I remember I waited and waited and waited until you both arrived about two hours later than advertised. You'd been in a pub somewhere, that was clear. No surprise really, given that Robert had become a sort of 'Mr UK Pub', as secretary of the All-Party Parliamentary Beer Group, which he had founded and steered to become the largest lobbying group in Parliament. So, when you arrived at the club you were both in high spirits. It was a fun evening. You did have verve – you still do.

This was in 1997. A genteel courtship commenced between us, though I confess I was tested to the limit in the early stages by that goody-two-shoes 'wellbeing' class your sister Sarah took you to, with me tagging along. I was very hesitant about this and my reservations grew when the two men running the course started to sing a song, which we all had to join in with, that went as follows: 'Doors are opening, doors are closing, we are safe, we are say-yay-yafe.' This was an extremely embarrassing moment for me and I immediately broke out in a sweat. When the leader said, 'We will now each hold a mirror up to our own faces and say, "I love you",' I found myself tripping and stumbling towards the exit door. I looked back to see you with a twisted smile and a little wave goodbye.

So, here we are, twenty years later, and while I readily admit that I'm not the most tolerant person in the world, I have identified a number of problem areas which I'd like to address:

1. I know you're the daughter of a farmer and you like to get up at milking time, whereas I'm happy to stay put for as long as possible, but what on earth do you do at 5:30 in the morning? When, in the middle of a deep sleep, I sense you easing out of bed before the sun has risen, I sometimes I ask you this and you reply, 'I have tasks to complete.' I have never fathomed what these tasks are. The problem is that I go to bed much later than you and, if I have something important to tell you, as I often do, you growl at me: 'No talking, I have to get up in five hours' time.'

2. Why do you have to be so *nice* to people you don't know?

3. Why do you always place your spectacles lens-down and grind them into the granite kitchen worktop? I can hardly see you for the scratches.

4. Why do you always insist on buying the cheapest electrical goods, all clearly made in China out of cigarette-packet foil and beer bottle tops when we know they'll only last six months? Buy cheap, buy twice. Moreover, you are an indecisive shopper. Speed up.

5. Why do you refuse to learn how to drive 'on the wrong side of the road' when we're abroad? Also, your car has a perfectly good electronic parking assist system, which you refuse to use, claiming that you need 'in-house training'. Please get some soon as your parking ability is shocking.

6. The Bricks & Mortar section of the *Sunday Times* is not suitable bedtime reading.

7. Stop being so annoyingly skilful at conflict resolution. Your patience tries my lack of patience. My bad temper and short fuse don't faze you. Give me a break, I want a row!

Some may wonder why I'm prepared to soldier on. The answer is that the list of plus points outweighs the disappointments that I've listed above. Thus:

1. I don't think you're checking up on me as I roam the globe. People are aghast when I tell them you conduct timed conversations – not only the time of the call but also its duration – with all members of your family, but our daily 6:00 p.m. phone call is the one certainty in my

life. For twenty years we have kept up this little ritual; we even managed it via sat phone when I was in the middle of the Gobi Desert.

2. Thank you for my pre-dinner party briefings, particularly for the lists of subjects to be avoided and subjects which *must* be mentioned.

3. Thank you for constantly reminding me not to pick my nose in public, a habit born out of my parents' refusal to furnish me with handkerchiefs when I was sent away to boarding school.

4. Thank you for running an amazingly efficient house and knowing where all the fuses are, when the oil was last topped up, and not relying on me for anything at all. You are very kind for never mentioning that I have not cooked a single meal in the past twenty years. And thank you for never being cross when I fail to turn up at exactly 8:00 p.m. for dinner. I gave you a little bell to ring but you have chosen, I suppose in an effort at imposing some self-discipline in me, never to ring it.

5. Thank you for allowing me to melt away whenever mice, pigeons, baby rabbits or the occasional pheasant is dragged into the house and slaughtered by the cat. Thank you for clearing everything up. You understand that I can't stand the sight of blood.

6. Thank you for caring for my dear Labrador Jasmine during my long absences. It's well known in the area that you don't like dogs and yet you looked after her even up to her death. I never quite understood why you always called her 'him'.

7. Thank you for the calm way you dealt with my children's rather graceless behaviour when one or other of

them turned all the framed photographs of you face down at the house in France all those years ago. I was so embarrassed, but you said, 'They're still quite young, it's a natural reaction.' And thank you for being such a welcoming presence when they and the grandchildren visit Rectory Farm.

8. Thank you for making me chuckle as you stride down the corridor in that funny, head down, purposeful, determined Muffin the Mule walk of yours.

9. Thank you for showing me how a truly good person behaves.

10. Thank you for your soft and delightful sense of humour; you make me giggle every day, and your quiet laugh is music to my ears.

11. Thank you for introducing me to alcohol. I rarely drank a drop before I met you. It's yet another pleasure that you have granted me and I have taken it up with gusto.

12. Thank you for giving me complete freedom and encouragement to roam the world. Shame you won't come too. But you keep the home fires burning so that whenever I return there's a warm welcome and a big hug. It's true, doors close and doors open, and I am safe, after all.

That's me done.
I now await your assessment with some anxiety.
Love, Nick

W

Where'd Ya Get That Hat?

A useful thing to take on a picnic

On a heavy oak beam in my house in France rests a collection
of more than twenty hats, each bought, begged or stolen in a
different country. The collection ranges from an exquisite, stiff
straw riding hat only to be seen in Andalucía, right through to
the native headgear worn in Romania, Hungary, Kazakhstan,
Kyrgyzstan, Russia, Mongolia and Georgia, and, especially
prized, a beige beret worn only by members of Britain's
Special Services. The beret was given to me (with its cap badge
removed) by my good friend Ged (*see* S: SIERRA LEONE),
when he and I took ourselves off to Romania to travel the
Transfagarasan Highway, a 60--mile stretch of hairpin madness in the Carpathian Mountains also known as Ceausescu's
Folly – the defunct dictator ordered its construction, at vast
expense, in case the Russians had a mind to invade.

The Transfagarasan turned out to be a rather boring drive
because the S-bends are so tight you can barely get out of

second gear, but the trip itself brought some light moments, mostly prompted by my search for Romanian hats. One night, on our way to dinner in Bucharest, we passed a brightly lit shop and I was amazed to see on display tall golden crucifixes, chasubles, monstrances, thuribles for burning incense, all manner of lavish ecclesiastical garments and, more importantly to me, row upon row of wonderful hats.

We entered the shop, and I expressed a desire to buy a couple of hats but was rebuked by the serious young manager who explained that everything in the shop was only available to members of the Russian Orthodox clergy. 'Oh, what a shame,' I pleaded. 'I particularly want to buy a hat as next week I shall be celebrating the birthday of the Father Rector of my religious school.' The cheerless manager said he would talk to the director. He disappeared, leaving me and a rather hungry Ged to feast our eyes. Returning a few moments later, the manager said that, under the circumstances, it had been decided that I should be allowed to purchase a few hats. I went about it with a will, picking the black velvet models of the lower orders of the clergy, right up to stovepipe numbers with crimson lining for the higher echelons of bishop and archbishop. The manager seemed surprised that I needed so many, but before he could demure, I snaffled half a dozen hats which were popped into a plastic bag, and Ged and I made off into the dark Bucharest night to find our restaurant.

Ged is one of those characters who likes a good night out and it wasn't until the next morning that I realised I had, in my tipsy state, left my precious cargo in the restaurant. I rushed back, only to be told that nothing had been handed in. The hats were gone. I retraced my steps back to the ecclesiastical outfitters and explained my plight, avoiding any reference to unseemly behaviour. The manager cocked his head to one side and closed one eye, the better to bore into my brain with the other one. 'You want to buy more hats?' he said, in a tone that served as due warning that he knew something was askew. 'Oh, please,' I begged. 'Could you possibly allow me to?' I flew back to London clutching my second batch, which I distributed liberally among my friends, though a bishop and archbishop made their way onto my oak beam.

I don't know when my obsession with hats began. Certainly, they were a prominent feature of my childhood, as they were much more commonly worn then. Even when I started work in London, you would still see troops of bankers and civil servants wearing bowler hats striding into the City and Westminster across London's bridges. My grandfather, who was a country vet and two-days-a-week hunting man, was not among them, though he did own a beautiful hunting bowler with a rein-forced crown, called a Coker, and a tall, black silk topper, valued at £5,000 according to my son, its current possessor.

The place to buy a bowler was – still is – at Lock & Co., the world-famous hat shop in St James's Street, where my grand-father's hat originated in 1849 when Edward Coke, nephew of the Earl of Lancashire, requested a close-fitting hard hat for his gamekeepers. Before paying his twelve shillings, Coke dropped it on the floor and stamped on it twice to test its strength. Lock's staff were well used to the demands of the upper classes. Some old belted earl, whose name has disappeared in the mists of time, who could not bring himself to enter a place of commerce, once kicked open the door and shouted, 'A hat!', to which the staff responded by thrusting him a series of hats as he waited on the threshold until he was satisfied and stalked off back to his gentlemen's club. There was no talk about payment. No doubt, a bill would fetch up at the ancestral home, to be dealt with years later.

In 2005, I found myself in Lock's when filming *The Apprentice*, following a ragtag string of candidates through the venerable green door in search of a bowler, one of the items to be sourced on that week's task. Sometime later, I took my friend Frances there. She was feeling a bit poorly at the time and in need of distraction, so I said I'd buy her a hat. There we were in mid-discussion about what would be most appropriate, the autumn sunlight pouring through the windows, when suddenly the shop was plunged into darkness. Surprised, we looked up to discover in the doorway an enormous shape that had blotted out the sun. As our eyes adjusted to the gloom, the shape revealed itself to be the massive frame of a man who was magnificently accoutred, from the black homburg to his grey spats, in between which he wore an exquisitely tailored, dove-grey three-piece suit with a silk handkerchief in the pocket; in one hand, he held a silver-top cane, and in the other, with great delicacy, a pair of grey kid gloves.

Silence fell over the shop. I turned, with a raised eyebrow, towards Frances and she murmured, 'I do believe that's the King of Tonga.' No sooner had the king been identified than the eclipse once again descended at the doorway, as an equerry followed on His Majesty's well-appointed heels. This man was also beautifully outfitted and sported a bowler hat. But for his height, he was the spitting image of the *Goldfinger* villain, Oddjob. The equerry's neck circumference, like the king's, was that of a Thames tug. Clearly, His Majesty was carrying his grandmother's genes: when somebody asked who was sitting next to the Queen of Tonga in an open carriage during Queen Elizabeth's coronation parade in 1953, the answer (wrongly attributed to Noël Coward) was, 'Oh, that's her lunch, my dear.' It was, in fact, the diminutive Haile Selassie.

The king murmured to the young Japanese assistant behind the reception desk, 'Ladies' hats? Upstairs?' Struck mute, she nodded furiously, and two enormous behinds disappeared up a narrow staircase. Frances and I busied ourselves at the back of the shop, but hurried forward when we heard the king's soft voice again. His Highness was now conferring with the Japanese assistant. He had chosen a Panama, but just as his equerry darted forward with a credit card, the king gently dismissed him, turning instead to the young lady to proffer a deck-full of credit cards, neatly arranged in two ladders on either side of a beautiful red Moroccan leather wallet. The assistant looked completely baffled, so the king took it upon himself to deftly extract a card which he then placed on the desk.

The card was processed swiftly, and the assistant then reached under the desk and produced a rather beautiful, bespoke cardboard tube. 'What is this?' the king asked, stepping back slightly. 'It's Lock's special tube for rolling one's Panama for travel,' she explained. 'All our clients use them.' 'Oh no, no,' came the reply. 'I don't need that.' The equerry's eyes began to lower as the king brought the discussion to a head. 'I always roll my Panamas and store them in those plastic boxes with the lid.' Here, he paused. 'You know, you can snap the lid shut.' He demonstrated with his thumbs, pressing down with a snapping motion. Another pause. 'You know, you can buy them in supermarkets to put sandwiches in when you're going on a picnic.' The assistant returned an uncomprehending stare.

Listening intently to this exchange while pretending to try on a hat or two, Frances and I, together with a couple of other visitors to the shop as well as two staff members, called out as one: 'Tupperware!' The king's head was thrown back to reveal a beaming smile, 'That's it, Tupperware!' The Japanese girl was now the only person in the shop not to have grasped the delicious little comedy that had just unfolded.

The king and his equerry made their gracious exit from the shop. Not wishing to lose contact with this extraordinary character, Frances and I followed them out onto the street to catch a last glimpse of the king as he picked his way up St James's and sank into the back seat of an elderly and vast Daimler limousine. The suspension sighed and sagged as the biggest monarch in the world got in. We stood and watched him go, with the equerry in close pursuit in a black Range Rover.

When King Siaosi (George) Tupou V died in March 2012, Frances and I raised a glass of champagne in thanks for that unforgettable moment.

X

'XX'

Double-cross and my friend the codebreaker

On reaching fifty years of age, I decided to plan for the future. My first act was to buy a burial plot. I had never liked the cemetery at Christ Church, next to my childhood home (*see* B: BOYHOOD), where my parents and grandparents lie buried. The bells, eulogised by Betjeman, are so loud they can, I believe, waken the dead; their sound blighted my childhood and I was determined they would not disturb me in my final resting place. So, I took myself to the tiny churchyard in the pretty village of Sevenhampton in Oxfordshire, where my great-great-grandparents, William and Mary, who farmed Manor Farm there in the 1840s, lie buried in what looks to be a roomy tomb. To add a bit of glamour, Ian Fleming lies next door. Having tracked down the churchwarden, asked about the forms and costs, I was on my way to securing the second prize, which was to do with getting on with life.

What better way to feel young than to mix with those

275

who are incredibly old? Simple: join a Pall Mall gentlemen's club. My old friend, journalist and author Mihir Bose (*see* T: TOTTENHAM) had invited me to tea at the Reform Club some weeks before my fiftieth birthday, and, noticing that my table manners were up to scratch and that I was not wearing brown shoes in town, he kindly asked if I would allow him to put me up for membership. I did not hesitate. The Reform was the first London club to admit women, definitely a bonus (who wants to mix only with men?), and it is surely the most spectacular building in club land, designed by the architect Charles Barry and inspired by the Farnese Palace in Rome. It stands in Pall Mall next to the Travellers, the haunt of spies galore, and the Travellers in turn sits next to the Athenaeum, a club chock-full of clergymen and Nobel Prize winners.

Sir Geoffrey Pattie, a member I had dealt with when he was a minister in John Major's government, kindly agreed to second my application and, after a decent wait and a chat with someone on the membership committee, I found myself in 'the book' and waited with bated breath to see if I would attract the sufficient signatures to secure admission to a club whose membership boasted pretty much everybody who was anybody over the last two centuries. Churchill's cigar lighter still sits perched by the door, next to the porter's lodge. It was from that lodge that a young porter, sometime in the 1800s, darted one morning to intercept the Lord Chancellor as he left. Although not a member, this grand panjandrum would pop into the club every morning on his way to Whitehall to relieve his bladder. The young porter wished to mention to his Lordship that the use of the club was reserved for members only. 'But I've always assumed that this place is a public convenience and I shall continue to treat it as such,' came the reply.

When I climbed the steps as a member for the first time, walked through the enormous dark-green doors, passed the porter's lobby and entered the glorious domed and galleried saloon, some friendly faces waved me over to join them at the bar and introduced themselves. A welcoming glass of champagne was put in my hand and I was toasted as a new member. Such a kind and friendly place, where for almost a quarter of a century I have made steadfast friends and sadly, given the average age, lost a few too. I put up my old pal Robert Humphreys (*see* B: BOYHOOD) for membership, and a few others. It has become my home from home and in the evenings, up in the smoking room (smoking no longer allowed), groups gather for lively conversation and heavy drinking. None is more active than what I have dubbed the Bad Boy Claret Circle, chaired by the wonderfully witty and learned Professor Lord Smith of Clifton, or simply Trevor, who conducts his seminars ruthlessly and can attract twenty or so members in a circle.

Another regular member, John Croft CBE, comes up from the country for his haircut by Wendy of Truefitt & Hill in nearby St James's Street. Diminutive, in his nineties, softly spoken, quite the sharpest brain I have ever encountered, a man whose gentle wit requires one to wonder whether what he has just said was intended to be funny and then you realise it was, by which time he has moved on. Much loved within the club, with seventy years' membership, he is officially the father of the Reform. Given his wartime career in military intelligence, some might say that John joined the wrong club, that the Travellers next door would have been more appropriate given its reputation as the spooks' hangout.

Fresh from chairing a session of the Cryptos conference on 'A Century of Signals Intelligence' at the Reform, John agrees to have lunch with me and be interviewed in Bath, where he lives. After sitting down in the restaurant, I switch on the tape machine as he studies the menu and announces that this is the perfect celebration for his ninety-fourth-and-a-half birthday – 'At my age,' he says, 'you count the halves.'

John was at Westminster School in the late 1930s, where he remembers Rudolf von Ribbentrop, son of the then German ambassador, Joachim von Ribbentrop, stripping down for a shower to reveal pink underwear. Another contemporary, the future British diplomat Brian Urquhart, later described Rudolf as 'surly and arrogant', arriving at school each day in a plum-coloured, chauffeur-driven Mercedes. Rudolf returned to Germany in 1938 when his father was recalled by Hitler and appointed Foreign Minister.

After Westminster, John went to Christ Church College, Oxford to read Modern History. There, he was enlisted as a Royal Fusilier and was expecting to be called up in the summer of 1942 and posted to an officer cadet training unit, when his tutor suggested he might be better suited to intelligence work. He was invited to meet the Master of Balliol for an interview. In a room in the Master's lodgings, which smelled strongly of tomcat, John was shown a German newspaper and asked if he could translate the headlines. Having passed this initial test, he was told to report to a hut on a playing field in Oxford, where he was interviewed by a Colonel Tiltman, who wore a toothbrush moustache and asked in clipped tones if John could do cross-word puzzles. John replied that this was not one of his interests. Could he play chess? Well, yes, he had played chess as a child. A few months later, in early autumn 1942, John reported to the Government Code and Cypher School in Bedford.

There, aged nineteen, he joined two dozen other men,

mostly his age and also interrupting their courses at Oxford or Cambridge, though there were also a few older men from the British Museum Reading Room (including the future novelist Angus Wilson) and a small group of crossword puzzle experts who could crack the fiendishly cryptic *Telegraph* crossword in under five minutes. Together, they were given a basic course in cryptography. 'There were no machine cyphers, just exercises in hand encryptions like the Double Playfair,' John recalls. 'What's that?' I ask. Apparently, it's a rather elementary 'substitution cypher', but John declines to explain how it works – not for secrecy reasons, but because he quite sensibly realises I do not have a brain for such riddles and he'd be wasting his time. Waiters hover around our table, and John turns to the wine list with interest.

After an intensive course in German – John is still unclear as to the usefulness of reading a German translation of Dostoevsky's letters to his wife – he was posted to Ralph Tester's section at Bletchley Park as a member of the small team working on decryptions of the Lorenz machines of the German High Command. The section was housed in a hut, divided into two parts. At the back of the hut was the machine for speeding up the process of decryption automatically, nicknamed the Heath Robinson. 'I'm the only person alive who remembers the Heath Robinson,' John says. 'It had tapes which kept on breaking and flashing lights that flashed when they shouldn't have done. Occasionally, Alan Turing would pop in to tinker with it. It was soon replaced by the Colossus, which was very much more sophisticated.'

'We had no idea what a Lorenz machine looked like, so in that sense we were working very much in the dark,' John continues. However, Tester's team did manage to diagnose the logical structure of the Lorenz machine three years before they actually saw one, and the German High Command never realised that its cyphers had been compromised. Although these cyphers yielded high-level strategic information that made a significant contribution to the Allied victory in Europe, John and his colleagues had to endure long periods of tedium reading about such things as the supply of lavatory paper to the German front. Night shifts were especially boring: 'German generals went to sleep at night, apparently, so there was very little traffic on the line. But there was one message which Tester tickled out, a personal message from Hitler himself demanding the capture of the Yugoslav partisan leader General Mihailovic and offering a reward of a large quantity of gold – *Eine grosse Menge Gold.*'

In late 1943, John was allocated to the research section at Aldford House, a 1930s block of flats overlooking Park Lane. Aldford House was an outpost of the Government Communications Bureau at nearby Berkeley Street, run by Commander Alastair Denniston, head of the Government Code and Cypher School (later renamed GCHQ). This outfit, John explains, handled all diplomatic and commercial communications of the Axis powers, 'but also those of neutral countries and indeed those of our allies. I remember being taken round the various sections and meeting the man who was reconstructing the United States' consular codebook; another man was reading the Papal Nuncio's enciphered correspondence with the Vatican.'

John was part of a small team that worked out of a flat on the top floor of Aldford House, which was strictly closed to visitors. The team had been assembled to crack the Morse Code signals that were being sent, from late 1943, between a control centre in or near Moscow and outposts in Eastern Europe, the Balkans, western France, Belgium and Norway. 'The significance of this network was established after one of our military outposts heard some messages coming out of Moscow and recognised the handwriting, or signalling habits, of one of the transmitters. This transmitter was recognised as an ex-Metropolitan Police officer and member of the British Communist Party who had gone to Russia in the mid-thirties. The Soviets had been using him to transmit messages out of Moscow for a long time.

'The Radio Security Service was intercepting the messages coming out, but the ones going back to Moscow from its agents in the field were much more difficult to intercept. And, of course, they meant nothing without breaking the encryption. We all had some difficulty breaking into it at all in the early days until, in early 1944, the head of section Bernard Scott, who eventually became Professor of Maths at Sussex University, took it home with him one evening (which he shouldn't have done, of course) and came back the next morning saying, "I've got into it." I said, "How?" "By algebraic means," he replied mysteriously, and we left it at that because he was a mathematician and I wasn't.'

John is now well into his main course – pan-fried fillet of lemon sole, carrot purée, artichokes *barigoule* – and gathering speed. I hastily check that I'm still recording him; I couldn't bear to lose this first-hand account. 'It's like a eureka moment. Once you've seen it, it becomes obvious. It was a substitution cypher in which, with the thirty-three letters of the Russian alphabet transposed as numbers, the message was set out in a sort of three-line grid: to this was added the key, and the result transmitted to the recipient. The key, the indicators of which were sent at the beginning of each encryption, was a text which was taken from an edition, in English, of Shakespeare. The indicators gave the page and line – "To be or not to be", say – with which to start both the encipherment and the decipherment.

'Bernard Scott and myself went off to the Reading Room in the British Museum to see if we could find the exact edition of Shakespeare they were using. It was a rather eerie experience because there was no one in the entire museum except for the director, and most of its contents had been evacuated to safer places outside London. Bernard and I searched the stacks, which still contained dozens of standard editions of Shakespeare, but we never found the one the Russians were using. Presumably it was a pirate edition. Had we found it, it would simply have speeded up the process somewhat.

'So, every Russian political agent who was in advance of the Russian lines was working from the same edition of Shakespeare. If they were arrested, it wouldn't have been odd to be carrying an English translation of Shakespeare; after all, Shakespeare was more international even than the Bible – and indeed it might've looked a bit odd if you were caught with a Bible in Church Slavonic. And you didn't need to be able to understand English to use that text to send or receive messages because you started off with line so-and-so, page so-and-so, and you were then simply transposing language into numbers. The problem, for the Soviets, was that once their agents had been given a copy of Shakespeare, they had limited means of getting anything else to them, so they couldn't easily change the text on which the encryptions were based.'

Following Scott's success in breaking into the cypher, the team on the top floor of Aldford House was enlarged to include about a dozen women (some 'in the background', others from MI5), four or five codebreakers, and one Russian expert, Felix

Fetterlein, who was brought out of retirement to translate the decrypts. He was one of two legendary Fetterlein brothers who in the 1900s had been employed in the Tsarist cryptographic agency. The decrypts were typed up and given top-security classification and a limited circulation. They also went straight to Churchill through a man called Major Morton, his aide in intelligence matters.

'We got a bit alarmed by that,' John recalls. 'There he was, reading these things in bed with a bottle of champagne, and Mrs Churchill next to him. I suppose no harm was done, though officially no one was allowed to talk about such things, even to the cat. It was rumoured, subsequently, that Clarissa, one of Churchill's nieces, might have been the Fifth Man, so to speak, but I don't know anything about that. Certainly, Churchill's knowledge of Stalin's intentions was helpful in advance of the Tehran Conference. Russia was our ally, we were reading their signals (and the American encryptions) – it's a bit odd if you think about it, but in a war the principle is, you watch your front but it's a good idea to watch your back as well.'

John remembers being introduced to Kim Philby in Aldford House. 'There was nothing odd about his occasional visits as he was in MI6 and, in that capacity, he read the decrypts. But he was never allowed access to the top floor. Our section was strictly off limits, except for Denniston himself and the officer in the Royal Signals who was in charge of the intercepts. Any communication between the section and Denniston or the Royal Signals was made through scramblers – black telephones with a green handset which were connected to a scrambling box parked on the floor next to one's desk. Every evening we all put the material we were working on in locked security cupboards. One morning, we arrived to find that Fetterlein's cupboard had been forced open and his papers disturbed, though nothing was taken. We reported the break-in, but I don't recall any follow-up or any inquiry at all. Some months later, the Russians changed the cypher – for obvious reasons, it couldn't have been changed in three minutes all across Europe. Much later, once Philby had been unmasked as a double agent, I assumed that it had been him behind the break-in: he must have tipped the Russians off.'

Our plates are swept away and the dessert menu is produced with a flourish. 'Oh dear,' says John. 'They've got my favourite thing, dark chocolate *délice*, white chocolate crunch, ginger, milk sorbet.' 'Why is that bad news? Are you not allowed to have it?' I ask. John pauses before replying, 'Well, I'm meant to be losing weight [he certainly doesn't look like he's packing extra pounds], but of course I'm allowed it.' The waiter scurries off.

John gazes out of the window and says, 'I remember being by myself in the top-floor flat at Aldford House – it must've been lunchtime – and the chief Alastair Denniston turned up and we were chatting casually when suddenly a V1 approached. It cut out, and both of us went flat on the floor, and the bomb dropped on Lansdowne House, a few streets away in Berkeley Square.' John and his parents had already been bombed out of their home in a block of flats in Baker Street in 1940. 'To hear a stack of bombs coming down is not a very pleasant experience. Later on, I was walking to work from my digs just off Oxford Street at about nine in the morning, and a V2 fell on Speaker's Corner in Hyde Park. You didn't hear it coming; you heard it coming after it had been. It was the biggest bang I've ever heard. Glass fell out of all the windows on Oxford Street. The strange thing was, there were no people running screaming through the streets. It was a terrible experience but there was no hysteria.'

The chocolate *délice* arrives. It occurs to me that John, who lived through those bombs and all the hardships of rationing during and after the war, has never lost the frisson of pleasure that chocolate can bring.

When the war ended, John was given a class release to complete his degree at Oxford. One day there was a knock at the door of his room and a military policeman came in. 'He very politely told me that I had been absent without leave. I was nominally a Royal Fusilier, but the brilliance of army records meant they had only just caught up with me. Problem was, I had been sworn to secrecy and couldn't tell him what I'd done in the war. He very kindly decided not to arrest me, after I suggested he take the matter up with the college authorities, who somehow or another sorted it out. Imagine my surprise when, seven years later, the Royal Fusiliers wrote to me saying that I needed to come back for a refresher course. I wrote and told them that as I had never been freshened I didn't see how I could be refreshed. Consternation all round.'

After he took his degree at Oxford, John contemplated taking a degree in the history of art at the Courtauld Institute, where he was seen by the director, Professor Anthony Blunt. They had a congenial conversation until Blunt asked John about his wartime career. 'I said that I had been employed by "a department of the Foreign Office", which was the stock answer to all such enquiries. Suddenly, the temperature in the room dropped, and Blunt became remote.' Blunt confessed to MI5 in April 1964 that he had been a Soviet spy.

At the Reform Club, John remembers seeing fellow member Guy Burgess 'lunging about in the saloon, completely drunk. I took great care to avoid him, I didn't like that kind of behaviour.' Burgess defected to the Soviet Union in 1951, taking with him a couple of books on loan from the Reform Club library (they eventually found their way back to the club, many years after Burgess's death in Moscow). 'Isn't it extraordinary that Burgess never betrayed himself when he was drunk?' I ask. 'He may have done,' John speculates. 'But he was part of the establishment – they all were – and that's why it took so long to detect them.'

John's run-ins with enemy spies lasted well into his career as a civil servant. While head of the Home Office Research Unit, he noticed that there were curious leaks in advance of the unit publishing its reports. 'I went to the government chief scientist and said, "Ought we to have a look at this?" And he said, "Oh no, I don't think we want to get involved in all that."' John is convinced that it was the East German security service, the Stasi, which had detected that the Research Unit was a 'weak point' in the Home Office set-up. 'The Stasi was acting on behalf of the Soviets in many cases, and they were very thorough. I was sure that there was something funny going on – there was no confidential information coming out of the unit, so it was simply to upset the apple cart a bit and show us they could do it.'

Over coffee, John muses on the usefulness of talking about all this. He says he is conflicted, that the historian in him believes it is important to record the facts, while as a codebreaker he recognises that secrecy is essential. 'Problem is, if you don't talk about it, a great deal of myth surrounds the whole thing.'

After lunch, we walk through the rain to a gallery near John's house, where he is exhibiting some of his paintings (his unproductive interview with Anthony Blunt all those years ago did not put him off his passion for art). I offer John my umbrella. 'I've no need for an umbrella, I've got a hat,' he says and walks on briskly. I hurry to catch up.

'When are you next up to see Wendy?' I ask.

'In two weeks' time,' he says. 'I'll get a message to you somehow.'

'Encrypted?' I whisper.

PS: Some weeks after my visit to Bath, I found myself idly leafing through a book on my old school, Harman Murtagh's *Clongownians of Distinction*. I came across the biography of Richard James 'Jim' Hayes, clearly a brainbox, having graduated from Trinity, Dublin with three honours degrees taken simultaneously before being appointed director of the National Library of Ireland in 1940. During the war, Hayes was seconded to the army as a codebreaker, running the library part-time. His linguistic skills, keen memory and organised mind led to major successes in intelligence work. He was, Murtagh writes, the first cryptologist to break the German multi-dot code, disclosing the whole Nazi intelligence network in Ireland. His greatest breakthrough was to unlock the complex, letter-based cyphers with which Bletchley Park had struggled. After the war, Cecil Liddell, head of MI5's Irish section, admitted that a 'whole series of cyphers couldn't have been solved without Hayes's input'. I rang John Croft, excited at the connection. 'Can't say that I've ever heard of him,' John replied softly, with just the tiniest hint of a sniff.

Y

Yikes

Scams and frauds

I imagine we've all chuckled at the audacity, or marvelled at the ingenuity, of a scam where someone has got the better of us. How about the young father who approached me in a café in Old Havana? He got over the pleasantries fairly quickly. 'So, how are you enjoying Cuba?' he enquired. I told him I liked Cuba a great deal. 'Yes, I suppose Cuba is enjoyable for those who do not have a baby daughter with a severe allergy to normal milk,' he muttered. I made all the right noises, at which point he asked whether I might offer to buy some 'special' milk from the pharmacy, which stood right beside the café. Next thing I knew, we were both queuing at the counter.

A soft plastic pouch or bladder of the special milk was produced and handed to the grateful father, who thanked me profusely before hurrying off to satisfy the hunger of his baby daughter. 'That'll be sixteen dollars,' the pharmacist said quietly but firmly. 'Very expensive,' I said. 'Very special milk,' he replied, hand outstretched. Oh, well, at least the baby will be fed, I thought, as I went back to my coffee. As I lifted the cup to my lips, I suddenly realised that there was no baby; it was a $16 scam, probably split fifty-fifty with the pharmacist who no doubt had already put the bladder of milk safely back in the fridge and was waiting for the next soft-hearted sucker. Was I cross? Not a bit. It was a clever little scam undertaken by a wily Cuban with little or no hope of any other income.

How about the chancer who scammed me one bright summer's day in St James's Square? We were walking towards each other on opposite sides of a narrow street and, somehow, he found a way of making eye contact. As we drew almost level, he gave a little gasp and with an exaggerated movement bent down and plucked, from between two paving stones, a gold ring. He held it up and beckoned me over. 'It is a great day for you and me,' he said excitedly. 'We have good fortune.' I said that it was *his* lucky day for he had found the ring. 'No, no, you must have it,' he insisted, and there commenced a toing and froing as to who should benefit from this good fortune, neither of us considering whether or not to drop it off at the local police station.

Eventually, he pressed me to take it, handed it over and made to walk away. 'No, no,' I insisted. 'Please take this ten-pound note, it would make me feel better.' He took it gently and suggested that £20 might be a better gesture and I agreed. As I passed a jeweller in nearby Jermyn Street, I popped in and asked what they thought of this ring, was it nine or eighteen carats? No carats at all, came the answer, at which point the penny dropped. And indeed, that was all the ring was worth – sometime later, a friend who knows about such things told me that if it is gold, you'll be able to tell from the sound it makes when you drop it on the tiled floor (trouble is, I can't remember *what* sound). Anyway, I went home and put the ring in a cufflink box. It was a scam, but so clever because the scammer never actually asked for anything; he somehow influenced me into offering him money, correctly assuming that I, like many people, was greedy. It is greed that normally motivates the victim to take the plunge, and the plunge inevitably gives the victim a good soaking.

I like to think that believing what we are told is a reasonable way to carry on (and not just because I was in PR for most of my career). To question every claim or promise would turn us all into cynics and that would be to the detriment of our way of interacting with one another. However, I did *not* believe Mike, a New York-based American investment manager with the so-called Taschen Bank on Wall Street, or so he claimed. I had sold my company in Garrick Street but retained an office there, when my direct line rang one morning. Mike announced himself and asked whether I had $20,000 to invest in a very promising young company, but stressed that I would have to hurry because the offer was closing that evening. I asked him to fax some details through (it was before the internet) as I would need to have a close look at the offer and discuss it at home. He berated me for not having the authority to invest my own money, for being under the thumb of my wife, and was I one of those weedy types?

My hackles were raised, but I was curious to know more about this hard-sell New Yorker who was calling me from his Wall Street office at 5:00 in the morning, local time, to sign me up for some non-existent shares. I told him I had to go into a meeting and hoped that he would call me at the same time the following day. There then followed the most amusing carousel of calls over the following three or four days, as I passed him over to former colleagues in the office, apologised that I was being called away to a meeting, and giving any number of other excuses. Having deduced he was a scam merchant, I also took to resting the telephone receiver on my desk for several hours rather than hanging up – in those days, a caller on a single line could not use it until the person receiving the call had hung up. 'Mike' became really quite desperate, still believing he had almost hooked me, until I finally came clean and asked him if he had run out of American mugs to dupe so had had to turn to Europe and try his luck here? I put the phone down to a barrage of abuse.

Years later, after recounting this tale to a policeman seconded to the City of London anti-scam force, he said, 'You don't really believe he was an American and in New York, do you? More likely, he was calling you from his mother's phone in Clapham.' So, I had fallen for part of the scam after all.

Things have moved on apace since then, mainly because the internet is a heaven-sent tool for the unscrupulous fraudster who is moving right along with the technological advances designed to keep your money safe. So, when I was approached three years ago by the Financial Conduct Authority to publicise their ScamSmart campaign, set up in 2014 to help identify scams and fake firms offering to invest your money (especially if you're over fifty), and a one-stop shop for reporting suspected fraudsters who contact you, I jumped at the chance. I now know more than I care to about phishing (fake emails), vishing (call centres), SMiShing (text alerts), cloned websites, malware, ransomware, even the trick of sending flowers on your wife's birthday to keep you comfortable that you're not being conned. The longer you don't know you're being scammed, the more money they can take before moving on. Yikes.

Here's a typical approach. Ring any bells?

'Hello, this is John from Barclays Bank. We've detected some unusual activity on your account, and in order to sort it out we need to go through some security details with you.' We should all know by now that this might well be a scam. And you'll know for certain that it is if they ask you to supply your pin number or your online password, or suggest you make a 'test transaction' online (by which you make an online transfer into a new 'safe account' which is actually the fraudster's), or even instruct you to hand over your 'faulty' credit card to an 'official courier' who will come to your home, show you his or her official identification, and deliver the card to the 'bank'.

Trouble is, they sound so convincing. This is why they're called confidence tricksters: they have an intuitive under-standing of behavioural psychology and have anticipated our suspicions, which are then deftly deflected. For instance, if you question John from Barclays Bank, asking how you can know if he is genuine, John will offer to 'prove' his identity by hanging up while you check the phone number of your bank. You then dial this real number, which is answered by an advisor, and you say you've been alerted by someone called John that there may be unusual activity on your account, and they say, yes, this is the case, and you then proceed to give over your account details and passwords. You think you've been speaking to your bank, but you haven't: the scammers haven't hung up the phone at all, they've actually just played a dial tone, and when you dial in, you're talking to the same gang. The best way out of this is to keep the scammer on the phone, then use a different phone to call your bank. Then call the police.

As a sort of ambassador for ScamSmart, I undertook what is known as a 'radio day', which means pitching up to a radio studio at 8:00 in the morning, where twenty or thirty interviews have been scheduled for the following four hours. In a break between interviews, the sound technician sitting behind the glass screen of my tiny, soundproofed cell, told me an alarming story. He had been scammed for £16,000 by giving out some key security facts, believing the scammer to be from his bank. The bank's response? 'We're sorry, but that one's on you.'

To add insult to injury, the scammer rang back a few days later, putting on a different voice and telling the sound engineer that he was speaking from the bank and that they had indeed traced the scammer and could get his £16,000 back, though there would be a small upfront fee of 10 per cent. My engineer had been warned about this scam 'extension', and when he accused the caller of being the original scammer, the crook laughed at him, saying, 'Yes, but you don't know where I am, do you, sucker?'

If you have fallen for a scam, should your bank reimburse you? Why should it when it was you who gave over your security details? That's why the cyber experts call this kind of scam 'cyber-enabled', as the victim enables the scam when tricked into giving out bank details. It's against you and not the bank. That's a long way from a hack, which is a so-called 'cyber-dependent' attack, in which your data is stolen without your knowledge or acquiescence. Cyber criminals can hack your network, control devices linked to a network (such as your printer), or even view what a computer user is doing by monitoring keyboard strokes or viewing what is shown on the monitor or a webcam. It's as if they were sitting right there beside you.

I mentioned SMiShing earlier, the use of fraudulent text (SMS) messages which appear to come from your bank.

Following headlines in 2016 and 2017, I presented a BBC *Watchdog* programme about a scam affecting customers of Santander bank. They complained that they were contacted by text asking them to respond to a certain phone number or click on a link to a website. Both phone number and link were fake and accounts were drained upwards of £10,000–£30,000. The bank was refusing to reimburse customers, arguing they had willingly given over their details. Technically, the bank did nothing wrong, as the accounts had not been hacked. The customers were furious and accused Santander of not doing enough to protect them from fraud, arguing that these texts came while they were already in contact with the bank so they had believed it was just part of the conversation; some claimed that the thread of legitimate texts was being hacked. Either way, they did not think to contact the bank directly on the number on the back of their card, or simply walk into a branch to double-check.

Through the ScamSmart initiative I have met with a few victims of financial fraud. They give good advice, hard won: be wary if you get a call out of the blue, if you're told it's a safe investment, if they call repeatedly, or tell you the offer is only available for a limited time. And always check the Financial Conduct Authority's website, which lists all the firms found to be suspected of fraud or who aren't properly registered with it, the regulator.

Many of these scams target victims over a long period and include friendly call centres, flashy websites, helpful texts and legitimate advice (gold is rising, sterling is weak, bamboo is the hottest thing at the moment). They might even return some of your initial investment as income earned to entice you to invest more. They often target older, more affluent people who are too embarrassed to tell the police (or, indeed, family or friends) when the scam becomes apparent.

Derek was one of those taken in. I met the retired pensioner, an experienced investor, after he contacted ScamSmart, and he told me that, having taken several calls from 'a very credible' young man offering him a high-interest, short-term investment, he agreed to put £3,000 into a non-regulated investment. Shortly after, he received a call from a 'senior broker' who said that he was negotiating with a FTSE 100 company and there would be a much higher return if he invested a further £3,000. Derek took the bait, and doubled up. The quick return was expected in October, then delayed until November, and then no more phone calls, no more brokers, no more £6,000. They'd left the boiler room and done a runner.

You could say Derek was fortunate. The FCA tell me the average scam is for £32,000, which means for every £6,000 from a Derek, someone else has lost almost £60,000. If it sounds too good to be true, it is too good to be true. If you're thinking of investing, get independent advice – never rely on the advice of the person who has contacted you unsolicited.

I bet we have all seen this: an email comes along from Amazon or Apple or eBay or PayPal saying there is a problem with your account, just click here and log on and let's sort it. The site looks valid, of course; if it didn't you wouldn't fall for it. But what could be wrong with your account? I often get emails to say my account has been frozen though I haven't been on that site for a while. That's the first hint – why would a free site like AOL freeze my account? AOL hasn't frozen it: the fake email wants my password because I may, just may, use the same password on another site with money attached to it, such as PayPal. Worse, if I do fall for it on a site like Apple or PayPal, I could be out of pocket immediately. Imagine if I did that with a fake bank website. Don't click on websites from emails. Go to the website itself.

Two hints: check where the email address is coming from. Just hovering your cursor over the address will reveal all of it and it's likely to be from a hacked account. Look for a clear address from a big company and then look for a lock symbol to the far left of the address, and an 's' in the hyper link – *https://* means it's a secure site. Secondly, look out for copycat sites and those that promise to help you navigate something you find terrifying, like a tax refund, or council tax. These sites might look like the real thing, or might purport to make your journey smoother, and they may not be illegal. They will simply charge you a hefty fee to input your data onto the proper site, and, of course, they could sell your data since you probably clicked on a 'Terms of Agreement' box that you didn't read properly.

While long-term financial scams in which the victim is ignorant work a treat for some fraudsters, others want you to know they've got you and you have two choices – pay up or lose your data. Ransomware has been in the headlines thanks to the targeting of big firms like Sony and HBO, the former to embarrass a big film producer and the latter for money – both firms had their data seized and released, in instalments, on the internet. What we don't know is how many large firms have paid up to have their data back (they don't want that kind of publicity, any more than negotiators do in cases of human ransom).

You are not a big firm and you don't have a lot of money, so you figure they won't come after you. Wrong. I met a working mum who forked out over £100 to get her daughter's computer unlocked. Her seventeen-year-old was attempting to stream a film from an illegal site when her computer was hijacked. A message flashed up with a phone number and a deadline to pay up, or the computer would remain locked. After a few tears, her mum got on the phone to a helpful 'call centre' and gave over her credit card details and, lo and behold, the computer was unfrozen.

This scam can only work if victims have a high degree of trust that, once they pay, they'll get their data back or their computer unfrozen. And often they do, but that doesn't mean they can't be ransomed again. The infection could lay dormant for years and be triggered on your computer at a whim; you won't know it is there until it's too late. Up to now, ransomware has been largely motivated by geopolitical reasons, publicity reasons, or for one big payoff. Soon, it could hit millions of us for smaller payoffs.

We are victims, but we are also enablers. We are amazingly careless with our data, all the time. A friend of mine is a heavy user of Facebook. His hobby is family history, and he has typed in the same four-digit pin code for decades. So, his new bank asked him for a pin code, and, as backup questions, his mother's maiden name, his first school, the first street he lived on and the name of a favourite pet. Guess what, all of that can be gleaned from a search of his Facebook page: he has a Friends Group from his first school, he reminisces about his old neighbourhood, he belongs to a genealogy group through which he's been researching his mother, using her maiden name. Every Chat, every Like, every Comment is there to be found. As for that pin code? Well, like many of us, he uses the same one for everything.

It's likely that eye scans will soon become part of the current trend of three-factor authentication – something physical (phone, computer, bank card reader, a bank card itself, key fob), something known (password, pin) and something unique to you (iris, fingerprint, facial recognition), so-called inherence factors. Realise that once you get used to one form of online protection, a new or enhanced one will be coming down the pike. Realise also that, no sooner have you embraced this protection, the scammers will be adjusting their sights. You are never not a target.

Finally, two scams, one outrageous and one that mystifies me to this day.

I went into a well-known jewellery shop and passed three well-dressed men descending the staircase. One of them told me that he would join me in a moment or so. I apologised for interrupting what was clearly an important sales meeting. All three laughed. When the chap returned, he told me the other two were policemen from the fraud squad who were on a mission to catch a couple of enterprising crooks. 'Tell me more,' I said. 'This subject is close to my heart.'

This is how the story unfolded. An elderly woman had come into the shop two days earlier, purchased a £12,000 watch on her debit card and left happy. The salesman was surprised to welcome her back the following day, when she declared that she wanted to buy another watch, this time a £15,000 model.

Our salesman was happy to facilitate the sale but the card rejected the purchase. The seventysomething-year-old lady was furious and rang her bank, who told her that if she delayed putting the card through for ten minutes, all would be all right. Unhappily, all was not all right, and so the lady, though irritated, retained her calm and put a call through to the bank for a second time. Now the bank said that they would stay on the line and 'escort' the payment through, and so it was that our customer left the store with another expensive little parcel in her bag.

So what was the scam? Unbelievably, the previous week, two suited characters had arrived on her doorstep claiming to be from the local police station, telling her that her bank account had been breached but that the police knew the identity of the culprits and they now needed her cooperation to nab the crooks. Would she go to the town's biggest jeweller and buy an expensive watch on her bank card? That would provide the evidence that they needed to catch the rotters. So, off she went to do their bidding and returned with the gold watch. The officers expressed delight, but were disappointed with the watch, claiming that its value was below the threshold required for a conviction. They would take the watch to the station as evidence and would she mind popping back to the shop and picking up another watch costing more than £15,000? Happy to help the police, the woman did as she was asked. The £15,000 little beauty was duly collected from her by the fraudsters posing as policemen (itself a criminal offence). That's the last anyone saw of the watches or the crooks, and our trusting victim had lost £27,000. Massive yikes.

To end on a lighter note, some years ago I was driving around Morocco in my Renault 4L and had pulled up on a road in the south of the country to consult a map. I was in near-desert without a soul or any habitation in sight, when I suddenly sensed I was not alone. Turning towards the passenger seat, I was surprised to see a woolly head stuck through the sliding window, so that the smiling face of an elderly man was just inches from mine.

He greeted me in almost perfect English, saying, 'As you are a doctor, I wonder if you could give me a prescription for my throat condition to take to my pharmacy.'

'But I'm not a doctor,' I replied.

'In that case, I am sorry to have troubled you,' he said, and, extracting his head from my car, he strolled off into the desert.

I still can't work out what the intended scam was. Or perhaps there was no scam, and this man was simply waiting for a doctor to materialise in the middle of nowhere and write him a prescription. That's the trouble with knowing too much about scams, you start looking for them where they might not be.

Z

Z-List

'Celebrity is a mask that eats into the face'

John Updike was not referring to today's cascade of ridiculous wannabes disgorged out of TV's mincing machine of entertainment; he was writing nearly thirty years ago, long before the fame disease became a pandemic, about the celebrity dust that falls on the shoulders of great writers as they edge to old age, and how it erodes their creative power. 'As soon as one is aware of being "somebody", to be watched and listened to with extra interest, input ceases,' Updike observed, 'and the performer goes blind and deaf in his over-animation. One can either see or be seen.'

I wonder what Updike would have made of today's celebrity-crazed world. His contemporary, Andy Warhol, grooving at Studio 54 at night and driving his assistants on at the Factory during the day, spoke of the fifteen minutes of fame that everybody would have – and how prescient he was. The ghastly Donald Trump was also at Studio 54, trying to shake off his

301

'bridge and tunnel' gawkiness, and sadly he has long since passed the quarter-hour he was promised. But today, fame is thought to beckon for every skinny kid who leafs through *Hello!* and *OK!*, the tabloids, and all the other crap magazines focusing on the dimwits' appetite for someone else's apparently gorgeous lifestyle. 'We can have it too,' they tell themselves. 'We just need the break and we'll kill to get it.'

Celebrity tapped me on the shoulder shortly after *The Apprentice* first aired in early 2005. It was a light tap-tap and I took no notice, but when the show was hoisted onto primetime mainstream BBC1, the tap-tap-tap became more insistent. Yet still I remained naively ignorant of the surging interest in the show and its key players. Alan Sugar was already well known, though not as loved as he is now. Margaret Mountford and I were puzzled. We were not, in all truth, part of gossip-loving, tabloid-reading, telly-sated Britain; we were not aware of how, as the popular media expanded in the 1980s, reality TV – cheap, populist, and spreading like a rash – was becoming the main driver of instant celebrity. One of Margaret's proudest boasts was that she didn't even own a television.

The god-awful *Big Brother*, coyly promised as a 'social experiment' at its baptism, quickly revealed itself to be little short of a gang of manipulative show-offs engaged in an interminable argument. The curtain was then raised on *I'm a Celebrity …Get Me Out of Here!*, born out of those 1980s Japanese game shows we viewed, astounded, from behind the sofa and which confirmed our perception that the Japanese were addicted to sadism. Look what they did in the war, we reasoned, and now they hang people upside down by their heels and beat them with stinging nettles to see who gives in first, and they call it entertainment? But before you can learn to spell Endemol, we now have people encased in Perspex coffins with a writhing ball of snakes for company while Ant and Dec roll their eyes at each other in mutual amazement at the stupidity of celebs who are desperate for either money or profile or probably both.

Was *The Apprentice* the first talent show? I'm not sure, but it certainly spawned many more and it now seems that every other show involves an elimination process, from the Simon Cowell stable through *The Voice* to the *Great British Bake Off*, and just about anything from sewing to pottery to keeping an allotment or building a Lego toy.

I like to think that *The Apprentice* (*see* A: THE APPRENTICE) has had a truly worthwhile impact on the perception of business and, together with *Dragons' Den*, has demystified business and created a belief that it's possible to start your own enterprise with very little capital. It's also the case that many candidates could never be described as 'Britain's brightest business hopefuls', and many might just have squirmed their way past the arduous audition process in the hope they would become instantly famous, be picked up by a smart and pushy agent, propelled into the national consciousness, regaled by adoring crowds, fall into the arms of fabulous women, or men, or both, get terribly rich and, above all, become an 'A-lister'.

So, as a Z-list celeb, how has modest fame changed my life? Mostly for the better, I would say: it's brought me all sorts of unexpected advantages and ego-massaging compliments and my pension fund is now secure. But as time went on I found myself worrying that I might be a little too attached to my own profile. The mask seemed to be nibbling at my face. When I began to mix with live audiences after I'd signed up to Jeremy Lee Associates, the biggest speaker agency in the UK, and found myself surrounded by hundreds of people who wanted selfies and autographs, I stepped out of the bubble that was *The Apprentice*, because of course that was a controlled environment; it was reality TV, but it wasn't real; you didn't really meet the public in volume, just the occasional van driver who would shout 'You're fired!' as he sped past, and the cabbie who would say, 'So what's Surralan really like then?'

I think it was the after-dinner speaker circuit that revealed to me the almost fanatical devotion to *The Apprentice*, and I was standing there as the representative of that programme. I'd done about four years of *The Apprentice* before I signed up with JLA, and I think I'd kept my feet more or less on the ground till that point. I didn't have an agent, and I was genuinely surprised by the success of the show and people's interest in me. Even my children were calling me more frequently, and initially seemed quite excited. I was being invited to film premieres, gallery openings, all sorts of receptions – Alan once joked, 'You'd go to the opening of an envelope, Nick.' I even found myself in the Royal Box at Wimbledon. It was all great fun, though I did always feel that there'd been some mistake and I'd be politely asked to leave once people realised I was a mere interloper.

I remember my first gig with the speaker agency. I found myself in Edinburgh, booked to address a rather exclusive gathering of local business, political and public service worthies, including the chief of police. Terrified, I paced the streets in an attempt to quell the terror rising to my dry mouth. It was time, and I climbed the stone steps to an elegant front door and rang the bell. Within minutes I was standing on a podium *entertaining* people. The organiser wrote a generous tribute which found its way onto the JLA website and suddenly I started to drag that same speech – a friendly, anecdotal, forty-minute roam through *The Apprentice* – all over the country.

Sensing that I was in increasing demand, JLA doubled my fee and we were, as they say, off to the races. I was amazed that I was able to carry it off as I'm certainly not, by nature, a confident or extrovert person, though gradually the exposure seemed to be strengthening my nerve. But there was one event which had me in a knot of anxiety, the annual Christmas lunch for the Chartered Institution of Highways & Transportation in the Great Room of the Grosvenor House Hotel, one of the largest venues in the country. The mid-December date was in the diary and a few days beforehand I leafed through the paperwork to check the timings and was horrified to note that the audience would be 1,750-strong. A Christmas lunch for 1,750 chaps from the manly, heavy-drinking, road-building and trucking industries? Who'd listen to some old bloke waffling about a reality TV show? I predicted a bloodbath with me gurgling down the plughole.

I slid early into the Great Room to get a view of the battlefield and was confronted by acres of empty tables, not just in the Great Room itself, but up on the balconies and back deep into the lobbies, where there was no chance of anyone seeing the speaker, so the walls had been lined with television screens. With a deep sense of foreboding, I joined the president of the CIHT at her drinks reception. I introduced myself, and she viewed me with a lack of interest. 'We're up to 1,820 guests now, so you'll have to speak up,' she said crisply, before turning to find somebody worth talking to.

Somehow, I carried it off, and, I confess, I was completely adrenalised by the applause, the requests for autographs and selfies. Intriguingly, I had accrued a reputation for being honest and (incredibly) of having considerable business acumen and good judgement. The weird thing was that people were ascribing to me insights and qualities I simply didn't possess. I didn't know whether the yen was rising against the Argentine peso, or whether commercial rental rates were likely to fall in the medium term. I thought, Why are people asking me these questions? And why, in the June 2017 general election, were the Labour Party and the Lib Dems badgering me for a public endorsement? Were they really that hard up that they had to turn to a Z-lister?

Year on year, audience ratings for *The Apprentice* grew, and before long I was also working on a series of Nick 'n' Margaret documentaries – informally known as Fruit 'n' Nut – on subjects as diverse as immigration, the state of the railways, the state pension and working into old age. Invitations arrived to appear on *Have I Got News for You*, *Would I Lie to You?*, *Question Time* and various other panel shows. I found myself presenting a series on farm diversification for BBC Northern Ireland, and hacking across Central Asia with Saira Khan, *The Apprentice* runner-up in Series 1. As one of six teams, we were taking part in *Around the World in Eighty Days* for BBC's Children in Need (*see* P: PROOF OF LIFE).

Then *Countdown* came along, 225 (now upped to 260) shows a year, initially overlapping with my last two series of *The Apprentice*. I look back and yet again consider how blessed the last fourteen years have been. By pure luck, without any training or talent, I have earned far more than I deserve and have been treated with nothing but kindness and consideration by those with whom I have worked as well as by complete strangers.

That said, being asked for a selfie in trains and airport check-in lines can be tricky and embarrassing with everybody looking on, but I overcome that by agreeing and then steering the 'fan' to the other side of a nearby pillar where things can be dealt with discreetly so that I do not look like some 'big shot'. I've only ever been shouted at once for begging to be excused and that was in the stifling taxi queue at Euston Station, one of the most polluted locations in Europe. It was a long queue and I was in the middle of it. A woman tugging her child puffed and panted up to me and rather abruptly demanded a selfie. Faced with a sea of onlookers and nowhere to deal with it quietly, I demurred as politely as I could. Red-faced, she shrieked for all to hear, 'But that's your job!'

And I agree, it is. Writing in the *Evening Standard*, Judge Rinder – a delightful fellow who works in an adjoining studio to *Countdown* in Salford's Media City – put it perfectly: 'On the very rare occasions that someone comes over to me and asks for a photo, I am only too happy to stand and smile vapidly at a selfie stick. It's the least I can do. I have zero tolerance for anyone in the public eye who dares to eye-roll at this sort of thing. By doing nothing you get to improve someone else's day so, as I recently said to someone rather well known who was complaining about the "exhaustion" she felt because people all have cameras these days, "Jolly well smile, be polite and keep whatever self-indulgent first-world issue you may have to yourself."'

The truth is, people can change for the worse as the mask of fame eats into them. I know of celebs who refuse to be photographed, who refer to the public as 'civilians', who stamp their feet if some junior production manager can't guarantee there's a car waiting for them outside whatever venue they've been booked for. And not any old car, mind – people carriers are a no-no, E Class Mercedes are only just acceptable, and, really, you could have sent an S Class. Coffee is another important punctuation mark for the day. I'm told of one middle-aged woman celeb, recently introduced to household-name fame, who has a standing order that the moment her chauffeur-driven S Class (yes) arrives at the studio, the door must be opened and a HOT latte thrust into her outstretched hand. And it's got to be HOT, otherwise there'll be a volley of abuse heading at the unfortunate junior.

I am not entirely blameless. I did once have a strop with my camera crew, though in mitigation, the circumstances were very overheated (*see* P: PROOF OF LIFE). And, to my discomfort, Catherine reminds me of the occasion when I was asked to judge the cake-baking competition at our local village fête. I was handed a microphone, and in the guise of a Mary Berry, I called upon the baker of a particular cake to make themselves known. A woman in the crowd excitedly raised her hand. I ventured that her cake was 'unusually dry', though of course I was joking. Catherine was disappointed at my lack of empathy, for not recognising that, while trying to be clever, I had in fact been cruel. My face fell like a soufflé.

This incident came back to haunt me recently, after national humiliation on Channel 4's 2018 *The Great Celebrity Bake Off*. When approached to participate, I readily agreed, delighted to know that the £10,000 fee would be going to a cancer charity and believing that baking, after all, was a little chemistry exercise and nothing more. What could possibly go wrong? Everything, simply everything, went terribly wrong and, no matter how hard I tried, my fellow contestants surged ahead, leaving my dismal efforts the subject of the judges' mounting derision.

Matters came to a crunch, literally, with the Showstopper, featuring a concoction centred on profiteroles, assembled to represent something important in the baker's life, in my case, being host of *Countdown*. Hurrying on (I can hardly bear to dwell on it), let me say that I enjoyed five disastrous attempts, employing nearly thirty eggs, ending with a batch of burnt biscuits pinned in place with cocktail sticks rather than the instructed caramel. A small splodge of cream added a bit of colour but not the satisfying filling that the recipe had promised.

'Nick, with flair and confidence, please bring up your Showstopper,' was the brisk instruction from co-host Sandi Toksvig, and as I began my walk of shame towards the judges' table, the crumpled face of my village fête victim swam into view. Despite my claim that my Showstopper was 'the new choux', a biscuit version that was all the rage in Italy which I was proud to introduce to Britain, the judges declared it, through tears of laughter, a complete failure. So when I was called to be a judge of cakes in Northamptonshire recently, you can be sure that I was generous and kind in my comments. Baking ain't a piece of cake.

Returning to the theme of bad manners, Catherine also recalls on my behalf that I once left her trailing, Melania-like, in my wake. It was the final of *The Apprentice*, recorded with a live audience, and we swept up in a car to be confronted by crowds waiting to enter the studio and a wall of photographers. I got out of the car and walked straight into the action, leaving Catherine/Melania behind looking like a bag-carrier. Catherine reminded me of the importance of good manners, and then went into one of her very occasional non-verbal modes. On another occasion, I was instructed to stop looking like I was actually enjoying having young girls draped all over me asking for a kiss.

Is celebrity really worth the candle? One of the strangest outcomes for me is the way that some family and close friends deliberately choose to ignore my good fortune and studiously refuse ever to mention whatever my most recent slight incursion into public consciousness happens to be. Even at the height of some *Apprentice* outrage, my children would make no reference to it, and friends at dinner would ask about everything other than that which had captured the public conversation just two days before. Catherine found the same, reporting that some friends had announced, in a sort of bored Islington way, 'We never watch the programme.' I find that unkind, mean-spirited, because I've always rejoiced wholeheartedly in the success of my friends. By contrast, my childhood pal Robert Humphreys (*see* B: BOYHOOD) has always been unstintingly generous, and I thank him for that. I also treasure a letter from my old friend and former colleague, Mary Pipes, whom I rarely see as she has lived in the Far East for many years. After meeting in London for a coffee recently, she wrote: 'I am glad that you are still, unwaveringly, the old Nick I used to know thirty years ago.'

The tragedy for the hugely ambitious though talentless, got-lucky celeb is that it's all a rather short ride. Agents are hired and fired, publicity stunts fall flat, outrageous statements are made to the tabloids in the hope of a photo on the showbiz page, celeb girls take their clothes off for a saucy spread in some cheap magazine, but inexorably the press loses interest, the circus has moved on and our poor celeb is back where he/she started – nowhere. Now that's what you call fifteen minutes of fame.

To avoid that fate, there are some who fight to keep in the limelight. Step forward Katie Hopkins. In Series 3 of *The Apprentice*, Miss Hopkins was notable for her sharp and cruel tongue as she steadily dissected her fellow candidates. Having missed out on the top job, she then had to appear before a live audience on the *You're Fired* follow-up programme. The producers had a habit of wheeling me in to calm down potentially difficult situations, and so I found myself knocking on Katie's dressing-room door. She had brought along a wing-woman and I spent some time assuring them both that the *You're Fired* programme was all about celebrating candidates' achievements on the show, rather than anatomising their failures. I felt I had achieved my objective, and sat on the panel with Michelle Mone, surely the quintessentially self-made celeb, who now graces the red benches in the House of Lords as Baroness Mone of Mayfair, having made a few quid in the brassiere business. The baroness rather lost her temper and accused Katie of being a disgrace to women in business, and I remarked that it was sad that her considerable intelligence should be spent on undermining everyone in her sights, and that, dressed in a white trouser suit and with her ruby red, sulky lips shaped for sin, as Betjeman put it in 'The Licorice Fields at Pontefract', she would eventually run out of road (*see* A: THE APPRENTICE). I remember well her very ordinary, West Country parents, and the look of horror on their faces as they anticipated their daughter's next caustic, brutal incursion. And indeed, her media career did come to a bumpy halt in 2017, though I wouldn't exclude the possibility that, in this age of trolling, she might rise again from this lowest of the low points.

During the latter stages of 2016, I had decided that it was time to shed the emperor's clothes of celebrity and face up to the fact that I'd got to say no to the opportunities that kept popping up lest I became addicted to the mask. The nibble had become a gnaw. No more speeches for me, I told myself, but I'll do the

Oxford Union, they've been after me for years. Remembering, beforehand, that Alan Sugar had also spoken in this famous debating chamber and that somebody had surreptitiously made a recording and sold it to the tabloids, I made a note to tape my speech lest the same should happen to me. As is often the case, this self-warning went by the way as I stood up in the debating chamber to deliver my friendly, affectionate sketch of ten years on *The Apprentice*.

I, who would never have made it to Oxford, was flattered by the applause of over two hundred Oxford undergraduates. But taking questions at the end, I noticed nearby a slightly older man who didn't seem to be a student. I made nothing of it but no doubt this was the person who taped my speech and delivered it to the red-tops which, in their noble tradition of distorting everything, turned a perfectly harmless, positive talk into a whistle-blowing exposé of the behind-the-scenes trickery of *The Apprentice*, where no such trickery existed.

Two days later, *The Sun* did a good job of turning my irreverent comments, delivered with affection and humour, into ungrateful gossip, apparently short-changing the show which had impacted my life so positively. I was stunned to see what I had said broken down and distorted into attention-grabbing, scandal-mongering headlines. It didn't take Alan long to address his five million followers on Twitter, reminding them of *The Sun*'s scandalous phone-hacking and their lies about the Hillsborough disaster. Together with my own Twitter counter-attack, this unleashed a torrent of abuse directed at *The Sun*. It wasn't long before the paper asked for a truce, with everybody pulling back, and I felt I had been strongly vindicated. But don't worry, given half a chance, *The Sun* will find a way to monster me again.

Must that be the price of celebrity? Clearly, by some perverted internal logic, it is. Perhaps, one day, Katie Hopkins might lurch on her killer stiletto heels into the realisation that fame is a mug's game. For myself, once this book has come and gone, I'm happy in the knowledge that consciously stepping back from it, and quietly dropping off the Z-list, means that I'll escape the worst ravages of the disease of celebrity and keep my face.

Acknowledgements

This book certainly had a difficult conception. The literary agent Heather Holden-Brown's first attempt at seduction was some years ago and, in the manner of the giant panda, I wanted nothing to do with her approaches. Thereafter, she mounted an annual campaign and still I resisted her on the grounds that I had nothing to write about and would she kindly go and pursue somebody more amenable to her charms. A year or two later, she returned with the loose idea of 'interviews' and, thinking a little more creatively, I thought that if I rummaged around in the attic of my memory, a series of 26 anecdotes might emerge. And they did, and here they are, so thank you for being so persistent, Heather.

My editor Ian Marshall at Simon & Schuster was clearly keen from the outset, fighting off, amazingly, several other publishers and he has been a pleasure to work with, as has my wonderful friend of more than thirty years, Frances Stonor Saunders, who adopted the role of slave driver to my lazy and ill-disciplined slave, and kept me at it and humoured me and tidied up my prose with elegant fastidiousness and saved me from myself on many occasions.

I am especially grateful to the architects of my good fortune over the past 20 years, particularly Lord Alan Sugar, Margaret Mountford, Patrick Holland, now controller of BBC Two, the brilliant Peter Moore, who set the tone of *The Apprentice*, the spirited Jay Hunt. Michele Kurland, never without a mobile in each hand, the wry Mark Saben, Andy Devonshire, series director of *The Apprentice*, then *GBBO* and more recently *Taskmaster*, the witty Claire Walls, all *Apprentice* pillars and the many other talented people who put that show together so expertly, Damian Eadie, Peter Gwyn and David Sayer, as well as, of course, Susie Dent and Rachel Riley of *Countdown*. Elsewhere, my thanks to Alan Watts of Herbert Smith Freehills, John Croft CBE, Dr Mary Pipe OBE, Professor Lord Smith of Clifton, Bob Borwick, Mihir Bose, John Kelleher, Harman Murtagh, Michael Deeny, Gerry Wilkinson, David Nelson, Declan O'Keeffe, Fr Michael Sheil SJ, Ged Healey, Wayne Cornish and, of course, Jo Brand, Gyles Brandreth and Michael Whitehall for their generous citations.

Index

INDEX

INDEX

INDEX

INDEX